political
parties in
america

political parties in america

CQ PRESS

A Division of Congressional Quarterly Inc.
Washington, D.C.

CQ Press
A Division of Congressional Quarterly Inc.
1414 22nd Street, N.W.
Washington, D.C. 20037

(202) 822-1475; (800) 638-1710

www.cqpress.com

Printed in the United States of America

05 04 03 02 01   5 4 3 2 1

Book designer: Debra Naylor

∞ The paper used in this publication meets the minimum requirements of the American National Standard for Information Sciences—Permanence of Paper for Printed Library Materials, ANSI Z39.48-1992.

Library of Congress Cataloging-in-Publication Data

Political parties in America
    p.   cm.
  Includes index.
  ISBN 1-56802-690-0 (alk. paper)
    1. Political parties—United States.

JK2261 .P636 2001
324.273—dc21   2001035186

contents

preface

Political parties are not directly mentioned in the U.S. Constitution, and early leaders of the country were suspicious of them. George Washington warned the nation about the "danger of parties" in his farewell address. Alexander Hamilton said, "Nothing could be more ill-judged than that intolerant spirit which has at all time characterized political parties." Thomas Jefferson in 1789 also strongly opposed parties: "If I could not go to heaven but with a party, I would not go there at all." Yet it was Jefferson who, as early as 1792, was credited with helping form one of the first political parties in the nation, the Democratic-Republicans.

Political parties emerged in short order to become and remain an integral part of the U.S. system of government. They did so because today, as well as in the early years of the Republic, they satisfy an important need for American democracy. Parties bring people with the same beliefs together to govern at the local and national levels. In something as unwieldy as the U.S. Congress, composed of 535 individualistic members representing a wide range of constituents, parties provide the organizational structure and leadership necessary for forging coalitions and ruling the nation.

At nearly every moment in U.S. history there have been two major political parties in operation. Jefferson's Democratic-Republicans, who believed in locating power in the agrarian strongholds of the states, faced off against the Federalists, led by Hamilton, who advocated a strong federal government. The political tranquility that ensued after the Democratic-Republicans emerged victorious was quickly shattered by the appearance of Andrew Jackson and his even more democratic view that the common people, not the wealthy elite, should have the dominant voice in government. Arising in opposition to the Jacksonian Democrats, the Whig Party was a coalition of business, merchant, and conservative interests that opposed Jackson and advocated modernizing American society. In the face of slavery, which polarized the nation, the Whigs faded as a party and the Democrats were split for a time into northern and southern wings. The political void was filled by the ascendant Republican Party, which opposed the expansion of slavery. Led by Abraham Lincoln, the Republicans took control of the White House, Congress, and the vanquished South at the end of the Civil War.

Since the Civil War, the Democratic and Republican parties have been the only two major parties in the nation. Although control of the presidency has more frequently rotated between them, control of Congress has been held by one of the two parties for longer periods of time. Between the Civil War and the Great Depression of the 1930s, Republicans generally held majorities in both the Senate and the House of Representatives. From 1932 through 1994, Democrats usually controlled both chambers. The Republican Party recaptured majority control in Congress in the 1994 elections and remained in control through the elections of 2000. As 2001 began, however, Congress perhaps had never before been so evenly divided between the parties. The Senate was exactly split 50–50 (although nominally in Republican hands, with Vice President Richard Cheney as presiding officer able to cast tie-breaking votes), and majority control of the House of Representatives hung by only 5 seats out of 435.

Although U.S. history has consistently been dominated by two major parties, third parties also have had an important role in the political process. Minor parties have provided the forum for radical ideas, not accepted by the ruling parties of the day, to take root. Ideas such as the abolition of slavery, women's suffrage, minimum wages, and Social Security were first advocated by third parties, such as the Populists and Progressives, before they were finally adopted by the major parties and accepted by the nation as a whole.

Third-party candidates, occasionally elected as members of Congress or as governors of states, can also affect presidential politics. Independent candidate Ross Perot, with his battle cry of eradicating the federal deficit and balancing the budget, won 19 percent of the popular vote in 1992. Although most political observers believe Perot did not affect the outcome of the presidential election that brought Bill Clinton to the White House, the two major parties clearly took note of his message. By 2000 the Democrats and

Republicans vigorously supported a balanced budget, and Perot's Reform Party had slipped to winning less than 1 percent of the presidential vote.

The election of 2000 offered other examples of how the presence of third-party choices could determine the eventual outcome of a presidential contest. Some political commentators point out that Green Party candidate Ralph Nader's 3 percent of the vote, although a slim amount by historical standards, may have been the deciding factor in the extremely close and controversial presidential election. In Florida, which eventually went for Republican candidate and presidential winner George W. Bush, the margin of victory was a mere 537 votes. Nader, whose supporters traditionally lean Democratic, received 97,400 votes in Florida. However, other analysts counter that Reform Party candidate Pat Buchanan, whose supporters traditionally lean Republican, may have prevented Bush from winning a number of close states (whose total electoral votes equaled the electoral votes of Florida) that went to Democratic candidate Al Gore.

Although the candidacies of Nader and Buchanan may have, in effect, canceled each other out, it is still surprising that seven other third parties on the ballot in Florida received more than 600 votes. Arguably, any one these parties could have decided the election.

Organization of the Book

Political Parties in America is divided into three parts. Part I provides a brief overview of the development of the major parties, from the time when Jefferson and Hamilton formed the first two parties in the early 1790s to the present day. Included in this introduction is a survey of influential third parties.

Part II, the heart of the book, is an encyclopedic presentation of all major parties and noteworthy third parties in U.S. history. This section examines the origins, development, and major policy ideas of more than forty of the most important American political parties. In addition to long essays on the Democratic and Republican parties, there are entries on such notable third parties as the Anti-Masonic Party of the 1830s, the Know Nothing Party of the 1850s, Theodore Roosevelt's Bull Moose Party of 1912, and the Green and Reform parties of today.

Part III examines aspects of campaigns and elections, the roads that parties follow to attain power. Campaigning has evolved into a distinctly American art form—candidates reaching out to voters through stump speeches, political buttons and slogans, and television ads. Political parties actively assist candidates with campaign advice and financial aid—which in the increasingly expensive modern era has become crucial for victory. This section discusses campaign finance, political action committees, and recent proposals for reform. It also takes a close look at significant presidential elections, those watershed and landslide events that have changed the course of American society.

Part III ends with two long discussions of presidential primaries and nominating conventions. Primaries, introduced early in the twentieth century to reduce the power of corrupt "party bosses" by giving the choice of the party nominee to party members as a whole, have had the unintended effect of weakening the parties. Because party leaders no longer control who runs for office, congressional and presidential candidates can bypass the established party leadership and appeal directly to voters. The final entry on nominating conventions briefly traces the history of such gatherings from their first appearance, in 1831, to the most recent, in 2000. Even though they no longer are crucial to the selection of the presidential ticket, conventions have endured because they continue to perform many needed functions—such as bringing the party together before a televised audience to nominate the presidential ticket, approve the platform, reconcile any internal party differences, and throw a huge political rally.

The appendix contains several helpful tables for quickly locating political facts on U.S. history, including a list of U.S. presidents and vice presidents; political party affiliations and election results in Congress and the presidency; and all presidential and vice presidential party nominees from 1831 to 2000. A detailed index completes the volume.

political parties in america

part I

political parties in america

Political Parties

Political parties are organizations that seek to gain control of government to further their social, economic, or ideological goals. The United States has usually had a two-party system, dominated since 1860 by the Democratic and Republican Parties. Yet more than eighty political parties have formed since the 1790s, and "third parties" have occasionally had a decisive impact on presidential elections. For example, in 1912 the "Bull Moose Party" of former president Theodore Roosevelt siphoned enough Republican votes from the incumbent, William Howard Taft, to enable the Democrat, Woodrow Wilson, to win the election.

The United States did not start out with a two-party system—or any parties at all. Initially there were no formal parties, and in the early 1820s the nation had in effect only one party. The Founders did not anticipate parties—which they derisively called factions—and this central aspect of American politics was unplanned and had no formal constitutional or legal status. Indeed, having seen the ill effects of overzealous parties in monarchical England and (beginning in 1789) revolutionary France, the Founders hoped to avoid similar pitfalls in the fledgling nation. Thus, in *Federalist 10* James Madison bragged that one of the Constitution's great virtues was that it would head off "the mischiefs of faction." In 1789 Thomas Jefferson declared: "If I could not go to heaven but with a party, I would not go there at all." Similarly, in his farewell address in 1796 George Washington warned that, in elective popular governments, the dangers of excess in the "spirit of party" demanded "a uniform vigilance to prevent its bursting into a flame."

By the time Washington issued his warning, he was the titular head of the Federalist Party, which faded after 1800 and, except for some local office-holders, was dead by 1821. Meanwhile, since 1794 Madison and Jefferson had been the leaders of another party, variously called the Democratic-Republicans, the Jeffersonian Democrats, and the Jeffersonian Republicans, but today understood as the kernel of what became the modern Democratic Party.

Political Issues and the Emergence of Parties

The debate over ratification of the Constitution led to the organization of factions but not parties. Future Democratic-Republicans and Federalists,

Political parties emerged in part from differences over policy in President George Washington's cabinet. Left to right: President Washington, Secretary of War Henry Knox, Secretary of the Treasury Alexander Hamilton, Secretary of State Thomas Jefferson, and Attorney General Edmund Randolph. *Library of Congress*

like Madison and Alexander Hamilton, worked together for ratification, just as future Democratic-Republicans and Federalists, like James Monroe and Samuel Chase, worked against ratification of the Constitution.

Ratification brought about a new national government, where parties were unknown. Presidential electors unanimously elected Washington as the first president, and nearly half of them supported Adams, who was easily elected vice president. Washington's cabinet included future leaders of the nation's first two parties: the future Federalist leader Alexander Hamilton and the future leader of the Democratic-Republicans, Thomas Jefferson.

By the end of Washington's administration two parties were fully engaged in politics. The parties differed over the nature of public policy and the interpretation of the Constitution. The Federalists, led by Hamilton, John Adams, and John Jay, favored a national government vigorously involved in economic development. Key to the Federalist program was the establishment of a national bank, federal funding at face value of all state and national bonds issued during the Revolution, and a flexible interpretation of the Constitution. The Federalists also wanted to strengthen diplomatic and commercial ties with England.

Jefferson's followers, called Democratic-Republicans at this time, opposed funding the war debts at par because many of the original bond holders had sold their bonds at depreciated values to speculators. Their hostility to commerce and business also led them to oppose the establishment of a national bank. Unsuccessful on these issues, the Democratic-Republicans were nonetheless able to thwart Hamilton's plan to use high tariffs to stimulate commerce and manufacturing in the new country. Jefferson and his followers wanted a strict interpretation of the Constitution, favored states' rights over national power, and in foreign policy supported France in its wars with England.

On issues involving race, slavery, and foreign policy, the parties also differed. The Federalists favored giving full diplomatic recognition to Haiti, a black republic in the Caribbean, and refused to seek the return of slaves who had escaped with the British at the end of the Revolution. Jefferson, by contrast, unsuccessfully demanded the return of the slaves but was successful as president in blocking any diplomatic ties to Haiti.

Presidents, Parties, and Policies, 1800–1860

By the time of Jefferson's election in 1800, ending twelve years of Federalist control, the party concept was entrenched in U.S. politics. Despite his previous denunciation of parties, Jefferson justified his own party leadership as a necessary opposition to the "Monocrats of our country." Jefferson's election by the House, after a tie electoral vote between him and Aaron Burr, led to adoption of the Twelfth Amendment to the Constitution in 1804. That amendment, which required electors to vote separately for president and vice president, further buried the likelihood of "partyless" U.S. elections.

Federalists nearly won the presidency in 1800 and 1812, but the party quickly withered after the War of 1812, when many party leaders opposed the war and flirted with secession, most notably at the Hartford Convention of 1814–1815. Federalists made a brief comeback in 1819–1820 during the debates over allowing slavery in Missouri on its admission to the

Union, but the party was effectively dead by the end of 1820, when James Monroe ran unopposed for reelection.

A system with only one party was less stable than a system with two or more parties. In 1824 four candidates competed for the presidency, with no one getting a majority of the popular or the electoral vote. The House of Representatives chose John Quincy Adams, who ran second in both categories. Andrew Jackson, who had led in popular and electoral votes, immediately began his campaign for the presidency, and he won in 1828. In 1832 the Anti-Masonic Party made its brief appearance, winning seven electoral votes, while Jackson was easily reelected. Jackson inherited the mantle of Jefferson and his party, while his political and personal opponents, such as Daniel Webster, Henry Clay, and John Quincy Adams, migrated in the 1830s to the newly formed Whig Party. In 1836 four Whigs, representing different regions of the country, competed for the presidency against Jackson's heir, Martin Van Buren.

The Whigs won the presidency in 1840 and 1848; Democrats won in 1836, 1844, 1852, and 1856. The Whigs favored a national bank, federal support for internal improvements, national bankruptcy laws, protective tariffs, and a relatively humane policy toward American Indians. The Democrats disagreed with all these positions. Whigs opposed territorial acquisition, especially by force, whereas Democrats annexed Texas and eventually pushed the United States into a war with Mexico to gain new territory in the Southwest, advocating that it was the "manifest destiny" of the United States to control the continent. The Jacksonian Democrats pushed for universal adult white male suffrage throughout the country, but at the same time worked to take the vote away from free blacks and to strengthen slavery at the national and local level. Jackson's presidency is most remembered for his veto of the rechartering of the Second Bank of the United States, his successful opposition to internal improvements, and his policy of Indian removal, which pushed almost all Native Americans in the east into the Indian Territory (present-day Oklahoma). On an important issue that seemed to transcend party politics, Jackson vigorously opposed extreme states' rights ideology when South Carolina attempted to nullify a federal tariff. However, following the nullification crisis, the Democrats became increasingly solicitous of states' rights and the southern demands for protections for slavery. Jackson and his fellow Democrats also accepted the South

Carolinians' critique of the tariff, even as they rejected the Carolinians' response, nullification.

The nation had two major parties in the 1840s, but third parties influenced some elections. In 1844 the antislavery Liberty Party won enough votes in New York to cost the Whigs the state and the presidential election, assuming all the Liberty voters would have supported the Whigs. The Whig candidate, Henry Clay, opposed expansion and was more moderate on slavery than his opponent, but it seems unlikely that the committed abolitionists who voted for the Liberty Party would otherwise have voted for the slave-owning Clay as the lesser of two evils. In 1848, however, the Free Soil candidate, former president Martin Van Buren, won more than 290,000 votes, many of which would have otherwise gone to the Democratic candidate, Lewis Cass of Michigan. As a result, the Whig candidate, Gen. Zachary Taylor, won the election. Equally significant, Free Soilers won state and local races, and in Ohio they held the balance of power in the state legislature and were able to elect an antislavery Democrat, Salmon P. Chase, to the U.S. Senate.

Yet the victorious Whigs of 1848 managed to carry only four states in 1852, and the party disappeared two years later. The 1856 election saw two new parties emerge: the Know Nothing (American) Party and the Republican Party.

The Know Nothing, or American, Party was a single-issue party, opposed to immigration in general and Catholic immigration in particular. The Know Nothings won a number of governorships and dominated a few state legislatures, including Massachusetts, in this period. In 1856 the Speaker of the House of Representatives, Nathaniel Banks, was a Know Nothing.

The Republican Party adopted many Whig policies but opposed the extension of slavery into the western territories. Many Republican leaders were former Whigs, including Abraham Lincoln and his secretary of state, William H. Seward. Others came from the antislavery wing of the Democratic Party, among them Lincoln's vice president, Hannibal Hamlin, and secretary of the Treasury, Salmon P. Chase. By 1858 many Know Nothings had also joined this party. In 1856 the Republican candidate, John C. Fremont, and the Know Nothing candidate, Millard Fillmore, together won about 400,000 more popular votes than James Buchanan, but Buchanan had the

Illustration of the Republican nomination convention of 1860 that chose Abraham Lincoln for president.
Library of Congress

plurality of popular votes and, more important, carried nineteen states to win the election. Buchanan was the first "sectional" president since 1824, as fourteen of the states he carried were in the South. This election underscored that the Democrats had become the party of slavery and the South.

The proslavery southerners who controlled the Democratic Party insisted on fidelity to their program to expand slavery into the territories. This arrangement unraveled in 1860, as the Democrats split into two parties—regular Democrats nominating Stephen A. Douglas of Illinois and southern Democrats nominating John C. Breckinridge of Kentucky. The Republican candidate, Abraham Lincoln, carried every northern state. Moderates in the North and the South supported the Constitutional Union Party, which hoped to hold the Union together by not discussing any of the key issues. The two Democratic parties and the Constitutional Unionists combined for more popular votes than Lincoln (who was not even on the ballot in many southern states), but Lincoln carried eighteen states and easily won a majority of the electoral college.

Parties in U.S. Politics since 1860

Lincoln's victory set the stage for Republican dominance in national politics for the next half-century. During this period the Republicans stood at various times for preservation of the Union, homestead laws to facilitate western settlement, federal support for a transcontinental railroad, protective tariffs, abolition of slavery, guarantees of African Americans' civil rights, and the suppression of Mormon polygamists in the West. Democrats favored lower tariffs; opposed emancipation and civil rights; and championed white immigrants (but not immigrants from Asia), labor unions, and (at the end of the century) small farmers in the South and West. In international affairs, the late-nineteenth-century Republicans favored expansion, ultimately leading to war with Spain and the acquisition of an overseas empire, while Democrats opposed these trends, with Grover Cleveland (the only Democratic president in this period) refusing to annex Hawaii.

From 1868 to 1908 various third parties—including the Liberal Republican, Greenback, Prohibitionist, Equal Rights, Anti-Monopoly, Workers, Socialist Labor, Socialist, United Christian, and Populist Parties—ran candidates. With the exception of the Populists in 1892, however, none ever won any electoral votes. Some of these parties did, however, elect candidates to state and local office and to Congress. James B. Weaver, for example, ran successfully for Congress on the Greenback ticket in 1878, 1884, and 1886; ran for president on the Greenback ticket in 1880; and ran for president on the Populist ticket in 1892.

In 1912 a third party determined the outcome of the presidential race. The Republicans split as former president Theodore Roosevelt tried, and failed, to gain renomination after a term out of the White House. Roosevelt thought that his successor, William Howard Taft, had abandoned the progressive goals of the party. Running on the Progressive ("Bull Moose") ticket, Roosevelt carried six states and won about half a million more popular votes than Taft. Together they outpolled Wilson, but Wilson carried forty states and won the election. The Socialist candidate, Eugene V. Debs, won nearly a million votes in the 1912 election, and, although he carried no states, Socialists won various local elections and sent some party members to Congress. Victor Berger of Milwaukee, for example, served in Congress as a Socialist from 1911 to 1913 and from 1923 to 1929. He was also

Franklin D. Roosevelt's presidential victory in 1932 ushered in an era of Democratic control of the federal government.   *File photo*

elected in 1918, but in that year Congress refused to allow him to take his seat because of his opposition to World War I.

Between the 1910s and the 1940s, Democrats became increasingly internationalist, while Republicans opposed American entrance into the League of Nations after World War I and were isolationist in the 1930s as the world moved toward a second world war. Democratic support came from labor, white southerners, and most northern urban immigrant groups. By the 1930s, blacks began to leave the Republican Party, forced out by "lily white" Republicans in the South and welcomed into the emerging New Deal coalition. The Republicans by this time had become the party of conservative business interests, white Protestants (outside the South), small town and rural northerners, and owners of small businesses.

Various third parties ran presidential candidates in the 1920s and 1930s, but only Robert M. La Follette, running as the Progressive Party candidate in 1924, won any electoral votes. In 1948, though, southern "Dixiecrats," who abandoned the Democratic Party to protest President Harry S. Truman's support for civil rights and racial equality, took four Deep South states. Some other Democrats supported former vice president Henry A. Wallace, running on the Progressive ticket that year. Despite these defections, Truman won. At the state and local level, third parties were sometimes successful, and various candidates running on socialist, communist, or various other tickets sporadically held office. For example, Wisconsin elected Progressives Robert M. La Follette Jr. to the Senate in 1934 and 1940 and Merlin Hull to the House from 1934 to 1944. Benjamin J. Davis, running as a Communist, served on the New York City Council as the "Communist Councilman from Harlem," while Vito Marcantonio, who had served one term in Congress as a Republican (1935–1937), served six terms in Congress (1939–1951) running on the ticket of the American Labor Party, which had Communist Party support. Independents also had some success; Henry F. Reams of Ohio, for example, served two full terms in the House (1951–1955).

By the 1960s, Republicans and Democrats had swapped places on the issue of African Americans' civil rights since a hundred years earlier. In 1964 large numbers of white southerners left the Democratic Party over President Lyndon Johnson's support for civil rights. Since then the Democratic constituency has generally comprised urban, northern, and far western liberals; Catholics and Jews; African Americans, Hispanics, Asian-Americans, and ethnic minorities; blue-collar workers; and the underprivileged. Republicans are viewed as conservatives, southerners, white Protestants, and the affluent.

Third parties continued to run presidential candidates, and in some places candidates for Congress and state and local offices. In the 1960s John Lindsey, a former Republican congressman, was elected mayor of New York City on the Liberal Party line, and in 1970 James L. Buckley won a U.S. Senate seat from New York, running on the Conservative Party line. But third-party candidates have also been spoilers, as in 1980 when incumbent Republican senator Jacob Javits of New York lost his party's nomination and ran as a Liberal Party candidate, dividing the votes of moderates, liberals, and Democrats and thus allowing for the election of conservative Republican Alfonse D'Amato.

George C. Wallace, running in 1968 as the presidential candidate of the segregationist American Independent Party, captured five states in the

South. Most of his supporters voted Republican in subsequent elections. In 1980 former U.S. representative John Anderson ran on the National Unity Party ticket and carried more than 5 million popular votes, but he did not affect the election of Ronald Reagan. In 1992 H. Ross Perot ran as an independent and won almost 20 million votes, and he may have cost the incumbent, George Herbert Walker Bush, a few states. Perot influenced policy in the 1990s by highlighting the importance of the national debt and thus nudging a change in policy that brought balanced budgets and a declining debt by the end of the decade. When he ran again in 1996, however, he had no effect on the election. In 1998 Jesse Ventura, a former professional wrestler running on Perot's Reform Party ticket, was elected governor of Minnesota. In 2000 Ralph Nader, running on the Green Party ticket, won enough votes in several states to give their electoral college votes to Gov. George W. Bush instead of Vice President Al Gore.

Party Systems

Historians and political scientists often use the concept "party systems" to refer to eras that more or less hang together in terms of major party alignment. The first, from 1789 to approximately 1824, marked the emergence of a two-party system and lasted from Washington's presidency through the end of the "Virginia Dynasty." The second, from 1828 through 1854, marked the years from Jackson's elections through the demise of the Whig Party. The third, from 1856 through 1896, marked the emergence of the Republican Party and its rise to dominance. The 1896 election marked a transition to a period that featured the Progressive era and persisted through World War I and the 1920s. The election of Franklin D. Roosevelt in 1932 marked another great electoral realignment, although the Democrats occasionally lost the presidency or one or both chambers of Congress in the years that followed.

In the sixty-eight-year period from 1933 through 2001, Democrats held the White House for forty years. The exceptions were the eight Eisenhower years (1953–1961), the eight Nixon-Ford years (1969–1977), and the twelve Reagan-Bush years (1981–1993). In Congress, Democratic dominance was even more striking. Democrats controlled the House for all but four years (1947–1949 and 1953–1955) from 1933 until the Republican takeover of both chambers in 1995. Democratic control of the Senate was

Shortly after the 1996 congressional elections, newly elected senators Robert Torricelli, D-N.J., and Susan Collins, R-Maine, shake hands as Senate Majority Leader Trent Lott, R-Miss. (center), and Minority Leader Tom Daschle, D-S.D. (right), look on.   *Scott J. Ferrell, Congressional Quarterly*

less consistent, with four periods of Republican majorities totaling sixteen years between 1933 and 2001. During this period third-party candidates became increasingly insignificant, although in 2000 one "socialist" and one "independent" served in the House.

Internal Party Politics

Although all presidents since 1852 have been either Democrats or Republicans, their parties have sometimes borrowed ideas from third parties that quickly faded from the U.S. political scene. For example, the Democrats under Andrew Jackson in 1832 followed the example of the Anti-Masons in holding a national convention to nominate their presidential candidate. Previously, party caucuses in Congress, called King Caucus, chose their nominees in secret meetings. The 1824 election of John Quincy Adams, nominated by the Massachusetts legislature, spelled the end of King Caucus. The House decided the election when none of the four candidates, all Democratic-Republicans, failed to win the required electoral vote majority. The 1828 election, won by Jackson, marked a transition to the as-yet-unborn convention system.

National nominating conventions have remained a staple of the political party system, but they have been more show than substance in the age of primaries and television. With the presumptive nominee known well in advance, the convention nomination is a formality, although the convention still has the important duty of writing a party platform.

The Democratic convention of 1952, which chose Adlai Stevenson to oppose Republican Dwight D. Eisenhower, was the most recent to require more than one ballot to select a nominee. Multiple ballots were common earlier, particularly at Democratic conventions because of the party's rule requiring a two-thirds majority for nomination. Democrats dropped the rule, never used by Republicans, in 1936.

The primary system was a creation of the Progressive era of the early twentieth century. Progressive governor Robert M. La Follette of Wisconsin pushed through a state primary law in 1905, but few other states followed suit until after 1968. Primary elections and caucuses became the de facto presidential nominating mechanisms after the tumultuous 1968 Democratic convention, won by Hubert H. Humphrey without entering any primaries. As the Democrats strengthened their primary rules in the 1970s and 1980s, primaries proliferated in both parties, and they came earlier and earlier in the election year. In 1996 more than forty states held presidential primaries, most of them before April. In 2000 Al Gore and George W. Bush had locked up their nominations early in the primary season.

Federal and state campaign finance reforms enacted since the 1970s have both helped and hindered political parties. Beginning in 1976 presidential candidates became eligible for public financing of their campaigns, which reduced their reliance on money from party coffers. However, the legislation allowed "soft money," contributions given directly to the parties, ostensibly for party building but often diverted to indirect support for the party's candidate. The reform legislation also permitted interest groups and candidates to form political action committees (PACs) to raise and spend money for campaigns. This further reduced candidates' dependence on the political parties, with the result that more and more campaigns are candidate-centered rather than party-centered.

Third Parties

Although the United States has always had a two-party system, third parties have frequently played a vital role in the political order. No third-party candidate has ever been elected to the presidency, but many have been elected to other federal, state, and local offices. The votes third parties have garnered have also been a crucial factor in the outcome of elections. Moreover, the issues spotlighted by minor parties have often ended up being co-opted into the platforms of the major parties.

Nineteenth-Century Third Parties

As the original party system of Hamiltonian Federalists and Jeffersonian Democratic-Republicans broke down, and the National Republican Party developed and transformed itself into the Whig Party, there also arose the Anti-Masonic Party, which ran William Wirt for president in 1832, gaining almost 8 percent of the popular vote. Nonetheless, they achieved some state and local offices, particularly in New York State, where the party originated.

In 1844 the Liberty Party, which opposed slavery, won 2.3 percent of the popular vote, although it did not affect the outcome of the election. In 1848, however, the less radical Free Soil Party, which was dedicated to stopping the spread of slavery in the territories, played the role of spoiler. Running former president Martin Van Buren, the party won enough votes, mostly from Democrats, to enable the Whig candidate, Zachary Taylor, to defeat the Democrat, Lewis Cass. It ran John P. Hale for president in 1852, obtaining 5 percent of the popular vote. The demise of the Free Soil Party was caused primarily by the rise of the Republican Party, which took up its stance in opposition to slavery in the territories.

In the 1850s the American Party, otherwise known as the Know Nothing Party, reaped large votes in Pennsylvania and New York and even briefly gained control over the Massachusetts government. The party's main goals were excluding Catholics from public office, enacting restrictive immigration laws, and establishing literacy tests for voting.

Parties such as the Greenback Party (1876–1884) and the Prohibition Party, which started in 1869 and has continued ever since, never attracted many votes on the national level, but their success rested in convincing one of the major parties to take up their cause. Eventually the Republican Party embraced Prohibition, while the Democratic Party espoused the expansion

William Wirt. *Library of Congress*

of the money supply, albeit with the free coinage of silver rather than by printing greenbacks.

The Populist (or People's) Party, which represented the interests of farmers and labor, arose in the South and West in the 1880s. Because it spoke for a perennial debtor class, the party tended to favor the free coinage of silver and backed free trade and the regulation of the railroads. The Populist platform would eventually be adopted by the Democratic Party under its 1896 presidential candidate, William Jennings Bryan.

Third Parties in the Twentieth Century

The Socialist Party came to prominence in the Progressive era, with members winning state and local offices and serving in Congress. In 1904 it ran Eugene V. Debs for president, winning 3 percent of the vote against the Republican incumbent Theodore Roosevelt and Alton B. Parker, the Democrat. Debs would run again in 1908, 1912, and 1920, and in this last election (campaigning from a federal penitentiary, where he was imprisoned for opposition to World War I) he tallied 915,490 votes (3.4 percent). Later, Norman Thomas would serve as the Socialist Party standard bearer in several elections, with his largest vote in 1932 when he won 884,649 votes (2.2 percent). Before World War I, socialist Victor Berger served as mayor of Milwaukee, and he served as a member of the House of Representatives from 1911 to 1913 and from 1923 to 1929.

Although they lack the long-term ideological impact of the third parties described above, some minor parties have served as vehicles for the candidacies of certain individuals. The Progressive (or Bull Moose) Party became a vehicle for Theodore Roosevelt's attempt to recapture the White House in

1912, running against Democrat Woodrow Wilson and Republican William Howard Taft. In that race, all three candidates were Progressives to an extent. When Taft's people prevented Roosevelt delegates from some states from being seated at the Republican convention, Roosevelt bolted the party and ran as a Progressive. The result was a split of the Republican vote and a victory for Wilson.

In 1924 the Progressive Party ran Robert M. La Follette for president, capturing 16.6 percent of the vote. In 1948, using the Progressive Party label, Henry A. Wallace, Franklin D. Roosevelt's former vice president and secretary of agriculture, scored 2.4 percent of the vote in a four-way race that saw Harry Truman reelected. Wallace ran to the left of Truman on both domestic and foreign affairs, where he pushed for greater cooperation with the Soviet Union. The 1948 election also saw the emergence of another third party, the States' Rights, or Dixiecrat, Party. The Dixiecrats ran J. Strom Thurmond, the governor of South Carolina, for president, opposing the Democratic Party's adoption of a civil rights plank in its 1948 platform. Thurmond won 2.4 percent of the vote.

In the close 1968 presidential race between Richard M. Nixon and Hubert H. Humphrey, George C. Wallace, the governor of Alabama, captured 13.5 percent of the popular vote and forty-six electoral votes. He ran on the American Independent ticket, pushing a conservative and somewhat racist agenda. In 1980 John B. Anderson ran on an independent line against Ronald Reagan and Jimmy Carter and received 6.6 percent of the

The Green Party candidacy of Ralph Nader (above) may have helped Republican George W. Bush defeat Democrat Al Gore in the close presidential race in 2000. *File photo*

popular vote but no electoral votes. In 1992 H. Ross Perot created the Reform Party and ran for president under its banner, receiving 18.9 percent of the vote but no electoral votes. This party has run candidates for state and local office across the country, and in 1998 Jesse Ventura was elected governor of Minnesota on the Reform Party line. In 2000 the Reform Party seemed destined for oblivion as it split down the middle over the contested nomination of Patrick J. Buchanan for president.

Today the Libertarian Party and the Green Party offer fairly consistent ideologies through their third-party movements. Because they are primarily ideologically based, however, they are the more likely to be absorbed eventually by a major party that has co-opted their ideas and raided their constituencies.

Finally, one must consider the regional and state-based third-party movements, although these are too numerous to consider in any detail. The Liberal, Conservative, and Right to Life Parties of New York State provide excellent examples of such movements. Each has had a significant influence on state politics, and the Conservative Party even elected James L. Buckley as U.S. senator in 1970. The Farmer Labor Party had similar success in the politics of Minnesota. Usually, however, such parties depend on the election law permitting cross-endorsements of candidates from the major parties.

part II

american parties a to z

American Independent Party (1968–) and American Party (1972–)

Both the American Party and the American Independent Party descended from the American Independent Party that served as the vehicle for George C. Wallace's third-party presidential candidacy in 1968.

Wallace, governor of Alabama (1963–1967; 1971–1979), burst onto the national scene in 1964 as a Democratic presidential candidate opposed to the 1964 Civil Rights Act. Entering three northern primaries—Wisconsin, Indiana, and Maryland—he surprised political observers by winning between 30 percent and 43 percent of the popular vote in the three states. His unexpectedly strong showing brought the term "white backlash" into the political vocabulary as a description of the racial undertone of the Wallace vote.

In 1968 Wallace broke with the Democrats and embarked on his second presidential campaign as a third-party candidate under the American Independent Party label. His candidacy capitalized on the bitter reactions of millions of voters, especially whites and blue-collar workers, to the civil rights activism, urban riots, antiwar demonstrations, and heavy federal spending on Johnson administration "Great Society" programs that marked the mid-1960s. With the help of his Alabama advisers and volunteer groups, Wallace was able to get his party on the ballot in all fifty states.

The former governor did not hold a convention for his party, but in October he announced his vice-presidential running mate (retired air force general Curtis LeMay) and released a platform. In the November election the

George Wallace. *File photo*

Wallace-LeMay ticket received 9,906,473 votes (13.5 percent of the popular vote), carried five southern states, and won forty-six electoral votes. The party's showing was the best by a third party since 1924, when Robert M. La Follette collected 16.6 percent of the vote on the Progressive Party ticket.

After his defeat in that election, Wallace returned to the Democratic Party, competing in Democratic presidential primaries in 1972 and 1976. Wallace's American Independent Party began to break into factions after the 1968 election but in 1972 united behind John G. Schmitz, a Republican U.S. representative from southern California (1970–1973), as its presidential nominee. Thomas J. Anderson, a farm magazine and syndicated news features publisher from Tennessee, was the party's vice-presidential candidate. In many states, the party shortened its name to American Party. In the November election, the Schmitz-Anderson ticket won 1,099,482 votes (1.4 percent of the popular vote) but failed to win any electoral votes. The ticket ran best in the West, taking 9 percent of the vote in Idaho, 7 percent in Alaska, and 6 percent in Utah.

In December 1972 a bitter fight occurred for the chairmanship of the American Independent Party between Anderson and William K. Shearer, the California chairman of the party. Anderson defeated Shearer, retaining control of the party but renaming it the American Party. Shearer, over the following four years, expanded his California-based group into a new national party. He had kept the name American Independent Party in California and made that the name of the new nationwide group.

By 1976 there were two distinct entities: the American Party headed by Anderson and the American Independent Party headed by Shearer.

The 1976 American Party convention was held in Salt Lake City, Utah, in June. Anderson was nominated for president and Rufus Shackleford of Florida for vice president.

The party's nomination of Anderson followed its failure to enlist a prominent conservative to lead the ticket. Both Gov. Meldrim Thomson Jr. of New Hampshire and Sen. Jesse Helms of North Carolina were approached, but both decided to remain in the Republican Party. With well-known conservatives declining the party's overtures, the convention turned to Anderson. He easily won the nomination on the first ballot by defeating six party workers.

Anderson's campaign stressed the "permanent principles" of the party, augmented by the 1976 platform. These principles included opposition to foreign aid, U.S. withdrawal from the United Nations, and an end to trade with or recognition of communist nations. The platform included planks opposing abortion, gun control, the Equal Rights Amendment, and government-sponsored health care and welfare programs. In general, the party favored limits on federal power and was against budget deficits except in wartime.

The American Party was on the ballot in eighteen states, including eight states where the American Independent Party was also. In seven of those eight states, Anderson ran ahead of the American Independent Party ticket. Anderson's strength was spread fairly evenly across the country. His best showings were in Utah (2.5 percent of the vote) and Montana (1.8 percent). Anderson's total of 160,773 popular votes (0.2 percent) placed him almost 10,000 votes behind the American Independent Party candidate nationally.

The American Independent Party convention met in Chicago in August 1976 and chose former Georgia governor Lester Maddox (1967–1971), a Democrat, as its presidential nominee and former Madison, Wisconsin, mayor William Dyke, a Republican, as its vice-presidential candidate. Maddox won a first-ballot nomination over Dallas columnist Robert Morris and former representative John R. Rarick, a Democrat of Louisiana (1967–1975).

At the convention, a group of nationally prominent conservatives made a bid to take over the party and use it as a vehicle to build a new conservative coalition. Richard Viguerie, a fund-raiser for Wallace and a nationally known direct mail expert, was the leader of the group. He was joined at the convention by two leading conservatives—William Rusher, publisher of the *National Review,* and Howard Phillips, the former head of the Office of Economic Opportunity (1973) and leader of the Conservative Caucus, an activist conservative group. Viguerie, Phillips, and Rusher all argued that the American Independent Party should be overhauled, changed from a fringe group to a philosophical home for believers in free enterprise and traditional moral values. They also hoped they could attract Sen. Helms, Gov. Thomson, or Rep. Philip M. Crane, R-Ill. When none of these men agreed to run on the American Independent Party ticket, Viguerie and his allies found themselves unable to promote Morris, a lesser-known substitute, successfully.

Many American Independent Party members favored Maddox because they saw him as a colorful personality, one capable of drawing media attention and perhaps of picking up the 5 percent of the national vote needed to qualify the party for federal funding. Maddox never came close to that goal, however, achieving only 0.2 percent of the national vote (170,531). It was 51,098 votes in California, where American Party nominee Anderson was not on the ballot, that enabled Maddox to run slightly ahead of Anderson nationally.

Despite the power struggle between Anderson and Shearer, there was little difference between their two party platforms. Like the American Party, the American Independent Party opposed abortion, gun control, forced busing, foreign aid, and membership in the United Nations.

By 1980 neither party was much of a force in American politics. Both retained the same basic platforms, but each was on the ballot in only a handful of states. The American Independent Party's nominee, former Democratic representative Rarick, ran in only eight states. Economist Percy L. Greaves Jr., the American Party candidate, was listed in just seven.

The American Independent Party did not field a presidential candidate in 1984, while the American Party placed Delmar Dennis, a book publisher from Pigeon Forge, Tennessee, on the ballot in six states.

Dennis also ran under the American Party banner in 1988 and, with his running mate, Earl Jeppson, received 3,475 votes. The American Independent Party fared better with their candidates, presidential nominee James C. Griffin and vice-presidential nominee Charles J. Morsa, receiving 27,818 votes.

By 1992 fortunes for both parties had dwindled. American Party presidential nominee Robert J. Smith and running mate Doris Feimer were on the ballot only in Utah, where they received 292 votes. In 1996 the American Party ticket of Diane Beall Templin and Gary Van Horn made the ballot in two states, Colorado and Utah, and collected a total of 1,847 votes. The American Independent Party did not appear on any presidential ballots in the 1990s.

Anti-Federalists (1789–1796)

Never a formal party, the Anti-Federalists were a loosely organized group opposed to ratification of the Constitution. With the ratification of the

Constitution in 1788, the Anti-Federalists served as the opposition to the Federalists in the early years of Congress.

Anti-Federalists were primarily rural, agrarian men from inland regions who favored individual freedom and states' rights, which they felt would be jeopardized by the new Constitution. After ratification, the efforts of the Anti-Federalists led to adoption of the first ten amendments, the Bill of Rights, which spelled out the major limitations on federal power.

As the opposition faction in Congress during the formative years of the Republic, the Anti-Federalists basically held to a strict interpretation of the Constitution, particularly in regard to the various economic proposals of Treasury Secretary Alexander Hamilton to centralize more power in the federal government.

Although never the majority faction in Congress, the Anti-Federalists were a forerunner of Thomas Jefferson's Democratic-Republican Party, which came into existence in the 1790s and dominated American politics for the first quarter of the nineteenth century.

Anti-Masonic Party (1828–1836)

Born in the mid-1820s in upstate New York, the Anti-Masonic Party focused the strong, antielitist mood of the period on a conspicuous symbol of privilege, the Masons. The Masons were a secret fraternal organization with membership drawn largely from the upper class. Conversely, the appeal of the Anti-Masonic movement was to the common man—poor farmers and laborers especially—who resented the secrecy and privilege of the Masons.

The spark that created the party came in 1826, when William Morgan, a dissident Mason from Batavia, New York, allegedly on the verge of exposing the inner workings of the order, mysteriously disappeared and never was seen again. Refusal of Masonic leaders to cooperate in the inconclusive investigation of Morgan's disappearance led to suspicions that Masons had kidnapped and murdered him and were suppressing the inquiry.

From 1828 through 1831, the new Anti-Masonic Party spread through New England and the Middle Atlantic states, in many places establishing itself as the primary opposition to the Democrats. In addition to its appeal to the working classes, particularly in northern rural areas, and its opposition to Masonry, the Anti-Masons displayed a fervor against immorality, as seen not only in secret societies but also in slavery, intemperance, and urban life.

In September 1831 the party held the first national nominating convention in American history. One hundred and sixteen delegates from thirteen states gathered in Baltimore, Maryland, and nominated former Attorney General William Wirt of Maryland for the presidency. In the 1832 elections, Wirt received only 100,715 votes (7.8 percent of the popular vote) and carried just one state, Vermont, but it was the first third party in U.S. politics to win any electoral college votes. The Anti-Masons did reasonably well at other levels, winning the Vermont governorship several years and competing in close elections in a few other states. In the U.S. House they had fifteen members in the 22nd Congress (1831–1833) and twenty-four in the 23rd Congress (1833–1835).

But the decline of Masonry, especially in New York, where the number of lodges dropped from 507 in 1826 to 48 six years later, robbed the Anti-Masons of an emotional issue and hastened their decline. The 1832 election was the high point for the Anti-Masons as a national party. In the 1836 campaign the party endorsed Whig candidate William Henry Harrison. Subsequently, the bulk of the Anti-Masonic constituency moved into the Whig Party. In 1836 the major parties also held their own conventions and wrote their own platforms. Despite its short life, the Anti-Masons were one of the most important American third parties, contributing to the openness of the system and establishing party platforms and conventions as part of modern political practices.

Breckinridge (Southern) Democrats (1860)

Agitation over the slavery issue, building for a generation, reached a climax in 1860 and produced a sectional split in the Democratic Party. Throughout the mid-nineteenth century the Democrats had remained unified by supporting the various pieces of compromise legislation that both protected slavery in the southern states and endorsed the policy of popular sovereignty in the territories. But in 1860 southern Democrats wanted the Democratic convention (meeting in Charleston, S.C.) to insert a plank specifically protecting slavery in the territories. When their plank was defeated,

delegates from most of the southern states walked out.

The northern wing of the party,
after recessing for six weeks, reconvened in Baltimore, where Illinois senator Stephen A. Douglas of
Illinois was nominated as its presidential candidate. Most of the
southern delegates, plus those
from California and Oregon, nominated their own ticket in a rump
convention held after Douglas's
selection. John C. Breckinridge
(1821–1875) of Kentucky, the incumbent vice president under President James Buchanan, accepted
the southern wing's nomination.
Joseph Lane, a states' rights advocate from Oregon, was selected as
his running mate. After the formation of the two sectional tickets,

John C. Breckinridge. *Library of Congress*

two separate Democratic national committees operated in Washington,
D.C., to oversee their campaigns.

The platforms of the Douglas and Breckinridge Democrats agreed that
the Fugitive Slave Law must be enforced, but the Breckinridge Democrats
also insisted on a federal slave code for the territories and on the right of
slaveholders to take their slave property into the western territories, decisions that the Douglas platform said it would leave to the Supreme Court
and that the Republican Party and its candidate, Abraham Lincoln, ab-
solutely opposed. The four-way election also included John Bell of the Constitutional Union Party.

The Breckinridge ticket placed third in popular votes behind Lincoln and
Douglas, receiving 848,019 votes (18.1 percent of the popular vote) and
winning eleven of the fifteen slave states, and second in electoral votes with
seventy-two. Although the combined Douglas-Breckinridge vote comprised
a plurality of the ballots cast, the split in Democratic ranks was a boon to
the campaign of the Republican candidate, Abraham Lincoln, who won

with less than 40 percent of the vote. Lincoln's victory in the electoral college, however, did not depend on a divided opposition, for he took an absolute majority in enough northern states to win regardless. Breckinridge's support came mostly from the South, although it did not necessarily reflect the degree of proslavery sentiment in the region, since some voters who later supported secession voted for Douglas or Bell, and many of Breckinridge's supporters were traditional Democrats who did not see themselves as voting on secession. Indeed, Breckinridge saw himself as the only candidate who could prevent secession, since if he won, the South would happily remain in the Union.

Lincoln's election led to secession by seven Deep South states, and four more joined the Confederacy soon after his inauguration. Before Lincoln's inauguration, Vice President Breckinridge worked with other Democrats in Washington to fashion a compromise that might prevent a civil war. On the main point of contention, however, slavery in the territories, Lincoln would not budge, so no settlement could be reached. Breckinridge, while still vice president, had been elected to the U.S. Senate, his term to begin when his vice presidency ended. As a senator in 1861 he defended the right of southern states to secede and opposed Lincoln's efforts to raise an army.

By late 1861 Union and Confederate forces alike had entered Kentucky, and Breckinridge offered his services to the Confederacy. He resigned from the Senate before it expelled him for his pro-Confederate behavior. He served as a major general in the Confederate army and then as Confederate secretary of war. During the war the Southern Democrats provided much of the leadership for the Confederate government, including its president, Jefferson Davis.

When the war ended with the Confederacy's defeat and slavery's abolition, the particular issues that had animated Breckinridge's presidential bid in 1860 no longer mattered. The Southern Democrats made no attempt to continue as a separate sectional entity and rejoined the national Democratic Party.

Citizens Party (1979–1984)

Organized in 1979 as a coalition of dissident liberals and populists, the first Citizens Party convention chose author and environmental scientist Barry

Commoner as its 1980 presidential candidate and La Donna Harris, wife of former Democratic senator Fred R. Harris of Oklahoma, as his running mate. The Citizens Party ticket ran on the central theme that major decisions in America were made to benefit corporations and not the average citizen. The party proposed public control of energy industries and multinational corporations; a halt to the use of nuclear power; a sharp cut in military spending; and price controls on food, fuel, housing, and health care.

Commoner ran in all of the large electoral vote states except Florida and Texas. He made his biggest push in California, Illinois, Michigan, New York, and Pennsylvania, where party leaders believed they could tap a "sophisticated working-class population" and appeal to political activists who had been involved in the environmental and antinuclear movements that sprang up in the late 1970s.

The Commoner-Harris ticket was on the ballot in twenty-nine states and the District of Columbia in 1980. Party leaders asserted that it was the largest number of ballot positions attained by any third party in its first campaign. In addition to its presidential ticket, the Citizens Party also fielded twenty-two candidates for other offices, including two for the U.S. Senate and seven for the House. The Citizens Party won 234,294 votes in the 1980 presidential election, or 0.3 percent of the vote.

As its 1984 presidential nominee, the Citizens Party chose outspoken feminist Sonia Johnson of Virginia. Johnson first attracted national attention in 1979, when the Mormon Church excommunicated her for supporting the Equal Rights Amendment (ERA). In 1982 she staged a thirty-seven-day hunger strike in an unsuccessful effort to pressure the Illinois legislature to approve the ERA. The Citizens Party selected party activist Richard J. Walton of Rhode Island to accompany Johnson on the ticket. Winning 72,200 votes in 1984, the ticket garnered 0.1 percent of the vote. That was the last year that the Citizens Party fielded a national ticket.

Communist Party (1919–)

In 1919, shortly after the Russian Revolution, Soviet communists encouraged American left-wing groups to withdraw from the Socialist Party and to form a communist party in the United States. The party arose at that time as part of the social and economic turmoil that followed World War I and the Bolshevik Revolution in Russia. Two major organizations emerged from the American Socialist Party: the larger Communist Party of American and the Communist Labor Party. But both were aggressively prosecuted by the U.S. government in the period around 1920, causing a drop in their already small membership and forcing them underground.

By the mid-1920s, the Communist Party of the USA was formed to implant the revolutionary aims of the Soviet Union in America. William Z. Foster, a labor organizer, was the party's first presidential candidate, in 1924. National tickets were run every four years through 1940 and from 1968 through 1984, but the party's peak year at the polls was 1932, when Foster received 103,253 votes (0.3 percent of the popular vote).

The Communists have a distinctive place in American political history as the only party to have had international ties. In 1929 a party split brought the formal creation of the Communist Party of the United States, with acknowledged status as a part of the worldwide communist movement (the Communist International).

The Communist International terminated during World War II, and in 1944 the party's leader in America, Earl Browder, dissolved the party and committed the movement to operate within the two-party system. In the 1944 campaign the Communists endorsed President Franklin D. Roosevelt, who repudiated their support.

However, with the breakup of the U.S.–Soviet alliance after World War II, the Communists reconstituted themselves as a political party. They supported Henry Wallace's Progressive Party candidacy in 1948 but were limited in the cold war period of the 1950s by restrictive federal and state legislation that virtually outlawed the party.

With the gradual easing of restrictive measures, the Communist Party resumed electoral activities in the late 1960s. In a policy statement written in 1966, the party described itself as "a revolutionary party whose aim is the fundamental transformation of society."

The party's success at the polls, however, continued to be minimal. Its presidential candidates in 1968, 1972, 1976, 1980, and 1984—the last year that they appeared on the ballot—each received less than one-tenth of 1 percent of the vote.

Conservative Party (1962–)

In 1962 the New York State Conservative Party began to take shape under the direction of J. Daniel Mahoney, a New York attorney, and his brother-in-law, Kieran O'Doherty. They were motivated primarily by the belief that real political alternatives were no longer being offered to the state electorate. They saw the three dominant parties in the state—the Liberal Party, the Democratic Party, and the Republican Party under Gov. Nelson A. Rockefeller and Sen. Jacob K. Javits—as offering a generally liberal agenda.

Although political commentators predicted the early demise of the party—particularly in the aftermath of Barry Goldwater's overwhelming defeat in the 1964 presidential elections—the party continued to grow both in membership and in candidate endorsements. In 1965 the nationally known columnist and intellectual William F. Buckley ran for mayor of New York City, generating national publicity for the party. One year later, the Conservative candidate for governor, Professor Paul Adams, outpolled Liberal Party candidate Franklin D. Roosevelt Jr., obtaining Row C of the ballot for the party. A party's position on the ballot is determined by the number of votes cast for its candidate for governor. Appearing in Row C is significant because the higher the row, the more notice voters are likely to take of the party's candidates. In 1970 James Buckley was elected to the U.S. Senate on Row C alone, and from the mid-1970s onward no statewide Republican candidate gained office without Conservative Party cross-endorsement.

Although the Conservative Party suffered some setbacks, such as the loss of Row C to the Independence (Reform) Party in 1996 and the siphoning off of some supporters to the Right to Life Party, it remains a major force in New York State politics. The Conservative Party has opposed abortion since it became a political issue; nonetheless, the party has occasionally backed prochoice candidates whose conservative credentials were otherwise satisfactory. The Right to Life Party never backs candidates who support abortion.

Even though some members of the Conservative Party are Protestant fundamentalists, the plurality of its membership and much of its leadership are traditionalist Roman Catholics. In a very real sense, the rise of the party has mirrored the rise of the conservative movement in America—from Goldwater's capture of the 1964 Republican nomination to Ronald Reagan's electoral triumphs in 1980 and 1984. In addition, the party has successfully fought the image of extremism while generally remaining true to its core principles—tax limitation, education reform, and tough anticrime policies.

Constitutional Union Party (1860)

The short-lived Constitutional Union Party was formed in 1859 to promote national conciliation in the face of rampant sectionalism, which included southern threats of secession. The party appealed to conservative remnants of the American (Know Nothing) and Whig parties, who viewed preservation of the Union as their primary goal.

John Bell. *Library of Congress*

The Constitutional Union Party held its first and only national convention in Baltimore in May 1860. For president the party nominated John Bell of Tennessee, a former senator and Speaker of the House of Representatives, who previously had been both a Democrat and a Whig. The convention adopted a short platform, which intentionally avoided controversial subjects, most notably the divisive slavery issue. Instead, the platform simply urged support for "the Constitution, the Union and the Laws."

In the fall election, Bell received 590,901 votes (12.6 percent of the popular vote) and won Kentucky, Tennessee, and Virginia. However, the Bell ticket finished last in the four-way presidential race and, together with the sectional split in the Democratic Party, was a prominent factor in the victory of Republican Abraham Lincoln.

In the months after the 1860 election the Constitutional Union Party continued to urge national conciliation, but with the outbreak of the Civil War the party disappeared.

Democratic Party (1828–   )

The Democratic Party is the oldest political organization in the United States. Indeed, a history of the party is in some ways a political history of the nation. In the first few years of the Republic, political parties did not exist, although factions tied to issues and the personal ambitions of political leaders influenced elections and policies. The Democratic Party traces its roots to this factionalism, beginning with opposition to the Federalist policies of Alexander Hamilton in the first administration of George Washington.

Origins of the Democratic Party

Opposition to Federalist policies, organized by U.S. Rep. James Madison and Secretary of State Thomas Jefferson, first coalesced around Hamilton's proposal for a national bank, which Congress passed and Washington signed, over the strenuous objections of Jefferson and Madison. The two Virginians were more successful in preventing the adoption of Hamilton's larger plan for federal support for the development of American industry. The Federalists, led by Hamilton and John Adams, favored a strong central government and a flexible interpretation of the Constitution. Key to their program was a national bank, which would facilitate economic growth and strengthen national and international commerce.

Jefferson's Democratic-Republicans advocated "strict construction" of the Constitution and opposed a national bank. Moreover, they favored friendly relations with France, while the Federalists sought to forge friendly diplomatic and commercial relations with England. Both parties had supporters throughout the country, but the Democratic-Republicans were strongest in the South and among slaveowners, and the Federalists were strongest in New England and among men with commercial and manufacturing interests. From the 1790s until the late 1820s various terms—Democratic-Republicans, Jeffersonian Republicans, Jeffersonian Democrats, and National Republicans—were applied to the people and leaders who, opposed to the Federalists, gradually became known as Democrats.

The Democratic-Republicans grew stronger as the Federalists began to fade during the presidency of John Adams. A new alliance of agrarian southerners and urban northerners helped Jefferson defeat Adams in 1800 and win reelection in 1804. After Jefferson the presidency went to his friends and allies, James Madison (1809–1817) and James Monroe (1817–1825). By 1820 the Federalist Party had all but disappeared, and James Monroe won reelection with no opposition.

Indicative of the change in the party of Jefferson was its attitude toward the Bank of the United States. In 1791 Jefferson and Madison had vigorously opposed the creation of this bank, arguing that establishment of such a bank was unconstitutional. We might date the development of the Democratic Party from that debate over the bank. In 1811 the bank's twenty-year charter expired, and the Democrats who controlled Congress and the presidency did not renew it. By 1816, however, Madison supported the creation of a new bank and renounced his former public policy and constitutional opposition to it. Congress, controlled by Democrats, passed the bill.

The inherent instability of one-party politics became clear in 1824, as four candidates—Andrew Jackson, John Quincy Adams, William Crawford, and Henry Clay, all claiming to represent the Jeffersonian tradition—ran for president. No candidate received a majority of popular or electoral votes, and the House of Representatives chose John Quincy Adams, although Andrew Jackson had received more popular votes and more electoral votes. After 1824 the old Jeffersonian party unraveled. Adams had broken with the Federalist Party during the War of 1812 and had served as Monroe's secretary of state, but he was never a true "Jeffersonian." By the end of his administration in 1829 he and supporters like Henry Clay emerged as members of a faction that eventually became the Whig Party.

The Jackson Legacy

War of 1812 hero Andrew Jackson defeated John Quincy Adams in 1828 and became the first president to represent the "Democratic Party." The party has maintained that name ever since, although it was often divided over issues such as slavery, economic policy, and national unity in the nineteenth century and foreign policy, civil rights, and economic policy in the twentieth.

Jackson, nominated in 1828 by the Tennessee legislature, led the Democrats into adopting a nominating convention as the method for choosing the party's future standard-bearers. The Democrats held their first national convention at Baltimore, Maryland, in 1832, eight months after the Anti-Masons held the first such convention, also in Baltimore. The 1832 Democratic convention adopted two rules that lasted more than a century. The two-thirds rule, requiring a two-thirds majority for nomination, led to numerous floor fights over the choosing of a Democratic presidential candidate. The unit rule allowed convention delegations to override minority objections within the delegation and to vote as a whole for one candidate or position.

From Jackson's election in 1828 through the end of James Buchanan's term in 1861, the Democrats dominated national

Andrew Jackson. *Library of Congress*

politics. In this period the Democrats opposed any national bank, high tariffs, internal improvements, and even a uniform bankruptcy law. High points of Jackson's presidency included his veto of bills to support internal improvements and to extend the charter of the Second Bank of the United States. Jackson and other Democrats in this period vigorously supported territorial expansion through Indian removal, the annexation of Texas, and ultimately the Mexican-American War. Their support for territorial gains followed Jefferson's expansionist policies that led to the peaceful acquisition of Louisiana from France in 1803. Most Democrats, and almost all party leaders, supported the demands of the South between 1828 and 1861 on issues involving slavery. Meanwhile, Jackson's opponents—led by Henry Clay, Daniel Webster, and William Henry Harrison—formed the Whig Party. The Whigs—who favored higher tariffs, a national bank, federally funded internal improvements, and a weak presidency—provided the main opposition to the Democrats until the emergence of the Republican Party in 1854.

Jackson's election ushered in an era known as "Jacksonian Democracy," which stressed political equality—for white men. Jacksonians throughout the country made war on black voters, taking away their voting rights in Pennsylvania, New Jersey, Tennessee, and North Carolina and opposing their voting rights elsewhere. Jackson himself led the movement to force Native Americans out of the states east of the Mississippi River.

Jefferson, already considered the "father" of the Democratic Party, had been the first president to remove officeholders and replace them with his supporters. Jackson renewed this policy through the "spoils system," a term that stemmed from the phrase "to the victors go the spoils." As the party in power during most of the period from 1829 to 1861, the Democrats controlled the growing bureaucracy and rewarded many supporters with patronage jobs.

Jackson's legacy was a Democratic Party that endured into the twenty-first century. Dominating national politics during the first half of the nineteenth century, the Democrats lost the presidential election only twice (in 1840 and 1848) between 1800 and 1856. From Jackson's inauguration in 1829 until the year 2001, the Democrats controlled the House of Representatives for fifty-five two-year sessions and the Senate for forty-six sessions; the Whigs or Republicans controlled the House for thirty-two sessions and the Senate for forty-one sessions.

Despite their long-term success, the Democrats barely survived their severest test, over slavery and secession. In 1846 northern Democrats supported the Wilmot Proviso, introduced in the House by Pennsylvania Democrat David Wilmot. The proviso would have prohibited slavery in any territory acquired during the Mexican-American War. Southern Democrats uniformly opposed the proviso. In 1848 many antislavery Democrats from New York, Pennsylvania, and New England voted for former president Martin Van Buren, who was running on the Free Soil Party ticket. These defections led to the election of the Whig candidate, Zachary Taylor. The Democrats regained the presidency in 1852, but slavery soon splintered the party. In 1856 Democrat Franklin Pierce became the first elected president denied renomination by his own party. He had alienated fellow northerners by signing legislation that allowed slavery into Kansas Territory, which in turn led it to become a battleground between pro- and antislavery forces. Another northerner, James Buchanan, won the nomination but also became a one-term president. By 1860 many northern Democrats, among them Sens. Salmon P. Chase of Ohio and Hannibal Hamlin of Maine, had joined the new Republican Party.

At the 1860 convention in Charleston, South Carolina, northern and southern Democrats were divided over how much support to give slavery in the territories. Northerners, backing Stephen A. Douglas of Illinois, favored opening all territories to slavery under a system of popular sovereignty, in which settlers would decide for themselves whether to permit slavery. Most of the southerners bolted after the defeat of platform planks endorsing a federal slave code for the territories and guaranteeing the right of slaveowners to carry their human property into all federal territories. The northern delegates nominated Douglas for president. The southern Democrats nominated John C. Breckinridge of Kentucky for president. Even had the Democrats remained united, it is doubtful they could have prevented the Republican candidate, Abraham Lincoln, from winning an electoral majority, as he swept every free state but New Jersey, which he split with Douglas. The split in the Democratic Party presaged the more important split in the nation, which occurred with the secession of eleven southern states in 1860–1861.

Decline and Resurgence

During the Civil War, northern Democrats remained divided. War Democrats generally supported the war effort and Lincoln's initial goal of bringing the South back into the Union, although they objected to Lincoln's emancipation policies and after 1863 were far less enthusiastic about the war or its goals. Throughout the war, by contrast, the Copperhead faction opposed the war effort and sought peace negotiations with the Confederacy.

Democrats came back together after the Civil War, but both their commitment to white supremacy and their image of disloyalty continued. During Reconstruction, Democrats opposed civil rights laws and the Fourteenth and Fifteenth Amendments, which were designed to establish blacks' citizenship, recognize blacks' civil rights, and guarantee blacks' voting rights. As late as the 1880s, the Democrats were termed the party of "rum, romanism, and rebellion," because of the party's opposition to temperance laws, its support among Irish Catholics, and the fact that much of its support came from former Confederates.

THE MODERN BALAAM AND HIS ASS.

In the first appearance of the Democratic donkey, this unfavorable 1837 political cartoon shows Martin Van Buren walking behind his predecessor, Andrew Jackson, who rides the donkey.
Library of Congress

In 1876 the Democratic governor of New York, Samuel J. Tilden, won the popular vote against Republican Rutherford B. Hayes, but Tilden lost the election when a congressional compromise awarded Hayes all the disputed electoral votes of three southern states. Election fraud, intimidation, and outright violence by white southern Democrats prevented thousands of blacks from voting. Had the election been run fairly, it is likely that Hayes would have won outright. As part of the compromise that brought Hayes to the White House, the new president promised to remove federal troops from the South, effectively ending Reconstruction. Their removal led to a gradual disfranchisement of blacks in the South, which soon became solidly Democratic and would remain largely so until the presidential election of 1964. Despite a virtual lock on all southern electoral votes, the Democrats captured the presidency only twice between 1860 and 1912; Grover Cleveland won in 1884 and 1892.

By the late nineteenth century the Democratic Party's policies had changed somewhat from the antebellum period. Still a "white man's party," it was hostile to African Americans' civil rights and to Chinese immigration. With slavery ended, however, the party had dropped its aggressive expansionism of the earlier period. Cleveland refused to annex Hawaii, and some Democrats opposed the Spanish-American War in 1898. Democrats remained hostile to high tariffs, but they split on the issue of an expansive monetary policy; western Democrats favored the free coinage of silver, and eastern Democrats, among them Cleveland, opposed it. Most southern whites gave their allegiance to the Democrats, but in the North by the 1890s, and especially following the 1893 depression, economic and cultural issues outweighed memories of Civil War enmity in voter choices between the two major parties.

The GOP continued to dominate presidential politics for twelve years into the twentieth century. In 1912 the Republicans split when former president Theodore Roosevelt failed in his attempt to gain his party's nomination over the incumbent, William Howard Taft. Roosevelt ran anyway, on the Progressive—or Bull Moose—ticket, winning six states and 4.1 million votes. Roosevelt came in second, and Taft a distant third, but Taft and Roosevelt combined for 1.3 million more popular votes than the Democrat, Woodrow Wilson. Had the Republicans been united, their candidate—either Roosevelt or Taft—would have won. But divided they enabled Wilson to carry forty states and the election, ending the Democrats' long presidential drought. Wilson demonstrated the Democrats' hostility to civil rights and racial equality, as he ordered the segregation of all federal facilities in Washington, D.C. He was a progressive reformer on many issues, however, and brought such innovations as the Federal Reserve System, in contrast to historic Democratic hostility to federal government intervention in the economy.

Wilson also led the Democrats away from their historic position on foreign policy. Before the Civil War, the Democrats, in part spurred by the demands of the South for more territory for slavery, had pursued an aggressive policy of land acquisition, ultimately leading to war with Mexico. Pre–Civil War Democrats had had little interest in international affairs beyond the Western Hemisphere, however. In 1917, by contrast, Wilson successfully asked Congress for a declaration of war, and he continued his internationalist policies after the end of World War I, as he vainly attempted to bring the United States into the League of Nations. For the next half-century the Democratic Party stood for intervention and international responsibility, while the Republicans retreated into a large measure of diplomatic isolationism.

After World War I the Republicans took back the White House in 1920, kept it in 1924, and won again with Herbert Hoover's 1928 victory over Democrat Alfred E. Smith, the first Roman Catholic presidential nominee. After the stock market crashed in 1929, however, the Great Depression paved the way for a new Democratic dominance in the White House and an even longer one in Congress.

New Deal to Great Society

The election of Franklin D. Roosevelt in 1932 made a dramatic and lasting change in American politics. Democrats sang "Happy Days Are Here Again" as they became the majority party and rallied behind FDR's bold New Deal programs. Democrats, long the party of states' rights and localism, became identified with national initiatives on economic and social issues. During the New Deal, rural electrification brought light and heat to much of the nation; a range of programs helped the poor and the unemployed; the nation's labor policy went through a sea change with the Wagner Labor Relations Act; and massive public works programs, such as the Tennessee Valley Authority, not only created jobs but constructed public buildings, roads, and dams. Once a party opposed to regulation, the Democrats helped create the regulatory state. Social programs, most notably Social Security, set the stage for the modern industrial state that provides a social safety net for citizens.

At Roosevelt's urging, the 1936 Democratic convention abolished the controversial two-thirds rule, which in effect had long given the South a veto in choosing the national party ticket. Southern delegates agreed to a compromise, basing the size of future delegations on a state's Democratic voting strength instead of population size.

During the Roosevelt years and after, for the first time in its history, the Democratic Party welcomed black support and even supported some civil rights legislation, and President Roosevelt and his successor, Harry S. Truman, issued executive orders to combat some types of racial segregation and other discrimination. The "New Deal coalition"—northern blacks,

Franklin D. Roosevelt and his New Deal brought about the realignment of the two major political parties in the 1930s. *Library of Congress*

southern whites, farmers, labor unionists, intellectuals, and ethnic urban voters—kept Roosevelt and Truman in office for twenty consecutive years, ending in 1953.

As Europe moved toward war in the 1930s and then fought in World War II, Roosevelt pushed an international agenda, building on Wilson's legacy. Here Roosevelt had the support of southern Democrats, who opposed some of his domestic agenda. Opposition came from Republican isolationists, but, unlike Wilson, FDR was able to bring the nation along with him, and thus the United States took the lead in establishing the United Nations (UN). Truman continued this internationalist policy, first with the Marshall Plan to help Europe recover from World War II and then with the development of NATO and other international defense pacts. In 1950 Truman pushed for UN intervention when North Korea attacked South Korea, and soon the United States was heavily involved in another war in Asia.

In domestic politics, Truman pushed an activist agenda that he called the "Fair Deal" and called for expanded enforcement of African Americans' civil rights. Running for another term in 1948, he confronted schisms within his party from two quarters: the South and the left. Displeased with Truman's civil rights plank, conservative southerners bolted the Democratic Party in 1948 and ran J. Strom Thurmond of South Carolina as the States' Rights Democratic (Dixiecrats) nominee. Under the Progressive Party banner, Henry A. Wallace also challenged Truman. Thurmond won four states; Wallace took none. Despite the split, Truman defeated Republican Thomas E. Dewey.

After Truman left office in 1953, a Republican, Dwight D. Eisenhower, served the next two terms, but then the Democrats took back the White House in 1960, as John F. Kennedy, the first Roman Catholic president, narrowly defeated Eisenhower's vice president, Richard Nixon. Kennedy's slogan, "New Frontier," mirrored traditional Democratic slogans, such as Wilson's "New Freedom," FDR's "New Deal," and Truman's "Fair Deal." Kennedy continued the Democratic agenda of internationalism, with the Peace Corps and aid to the pro-Western regime in South Vietnam, and of federal support for domestic improvements, with a massive tax cut and federal programs in housing. Kennedy made tentative moves toward an expanded role for the national government in civil rights, but he moved cautiously because of the power of southern whites within his party.

After Kennedy's assassination in 1963, President Lyndon B. Johnson completed much of Kennedy's "New Frontier" agenda and called for additional programs in pursuit of the "Great Society," including a civil rights program that was termed by some a "Second Reconstruction." Applying all the skills he had learned as Senate majority leader, Johnson pushed through the Civil Rights Act of 1964. Johnson's support for civil rights ended the "solid South" as a Democratic stronghold. In 1964 Johnson won in a landslide. Carrying all but five states, he took 61.1 percent of the popular vote, the largest popular victory of any presidential election in U.S. history. The Deep South, however, supported Republican Barry Goldwater, who had opposed the Civil Rights Act of 1964 and had flirted with the ultraright John

Birch Society and segregationist White Citizens' Councils. Johnson's mandate enabled him to win passage of the Voting Rights Act of 1965, further solidifying Democratic support among African Americans while further undermining Democratic power among white southerners.

Johnson expanded U.S. involvement in an increasingly unpopular war in Vietnam, thereby splitting the party and prompting his decision against running for reelection in 1968. Two antiwar candidates, Sen. Robert F. Kennedy of New York, brother of the slain president, and Sen. Eugene McCarthy of Minnesota, dueled for the nomination in primaries across the nation. But Kennedy was assassinated the night he won the California primary, and McCarthy was outmaneuvered by party insiders. The Democratic convention that year, held in Chicago, was marred by police violence against antiwar demonstrators. Hubert H. Humphrey, nominated without entering any primaries, also faced competition in November from the American Independent candidacy of George C. Wallace, former Democratic governor of Alabama. All these divisive factors contributed to Humphrey's narrow defeat by Republican Richard Nixon.

The Democratic Party since 1968

Still chafing from the dissension and bossism at the 1968 convention and the subsequent loss to Nixon, the Democrats in the 1970s drastically reformed their delegate-selection and nominating rules, encouraging minority representation, dividing delegations equally between men and women, and awarding delegates to candidates in proportion to their primary votes. The party's 1972 candidate, George S. McGovern, led many of the reforms, most of which took effect in 1980. The changes enhanced the role of primaries in the nominating process, leading to more primaries and fewer state caucuses.

The 1972 election was the last privately financed presidential election. Nixon raised $61.4 million versus McGovern's $21.2 million. McGovern, running as a peace candidate with a commitment to massive domestic spending, lost to Nixon in a landslide. The election-related Watergate scandal, however, drove Nixon from office two years later and brought Vice President Gerald R. Ford to the presidency. Evidence from the Watergate investigation showed that Nixon's operatives had used "dirty tricks" in the Democratic primaries to sabotage the candidacy of Edmond S. Muskie, who might have been a more formidable candidate than McGovern.

Skillful use of the primaries, as well as Ford's unpopular full pardon of President Nixon for his criminal activities in the Watergate cover-up, helped the relatively unknown Jimmy Carter of Georgia defeat incumbent Ford in 1976. Carter's primary strategy also served him in 1980, staving off a renomination challenge from Sen. Edward M. Kennedy, brother of the late president. But Carter's inability to curb inflation or obtain the release of American hostages held in Iran for 444 days doomed him to a one-term presidency and to defeat at the hands of Republican Ronald Reagan.

Although the popular Reagan handily won reelection in 1984, his vice president and successor, George Herbert Walker Bush, fell victim in 1992 to Bill Clinton of Arkansas, as Democrats returned to the White House after twelve Republican years. As a presidential candidate Clinton addressed economic worries. His advisers reminded campaign workers, "It's the economy, stupid," and the strategy worked. He was the first Democrat to win without taking Texas and, with Al Gore of Tennessee as his running mate, the first president elected on an all-South ticket since 1828.

President Bill Clinton vetoes a budget bill in 1995. *Congressional Quarterly*

Clinton won as a moderate, declaring that "the era of big government is over." Behind him was a modified New Deal coalition that included "Reagan Democrats," union members, women, African Americans, Hispanics, Jews, a majority of Roman Catholics, public sector employees, and intellectuals. In one of his first acts he instituted a "don't ask, don't tell" policy toward homosexuals in the military. Although Clinton's convention call for a "new covenant with the American people" never caught on as a slogan, and although he and Hillary Rodham Clinton failed in an abortive attempt to reform the nation's health system, peace and an improved economy soon had the Democratic administration basking in high approval ratings in public opinion polls. Nevertheless, the voters in 1994 broke the Democratic lock on Congress, turning both chambers over to Republican control.

Two years later the electorate opted to continue a divided government, giving Clinton another four-year term in 1996 while leaving Congress in GOP hands. Although he was the first Democrat elected to a second full term since Franklin Roosevelt, Clinton again won with less than a majority of the popular vote. For the moment, Clinton's victories eased doubts that the Democrats' once-solid South had become a Republican bastion. Of the eleven states of the Old Confederacy, the Clinton-Gore ticket won four in 1992 and four in 1996. Unfortunately for the Democrats that success did not hold up four years later.

Democrats made history on various fronts from 1960 through the end of the century. In 1960 the party ran the nation's first successful Catholic presidential candidate, John F. Kennedy. In 1968 New York voters elected Democrat Shirley Chisholm as the first black woman member of the U.S. House, and in 1992 another Democrat, Carol Moseley-Braun of Illinois, became the first black woman U.S. senator. When former vice president Walter F. Mondale chose Geraldine A. Ferraro as his running mate against Reagan in 1984, she became the first woman in U.S. history to run on a major-party ticket. In 1989 L. Douglas Wilder of Virginia became the first African American to be elected state governor. In 2000 the Democratic nominee for president, Vice President Al Gore, chose Sen. Joseph Lieberman as his running mate. This was the first time a Jew was on a national ticket. Also in 2000, Hillary Rodham Clinton became the first presidential wife to seek a major elective office, a U.S. Senate seat from New York, which she won.

Nevertheless, the 2000 elections were a major disappointment for Democrats. Gore lost a disputed election to Republican George W. Bush, son of the former president. Moreover, the Republicans retained control of both houses of Congress, although by the narrowest of margins. Still, it gave the GOP full control of the federal government for the first time since 1953 and sent the Democrats to the sidelines as loyal opposition but with little leverage to block the GOP program much less advance their own.

The 2000 presidential elections reasserted trends many noted in recent years. As political analyst Rhodes Cook put it: "Exit polls showed men favored Bush, women favored Gore; whites preferred Bush, non-whites preferred Gore; the more affluent voted strongly for Bush, the less affluent heavily favored Gore; rural and small town America went for Bush, urban America for Gore." In the South, the Republicans reasserted primacy, showing that this region was not the center of the party. Bush won the entire South—the eleven states of the Old Confederacy plus Kentucky and Oklahoma, carrying the region of 3.7 million votes. Bush even won Gore's home state of Tennessee and Clinton's home state of Arkansas. The Democrats' strength, reflected in both the presidential and congressional elections of 2000, was on the west and east coasts, north of Virginia, and into the industrial heartland. The Republicans dominated everywhere else—a giant "L"-shaped area from the South through the Plains states and Southwest and into the Mountain states, plus Alaska.

Democratic-Republican Party (1792–1828)

The Democratic-Republican Party developed in the early 1790s as the organized opposition to the incumbent Federalists and successor to the Anti-Federalists, who were a loose alliance of elements initially opposed to the ratification of the Constitution and subsequently to the policies of the George Washington administration, which were designed to centralize power in the federal government.

Thomas Jefferson was the leader of the new party, whose members as early as 1792 referred to themselves as Republicans. This remained their primary name throughout the party's history, although in some states they became known as Democratic-Republicans, the label used frequently by historians to avoid confusing Jefferson's party with the later Republican

Party, which began in 1854. Party members were called Jeffersonian Republicans as well.

The Democratic-Republicans favored states' rights, a literal interpretation of the Constitution, and expanded democracy through extension of suffrage and popular control of the government. The party was dominated by rural, agrarian interests, intent on maintaining their dominance over the growing commercial and industrial interests of the Northeast. The principal strength of the party came from states in the South and Middle Atlantic.

The Democratic-Republicans first gained control of the federal government in

Thomas Jefferson. *Library of Congress*

1800, when Jefferson was elected president and the party won majorities in both houses of Congress. For the next twenty-four years the party controlled both the White House and Congress, the last eight years virtually without opposition. For all but four years during this twenty-four-year period, there was a Virginia–New York alliance controlling the executive branch, with all three presidents from Virginia—Jefferson, James Madison, and James Monroe—and three of the four vice presidents from New York. Lacking an opposition party, the Democratic-Republicans in the 1820s became increasingly divided. In 1824, when four party leaders ran for president, John Quincy Adams won the election in the House of Representatives, although Andrew Jackson had received more popular votes.

The deep factionalism evident in the 1824 election doomed the Democratic-Republican Party. The two-party system revived shortly thereafter with the emergence of the National Republican Party, an outgrowth of the

Adams faction, and the Democratic-Republican Party, the political organization of the Jackson faction. After 1830 the Jacksonians adopted the name Democratic Party.

Dixiecrats (States' Rights Party) (1948)

The States' Rights Democratic Party was a conservative southern faction that bolted from the Democrats in 1948. The immediate reason for the new party, popularly known as the Dixiecrats, was dissatisfaction with President Harry Truman's civil rights program. But the Dixiecrat effort to maintain a segregated way of life was also an attempt to demonstrate the political power of the twentieth-century southern Democrats and to reestablish their importance in the Democratic Party.

Strom Thurmond. *File photo*

The Mississippi Democratic Party's state executive committee met in Jackson in May 1948 to lay the groundwork for the Dixiecrat secession. The meeting called for a bolt by southern delegates if the Democratic National Convention endorsed Truman's civil rights program. When the convention did approve a strong civil rights plank, the entire Mississippi delegation and half the Alabama delegation left the convention. Gov. Fielding L. Wright of Mississippi invited all anti-Truman delegates to meet in Birmingham three days after the close of the Democratic convention to select a states' rights ticket.

Most southern Democrats with something at stake—national prominence, seniority in Congress, patronage privileges—shunned the new

Dixiecrat Party. The party's leaders came from the ranks of southern governors and other state and local officials. The Birmingham convention chose two governors to lead the party: J. Strom Thurmond of South Carolina for president and Wright of Mississippi for vice president.

Other than the presidential ticket, the Dixiecrats did not run candidates for any office. Rather than try to develop an independent party organization, the Dixiecrats, whenever possible, used existing Democratic Party apparatus.

The party was on the ballot in only one state outside the South and in the November election received only 1,157,326 votes (2.4 percent of the popular vote). The Thurmond ticket carried four Deep South states where it ran under the Democratic Party label, but it failed in its basic objective to prevent the reelection of President Truman.

After the election the party ceased to exist almost as abruptly as it had begun, with most of its members returning to the Democratic Party. In a statement upon reentering the Democratic fold, Thurmond characterized the Dixiecrat episode as "a fight within our family." (While serving in the U.S. Senate sixteen years later, Thurmond switched to the Republican Party.)

Federalists (1792–1816)

Two related groups in late-eighteenth-century American politics called themselves *Federalists*. First were the proponents of ratifying the Constitution as framed in 1787, chief among them Alexander Hamilton and James Madison. They won. Next was the group that dominated national politics in the 1790s, as Americans began to form political parties.

The two groups were not identical. Madison, successful in promoting adoption of the new Constitution, led a political opposition that emerged in 1792. He, along with fellow Virginian Thomas Jefferson, argued for strict construction, or a narrow interpretation, of the powers of the new national government and organized a rival political party, the Democratic- (or Jeffersonian) Republicans, which came to power with Jefferson's election in 1800.

The Federalist Party, led by Hamilton as President George Washington's secretary of the Treasury, dominated national politics during the adminis-

Alexander Hamilton. *Library of Congress*

trations of Washington and John Adams. The Federalists wanted to make the national government stronger by assuming state debts, chartering a national bank, and supporting manufacturing interests. In foreign affairs, they pursued policies that would protect commercial and political harmony with Britain, goals that led to ratification of Jay's Treaty in 1795. Under the treaty, Britain withdrew the last of its troops from American outposts and the United States agreed to honor debts owed to British merchants.

Though committed to a republican form of government, Federalists believed society to be properly hierarchical. Federalists such as William Cooper of New York and Henry Knox of Massachusetts professed that politics was an arena best left to the "natural aristocracy" of wealthy and talented men. Consequently, Federalists generally sought to limit suffrage, tighten naturalization policy, and silence antiadministration opinions. Recent examinations of the Federalists have disclosed a softer side to their conservatism, showing that, as self-proclaimed protectors of society, they sometimes sought to protect the basic rights of minorities. They tended to be more sympathetic than their Jeffersonian opponents to the plight of Native Americans and African Americans and less resistant to the inclusion of women in political processes.

Federalists drew their support primarily from the Northeast, where their procommercial and promanufacturing policies attracted merchants and businessmen. Although they had some southern strongholds in parts of Virginia and the Carolinas (especially Charleston), Federalists had considerably less success in attracting the support of western farmers and southern planters who opposed their elitism, antislavery bias, and promanufacturing economic policies.

Several factors contributed to the demise of the Federalist Party. Its passage of the highly unpopular Alien and Sedition Acts of 1798 served as a rallying cry for Jeffersonian Republicans. A more important factor may have been the Federalists' sharp division in the 1800 elections over Adams's foreign policies. Second-generation Federalists continued to mobilize regional support, mainly in New England, and, after Jefferson's unpopular embargo forbidding exports (1807–1809), they made something of a national comeback in the 1808 and 1812 elections. Many Federalists opposed the War of 1812, however, and in 1814 the Hartford Convention, a meeting of arch-Federalists, considered secession from the union, thereby permanently tainting the Federalist name and ending the party's legitimacy at the national level. Federalists continued to play a limited, though sometimes important, role in state and local politics into the 1820s, challenging for key offices in several states.

Federalist leadership during the nation's critical early years contributed greatly to preserving the American experiment. In large part they were responsible for laying the foundation for a national economy (later carried forward by National Republicans and then the Whigs), a national foreign policy agenda, and creating a strong national judicial system. The last of these was perhaps the Federalists' most enduring legacy as John Marshall used his position as chief justice (1801–1835) to incorporate Federalist principles into constitutional law.

Free Soil Party (1848–1852)

Born as a result of opposition to the extension of slavery into the newly acquired southwest territories, the Free Soil Party was launched formally at a convention in Buffalo, New York, in August 1848. The Free Soilers were composed of antislavery elements from the Democratic and Whig parties as well as remnants of the Liberty Party. Representatives from all the northern states and three border states attended the Buffalo convention, where the slogan "Free Soil, Free Speech, Free Labor and Free Men" was adopted. This slogan expressed the antislavery sentiment of the Free Soilers as well as the desire for cheap western land.

Martin Van Buren. *Library of Congress*

Former Democratic president Martin Van Buren (1837–1841) was selected by the convention as the party's presidential candidate and Charles Francis Adams, the son of President John Quincy Adams (1825–1829), was chosen as his running mate.

In the 1848 election the Free Soil ticket received 291,501 votes (10.1 percent of the popular vote) but was unable to carry a single state. The party did better at the congressional level, winning nine House seats and holding the balance of power in the organization of the closely divided new Congress.

The 1848 election marked the peak of the party's influence. With the passage of compromise legislation on slavery in 1850, the Free Soilers lost their basic issue and began a rapid decline. The party ran its second and last national ticket in 1852, headed by John Hale, who received 155,210 votes (4.9 percent of the popular vote). As in 1848, the Free Soil national ticket failed to carry a single state.

Although the party went out of existence shortly thereafter, its program and constituency were absorbed by the Republican Party, whose birth and growth dramatically paralleled the resurgence of the slavery issue in the mid-1850s.

Green Party (1996–)

With famed consumer activist Ralph Nader heading its ticket, the Green Party made an impressive debut in U.S. presidential politics in 1996. Nader received 685,040 votes (0.7 percent of the popular vote) to finish fourth, albeit a distant fourth, behind the Reform Party's Ross Perot. Four years later, he made an even more impressive showing, winning 2.9 million votes (2.7 percent of the total vote), and finished third, well ahead of other third party candidates in the race. His showing probably tipped the outcome to the Republican Party in one or two states.

Nader received votes in every state except three (South Dakota, North Carolina, and Oklahoma), a significant increase from four years earlier when he was on the ballot in twenty-two states. As before, he ran best in western states but also drew a strong following in a few northeastern states. His running mate was Winona LaDuke of the White Earth reservation in Minnesota. A Harvard graduate, LaDuke was active as an advocate and writer on human rights and Native American environmental causes.

Although new to the United States, the Green Party was part of a decentralized worldwide movement for peace, social justice, and the environment. Until the collapse of international communism and the fall of the Berlin Wall, the Greens were best known for their political inroads in Germany. But the party lost ground after opposing reunification and it only recently has returned to the German parliament.

Unlike four years earlier, Nader and LaDuke in 2000 ran an aggressive and active campaign. He took his populist, anticorporate campaign to a variety of venues, ranging from TV studios to union meetings, in a bid to put together what he described as a "blue-green" coalition of disaffected voters. Nationwide polls in the summer of 2000 showed Nader drawing roughly 5 percent of the vote, and even more than that in several battleground states, including California. In the end, however, he received far fewer votes nationwide than expected. Nader was on the ballot in a number of closely contested states but most were won by the Democratic nominee, Al Gore, who was seen by analysts as the candidate most likely to be hurt by Nader's presence in the contest. Of these states, none was more important than Florida. In that state, Nader took more than 97,400 votes in a contest decided by a few hundred in favor of Republican George W. Bush. That win put Bush over the top in electoral votes and gave the White House back to the Republicans. Some political observers thought that had Nader not been on the ticket, Gore would have won Florida and the White House.

Greenback Party (1874–1884)

The National Independent or Greenback-Labor Party, commonly known as the Greenback Party, was launched in Indianapolis in November 1874 at a meeting organized by the Indiana Grange. The party grew out of the Panic of 1873, a post–Civil War economic depression, which hit farmers and industrial workers particularly hard. Currency was the basic issue of the new party, which opposed return to the gold standard and favored retention of the inflationary paper money (known as greenbacks), first introduced as an emergency measure during the Civil War.

In the 1876 presidential election the party ran Peter Cooper, a New York philanthropist, and drafted a platform that focused entirely on the currency issue. Cooper received 75,973 votes (0.9 percent of the popular vote), mainly from agrarian voters. Aided by the continuing depression, a Greenback national convention in 1878 effected the merger of the party with various labor reform groups and adopted a platform that addressed labor and currency issues. Showing voting strength in the industrial East as well as in the agrarian South and Midwest, the Greenbacks polled more than one million votes in the 1878 congressional elections and won fourteen seats in the U.S. House of Representatives. This marked the high point of the party's strength.

Returning prosperity, the prospect of fusion with one of the major parties, and a split between the party's agrarian and labor leadership served to undermine the Greenback Party. In the 1880 election the party elected only eight representatives and its presidential candidate, Rep. James B. Weaver of Iowa, received 305,997 votes (3.3 percent of the popular vote), far less than party leaders expected.

The party slipped further four years later, when the Greenbacks' candidate for president, former Massachusetts governor Benjamin F. Butler, received 175,096 votes (1.7 percent of the popular vote). With the demise of the Greenbacks, most of the party's constituency moved into the Populist Party, the agrarian reform movement that swept the South and Midwest in the 1890s.

Know Nothing (American) Party (1856)

The Know Nothing Party of the 1850s was the most formidable nativist political organization in American history; for two years in mid-decade it was the nation's second-largest party. Nativism involved the fear of aliens and opposition to an internal minority believed to be un-American. Members of the American Party would be called Know Nothings because when asked about their organization they were instructed to say, "I know nothing." For them, fear and hatred of Catholics, particularly "papist conspirators," created this need for secrecy.

The Know Nothings emerged from one of the many nativist secret societies proliferating in the pre–Civil War period. The migration of millions of Catholics from Ireland and Germany stimulated an intense antialien activism in the United States. Key leaders of the Order of the Star Spangled Banner saw their group as a useful instrument for shaping a new

An 1854 political cartoon depicting the Know Nothing Party. *Library of Congress*

political party in 1853. Like nativists of earlier decades, leaders of the Know Nothing Party accused Catholics of undermining the public school system and of being responsible for a host of social problems accompanying the influx of so many poverty-stricken newcomers in the great port cities.

The party emerged at a critical moment in American political history. The slavery controversy was ripping apart the Whig Party, and the Democratic Party was suffering fissures in different states and sections. Out of this turmoil came a flood of members to the new nativist movement. For many people, a party organized around nativist themes—one that advanced "American" interests and stood for stability and union—offered a way out of the conflict between northerner and southerner, abolitionist and slaveholder. A common crusade against foreigners, they thought, could cement broken institutions and warring people.

The political divisions of the day meant that Know Nothing membership varied from section to section. In New York, where the party was born and had its strongest support, the leadership was composed of conservative Whig refugees, men who opposed free soil and antislavery elements in their former party. These included James Barker and Daniel Ullmann, the party candidate in the New York gubernatorial race in 1855. In New England the antislavery wing of the former Whig Party, "Conscience Whigs," played the key role. Leaders in Massachusetts included Henry Wilson, president of the state senate who was a U.S. senator in 1855, and Henry J. Gardner, elected state governor in the Know Nothing landslide that year. Also swelling the party rolls in New England were abolitionists from the other major party, anti–Nebraska Act Democrats.

In the West, where Know Nothings struggled to find support, nativists sought fusion with "Free Soil" activists in Indiana and Illinois, but in Wisconsin two factions (the Sams and the Jonathans) shared antialien attitudes yet split over slavery.

In the South, which contained a small immigrant population, nativism appealed to those who viewed "aliens" in the Northeast and West as threatening to the southern way of life because it was assumed that newcomers would be opposed to slavery. The nativist party in the South represented an escape from the divisive struggle that threatened civil strife, but it had only limited impact.

Despite its political success in 1854 and 1855, the national Know Nothing Party could not survive the antislavery controversy. At the party gathering in Philadelphia in June 1855, a proslavery resolution led to wild debate and a massive defection led by Massachusetts nativists but including representatives from many states. Further divisions in the party, including personal rivalries between New York leaders Barker and Ullmann, created more problems.

In 1856 the party nominated former president Millard Fillmore as presidential candidate. But Fillmore—who had joined a Know Nothing lodge as a political maneuver and had never been a real nativist—failed at the polls, trailing in a three-way race with only 22 percent of the popular vote and taking only Maryland's eight electoral college votes. The Know Nothings did not recover, losing members rapidly in subsequent months. In 1857 the party held its last national council.

Liberal Party (1944–)

New York State's Liberal Party was founded in 1944 by anticommunist trade unionists and other politically liberal individuals who left communist-dominated political parties. The party in 2000 described itself as providing an "alternative to a state Democratic Party dominated by local party machines rife with corruption and a Republican Party controlled by special interests." Many of the state's labor and educational leaders were instrumental in creating the party, which calls itself the nation's "longest existing third party."

The Liberal Party has played a major role in several elections. It provided crucial support for Franklin D. Roosevelt in 1944 and John F. Kennedy in 1960. Some political historians believe Roosevelt and Kennedy owed their national victories to the Liberal Party vote that carried New York State for them. John Lindsay, nominally a Republican, won reelection in New York City's 1969 mayoral race as the Liberal Party candidate. In 2000 Democrat Hillary Rodham Clinton won the Liberal line in her campaign for the U.S. Senate.

The party proclaims to nominate candidates on the basis of "merit, independence, and progressive viewpoints." Many of the state's most prominent liberal politicians have sought and won the party's nomination for New York City mayor, governor, and U.S. senator, regardless of their major party affiliation. When the party has not run candidates of its own, it has usually been supportive of Democrats. Sometimes, however, the party's role has been that of a spoiler, particularly in close races, where its support represents the balance of power. In modern Senate races, for example, political analysts say Liberal Party endorsement of moderate or liberal candidates has sometimes drawn enough votes from Democratic candidates to throw the election to conservative Republicans.

The party is active in pushing its political agenda, which is pro-choice, pro-universal health care, and pro-public education (it has aggressively opposed school voucher programs, for example). Its successful Supreme Court suit for congressional reapportionment contributed to the 1968 election of Shirley Chisholm of New York, the first African American congresswoman.

Through the latter part of the twentieth century, the Liberal Party served as a counterweight in Empire State politics to New York's Conservative

Party. In 1966, for instance, each party's gubernatorial candidate drew over a half million votes. The Liberal nominee was Franklin D. Roosevelt Jr.

Both parties have lost ground at the polls since then, the Liberals a bit more than the Conservatives. In 1998, for instance, the Liberal Party's gubernatorial nominee drew fewer than 80,000 votes, while the Conservative Party line provided Republican incumbent George E. Pataki with nearly 350,000 votes.

Liberal Republican Party (1872)

A faction of the Republican Party, dissatisfied with President Ulysses S. Grant's first term in office, withdrew from the party in 1872 to form a new party. Composed of party reformers, as well as anti-Grant politicians and newspaper editors, the new party focused on the corruption of the Grant administration and the need for civil service reform and for an end to the Reconstruction policy in the South.

The call for the Liberal Republican national convention came from the state party in Missouri, the birthplace of the reform movement. The convention, meeting in Cincinnati, Ohio, in May 1872, nominated Horace Greeley, editor of the *New York Tribune,* for president and Missouri governor B. Gratz Brown as his running mate. Greeley, the choice of anti-Grant politicians but suspect among reformers, was not popular among many Democrats either, who recalled his longtime criticism of the Democratic Party.

With the hope of victory in the fall election, however, the Democratic National Convention, meeting in July, endorsed the Liberal Republican ticket and platform. The coalition was an unsuccessful one, as many Democrats refused to vote for Greeley. He received 2,834,761 votes (43.8 percent of the popular vote) but carried only six states and lost to Grant by more than 750,000 votes out of nearly 6.5 million cast. Greeley died shortly after the election.

Underfinanced, poorly organized, and dependent on the Democrats for their success, the Liberal Republicans went out of existence after the 1872 election.

Libertarian Party (1971–)

In the brief period of four years, 1972 to 1976, the Libertarian Party leaped from a fledgling organization on the presidential ballot in only two states to the nation's largest third party. In the presidential election of 2000, although the party's candidate ran fifth in the race and won fewer popular votes than four years earlier, the Libertarians still claimed to be the third largest party in the nation.

Formed in Colorado in 1971, the party nominated John Hospers of California for president in 1972. On the ballot only in Colorado and Washington, Hospers garnered 3,673 votes (including write-in votes from other states). But he received a measure of national attention when a Republican presidential elector from Virginia, Roger MacBride, cast his electoral vote for the Libertarian presidential nominee.

MacBride's action made him a hero in Libertarian circles, and the party chose him as its 1976 standard-bearer at its August 1975 convention in New York City. MacBride had served in the Vermont legislature in the 1960s and was defeated for the Republican gubernatorial nomination in that state in 1964. In the 1970s he settled on a farm near Charlottesville, Virginia, and devoted himself to writing and party affairs. He was cocreator of the television series *Little House on the Prairie*.

Making a major effort in 1976, the Libertarians got on the ballot in thirty-two states, more than Eugene J. McCarthy—who ran independent of any political party—or any other third-party candidate. The reward was a vote of 173,011, more than for any other minor party candidate but far below McCarthy's total and only 0.2 percent of the national vote. MacBride's strength was centered in the West; he received 5.5 percent of the vote in Alaska and 1.0 percent or more in Arizona, Hawaii, and Idaho. He also ran well ahead of his national average in California (0.7 percent) and Nevada (0.8 percent). His running mate was David P. Bergland, a California lawyer.

In 1980 the Libertarian Party appeared on the ballot in all fifty states and the District of Columbia for the first time. The party also fielded about 550 candidates for other offices, a number that dwarfed other third-party efforts. The party nominees, Edward E. Clark of California for president and

David Koch of New York for vice president, garnered 921,299 votes or 1.1 percent of the vote nationwide. As in previous elections, the major support for the Libertarians came from western states.

Of all minor-party presidential candidates running in 1984, the Libertarians appeared on the greatest number of ballots: thirty-eight states and the District of Columbia. David Bergland, who had run in 1976 for the second slot, was the party's presidential candidate, and Jim Lewis, a Connecticut business executive, his running mate. In 1988 the Libertarian presidential and vice-presidential nominees—Ron Paul and Andre V. Marrou, respectively—were on the ballot in all fifty-one jurisdictions save four and received 432,179 votes.

In 1992 Nevada real estate broker Marrou was the presidential nominee with running mate Nancy Lord, a lawyer from Georgia. The pair was on the ballot in all states and the District of Columbia and had a campaign budget of $1 million. Marrou received 291,627 votes in a fourth-place finish behind Ross Perot, who stole most of the third-party candidates' thunder that year. The Libertarians maintained their strong base in the West, especially in California, Nevada, and Hawaii, where they also ran candidates in 1992 for most House seats.

In 1996 the Libertarians regained voting strength but nevertheless dropped to fifth place in the presidential race behind Ralph Nader of the newly formed Green Party. The Libertarian candidate, financial analyst Harry Browne of Tennessee, and running mate Jo Anne Jorgensen of South Carolina drew 485,798 votes or 0.50 percent of the total. It was the party's best showing since 1980.

The story in the 2000 presidential race was similar but not as favorable. The party won votes in forty-nine states, but its candidates, again Browne and running mate Art Olivier of California, won just 386,024 votes, or 0.37 percent of all votes, down 20 percent from four years earlier.

Individual responsibility and minimal government interference are the hallmarks of the Libertarian philosophy. The party has favored repeal of laws against so-called victimless crimes—such as pornography, drug use, and homosexual activity—the abolition of all federal police agencies, and the elimination of all government subsidies to private enterprise. In foreign and military affairs, the Libertarians have advocated the removal of U.S. troops from abroad, a cut in the defense budget, and the emergence of the

United States as a "giant Switzerland," with no international treaty obligations. Libertarians also have favored repeal of legislation that they believe hinders individual or corporate action. They have opposed gun control, civil rights laws, price controls on oil and gas, labor protection laws, federal welfare and poverty programs, forced busing, compulsory education, Social Security, national medical care, and federal land-use restrictions.

Liberty Party (1839–1848)

Born in 1839, the Liberty Party was the product of a split in the antislavery movement between a faction led by William Lloyd Garrison that favored action outside the political process and a second led by James G. Birney that proposed action within the political system through the establishment of an independent antislavery party. The Birney faction launched the Liberty Party in November 1839. The following April a national convention with delegates from six states nominated Birney for the presidency.

Although the Liberty Party was the first political party to take an antislavery position, and the only one at the time to do so, most abolitionist voters in the 1840 election supported the Democratic or Whig presidential candidates. Birney received only 6,797 votes (0.3 percent of the popular vote).

Aided by the controversy over the annexation of slaveholding Texas, the Liberty Party's popularity increased in 1844. Birney, again the party's presidential

James Birney. *Library of Congress*

nominee, received 62,103 votes (2.3 percent of the popular vote) but again, as in 1840, carried no states. The peak strength of the party was reached two years later in 1846, when in various state elections Liberty Party candidates received 74,017 votes.

In October 1847 the party nominated New Hampshire senator John P. Hale for the presidency, but his candidacy was withdrawn the following year when the Liberty Party joined the broader-based Free Soil Party.

National Democratic Party (1896)

A conservative faction in favor of the gold standard, the National Democrats bolted from the Democratic Party after the 1896 convention adopted a prosilver platform and nominated William Jennings Bryan for president. With the nation in the midst of a depression and the Populists in the agrarian Midwest and South demanding monetary reform, currency was the dominant issue of the 1896 campaign. This produced a brief realignment in American politics.

The Republican Party was controlled by leaders who favored maintenance of the gold standard, a noninflationary currency. Agrarian midwestern and southern Democrats, reflecting a populist philosophy, gained control of the Democratic Party in 1896 and committed it to the free coinage of silver, an inflationary currency demanded by rural elements threatened by debts. The Democrats attracted prosilver bolters from the Republican Party, but gold standard Democrats, opposed to the Republicans' protectionist position on the tariff issue, established an independent party.

Meeting in Indianapolis in September 1896, the National Democrats adopted a platform favoring maintenance of the gold standard and selected a ticket headed by seventy-nine-year-old Illinois senator John M. Palmer.

Democratic president Grover Cleveland and leading members of his administration, repudiated by the convention that chose Bryan, supported the National Democrats. During the campaign the National Democrats encouraged conservative Democrats to vote either for the National Democratic ticket or for the Republican candidate, William McKinley. The Palmer ticket received 133,435 votes (1.0 percent of the popular vote), and McKinley defeated Bryan.

William Jennings Bryan. *Library of Congress*

In the 1890s returning prosperity and the Spanish-American War overshadowed the currency issue, and the intense Democratic Party factionalism that produced the National Democratic Party ended.

National Republican Party (1828–1832)

The Democratic-Republican Party splintered after the 1824 election into two factions. The group led by Andrew Jackson retained the name Democratic-Republicans, which eventually was shortened to Democrats; the other faction, headed by President John Quincy Adams, assumed the name National Republicans. Reflecting the belief of President Adams in the establishment of a national policy by the federal government, the new party supported a protective tariff, the Bank of the United States, federal administration of public lands, and national programs of internal improvements.

But Adams's belief in a strong national government contrasted with the period's prevailing mood of populism and states' rights.

The Adams forces controlled Congress for two years, 1825 to 1827, but as party structures formalized the National Republicans became a minority in Congress and suffered a decisive loss in the 1828 presidential election. Running for reelection, Adams was beaten by Jackson. Adams received 43.6 percent of the popular vote and carried eight states, none in the South. Henry Clay, the party's candidate against Jackson four years later, had even less success. He received only 37.4 percent of the popular vote and carried just six states, none of which, again, were in the South.

Poorly organized, with dwindling support and a heritage of defeat, the National Republicans went out of existence after the 1832 election, but their members provided the base for a new anti-Jackson party, the Whigs, which came into being in 1834.

National Unity Party (Independent John B. Anderson) (1980–1988)

Republican representative John B. Anderson of Illinois formed the National Unity Campaign as the vehicle for his independent presidential campaign in 1980. Anderson began his quest for the presidency by trying to win the Republican Party nomination. But as a liberal in a party coming under conservative control, he won no primaries and could claim only fifty-seven convention delegates by April 1980. Anderson withdrew from the Republican race and declared his independent candidacy.

Anderson focused his campaign on the need to establish a viable third party as an alternative to domination of the political scene by the Republican and Democratic parties. The National Unity Campaign platform touted the Anderson program as a "new public philosophy"—more innovative than that of the Democrats, who "cling to the policies of the New Deal," and more enlightened than that of the Republicans, who talk "incessantly about freedom, but hardly ever about justice." Generally, the group took positions that were fiscally conservative and socially liberal. Anderson and his running mate, former Democratic governor Patrick J. Lucey of Wisconsin, tried to appeal to Republican and Democratic voters disenchanted with their parties and to the growing bloc of voters who classified themselves as independents.

The National Unity Campaign ticket was on the ballot in all fifty states in 1980, although Anderson had to wage costly legal battles in some states to ensure that result. In the end, the party won 6.6 percent of the presidential vote, well over the 5 percent necessary to qualify for retroactive federal campaign funding.

In April 1984 Anderson announced that he would not seek the presidency in that year. He said that instead he would focus his energies on building the National Unity Party, which he established officially in December 1983. He planned to concentrate initially on running candidates at the local level. In August Anderson endorsed Walter F. Mondale, the Democratic nominee for president, and his running mate, Geraldine A. Ferraro.

John Anderson. *File photo*

The National Unity Party did not run a presidential candidate in the 1988 race and by 1992 was no longer a political party.

Natural Law Party (1992–)

The Natural Law Party, which in its second presidential campaign in 1996 won 113,668 votes nationwide, experienced a large decline in voter support in 2000. Its presidential candidate, John Hagelin of Fairfield, Iowa, received 83,520, down almost 27 percent from four years earlier. In 1992 Hagelin won a total of 39,179. Among third parties, Hagelin's vote was seventh highest in 2000.

Hagelin was on the ballot in thirty-eight states in 2000. Because the Natural Law Party fulfilled the necessary requirements, it was assured automatic ballot access in ten states in the next presidential election in 2004. Hagelin not only was the Natural Law nominee again in 2000, but he challenged Patrick J. Buchanan for the Reform Party nomination. Losing that nomination, Hagelin and his Reform Party supporters set up a splinter Reform Party that later joined in coalition with the Natural Law Party.

Hagelin, a Harvard-trained quantum physicist, was born in Pittsburgh in 1954 and grew up in Connecticut. He became associated with Maharishi International University in Iowa in 1983. His running mate was fellow Maharishi scientist Mike Tompkins, a Harvard graduate and specialist in crime prevention programs.

The Natural Law Party has described itself as "the fastest growing grassroots party," standing for the environment, education, economic growth, job creation, and lower taxes. Despite its title, the party seemed to have little connection with the philosophic concept of natural law, which holds that some rules of society—such as the prohibition against murder—are so basic and inherent that they must be obeyed whether or not they are legislated.

Hagelin and the party have advocated prevention-oriented government and meditative, tension-relieving programs "designed to bring national life into harmony with natural law."

New Alliance Party (1988–1992)

The New Alliance Party formed in the late 1980s to promote a combination of minority interests. Self-described as "black-led, multiracial, pro-gay and pro-socialist," the party aggressively filed lawsuits to attain ballot access. In 1988 presidential candidate Lenora B. Fulani, a New York psychologist, drew 217,219 votes nationwide for a fourth-place finish. Her best showing was in the District of Columbia, where she received more than 1 percent of the vote.

In 1992, with the party qualifying for $1.8 million in federal matching funds, Fulani ran again, this time with California teacher Maria Munoz as a running mate. Fulani campaigned for equal employment for all. "I believe that a job at a union wage is the right of all Americans," she said. The New Alliance ticket appeared on the ballot in thirty-nine states and the District of Columbia and received 73,714 votes, slightly less than 0.1 percent nationwide.

Peace and Freedom Party (1967–   )

Although founded in Michigan, the radical Peace and Freedom Party has been active largely in California—the only state where it appeared on the ballot in 1996.

From the outset, the party worked with the California Black Panther Party to oppose U.S. involvement in the Vietnam War and espouse black nationalism and other so-called New Left causes. The first Peace and Freedom nominee for president, in 1968, was Black Panther leader Eldridge Cleaver. Running with various vice-presidential candidates, Cleaver received 36,563 votes.

Cleaver's autobiographical, antiracist polemic, *Soul on Ice,* was published in 1968. After the election Cleaver, a paroled convict awaiting trial for murder, went into exile. On his return years later, he became a born-again Christian.

Before the 1968 election, black activist-comedian Dick Gregory broke with the Peace and Freedom Party and set up the similarly named Freedom and Peace Party with himself as the presidential nominee. He received 47,133 votes.

After 1968 no Peace and Freedom candidate attracted significant numbers of presidential votes until 1980, when Maureen Smith and Elizabeth Barron received 18,116. In 1972, however, noted pacifist and pediatrician Benjamin Spock, the People's Party nominee, ran under the Peace and Freedom banner in California. He received 55,167 votes there and 23,589 votes in other states.

In 1974 the California Peace and Freedom Party declared itself to be socialist. In recent elections its presidential ticket has received at least 10,000 votes: 1988, Herbert Lewin and Vikki Murdock, 10,370; 1992, Ron Daniels and Asiba Tupahache, 27,961; and 1996, Marsha Feinland and Kate McClatchy, 25,332. In 2000 the party ran no presidential candidates.

People's Party (1971–)

Delegates from activist and peace groups established the People's Party at a November 1971 convention held in Dallas, Texas. The initial cochairmen were pediatrician Benjamin Spock and author Gore Vidal.

The People's Party first ran a presidential candidate in 1972. They chose Dr. Spock for president and black activist Julius Hobson of Washington, D.C., for vice president. Despite hopes for widespread backing from the poor and social activists, the ticket received only 78,756 votes, 0.1 percent of the national total. A total of 55,167 of those votes came from California alone.

At its convention, held in St. Louis, Missouri, August 31, 1975, the People's Party chose black civil rights activist Margaret Wright of California for president and Maggie Kuhn of Pennsylvania, a leader in the Gray Panthers movement for rights for the elderly, for vice president. Kuhn, however, declined the nomination and was replaced on the ticket by Spock.

The party platform focused on cutting the defense budget, closing tax loopholes, and making that money available for social programs. Other planks included redistribution of land and wealth, unconditional amnesty for war objectors, and free health care. In her campaign, Wright stressed the necessity for active participation by citizens in the governmental process, so that institutions and programs could be run from the grass roots up rather than from the top down.

As in 1972, the party's main backing came in California, where it was supported by the state Peace and Freedom Party. Wright's total national vote in 1976 was 49,024, and 85.1 percent (41,731 votes) of those votes came from California. The party has not fielded presidential candidates since 1976.

Populist (People's) Party (1891–1908)

The Populist (or People's) Party, a third party founded in May 1891 in Cincinnati, Ohio, grew out of a period of agrarian revolt and remained politically active until 1908.

Following the Civil War, farmers battled falling commodity prices, high railroad rates, and heavy mortgage debt. The Patrons of Husbandry (the Grange), organized in 1867 by Oliver Kelley, began as a group intent on improving educational and social opportunities for farm men and women but soon adopted economic and political initiatives such as the cooperative movement of the 1870s. The inability of the Grange to give farmers an effective political voice led many Grangers, in the 1880s, to join the Farmers' Alliance, a precursor to the Populist Party. More aggressive and politically oriented, the Farmers' Alliance considered all agricultural problems as economic and pursued remedies such as political education and cooperative marketing, particularly in the South, as a means to break the grip of the furnishing merchants, who extended credit through crop liens.

Women, while active members, held far fewer offices in the Farmers' Alliance than those in the Grange. Existing racial prejudices led to the separate creation of a Colored Farmers' National Alliance in 1888.

In June 1890 Kansas farmers founded the People's Party based on the Southern Alliance platform, which included government ownership of railroads, free and unlimited coinage of silver, and a subtreasury (a system by which farmers could turn over a staple crop to a government warehouse and receive a loan for 80 percent of its value at 2 percent interest per month). As a national third party in 1891, the Populists also sought a farmer-laborer political coalition that championed the belief, expressed by Minnesota Populist Ignatius Donnelly, that the "public good is paramount to private interests."

For a time, the party attempted to bridge the racial gulf and recruited black farmers as well as white. Populism in the South, however, became mired in the volatility of race, epitomized by Georgia's Tom Watson and South Carolina's Benjamin Tillman. Although not immune to the negative racial and ethnic overtones of the period, the Populist Party was nevertheless more concerned with achieving economic reforms, a humane industrial society, and a just polity than it was with attacking cultural issues. The party's greatest support came from white land-owning cotton farmers in the South and wheat farmers in the West.

The Populists rallied behind a policy of monetary inflation in the expectation that it would increase the amount of currency in circulation, boost

James Weaver. *Library of Congress*

commodity prices, and ease farmers' indebtedness. In 1892, when the People's Party nominated James B. Weaver of Iowa as its presidential candidate, its demands included a graduated income tax, antitrust regulations, public ownership of railroads, and unlimited coinage of silver and gold at a ratio of sixteen to one. Democrat Grover Cleveland was elected to a second term, with Weaver carrying only four states in the West. In 1896 the Populists nominated William Jennings Bryan, a free-silver candidate from Nebraska who was also the Democratic nominee, but the Republicans won with William McKinley.

Having lost on the silver issue and having lost their identity through a "fusion" with the Democrats, the Populists declined in strength and influence, particularly as new discoveries of gold eased the monetary crisis and agricultural conditions improved. Although the People's Party receded, some of the reforms it had championed, including a graduated income tax, were instituted during the Progressive era. The Populists' main significance lay in their visionary use of politics to turn a spotlight on the conditions facing farm families and thereby seek more democratic reform measures.

Progressive (Bull Moose) Party (1912)

A split in Republican ranks, spurred by the bitter personal and ideological dispute between President William Howard Taft (1909–1913) and former president Theodore Roosevelt (1901–1909), resulted in the withdrawal of the Roosevelt forces from the Republican Party after the June 1912 convention and the creation of the Progressive Party two months later. The new party was known popularly as the Bull Moose Party, a name resulting from Roosevelt's assertion early in the campaign that he felt as fit as a bull moose. While the Taft-Roosevelt split was the immediate reason for the new party, the Bull Moosers were an outgrowth of the Progressive movement that was a powerful force in both major parties in the early years of the twentieth century.

Although in 1908 Roosevelt had handpicked Taft as his successor, his disillusionment with Taft's conservative philosophy came quickly, and with the support of progressive Republicans

Theodore Roosevelt. *Library of Congress*

Roosevelt challenged the incumbent for the 1912 Republican presidential nomination. Roosevelt outpolled Taft in the presidential primary states. Taft nevertheless won the nomination with nearly solid support in the South and among party conservatives, providing the narrow majority of delegates that enabled him to win the bulk of the key credentials challenges.

Although few Republican politicians followed Roosevelt in his bolt, the new party demonstrated a popular base at its convention in Chicago in August 1912. Thousands of delegates, basically middle- and upper-class reformers from small towns and cities, attended the convention that launched the party and nominated Roosevelt for president and California governor Hiram Johnson as his running mate. Roosevelt appeared in person to deliver his "Confession of Faith," a speech detailing his nationalistic philosophy and progressive reform ideas. The Bull Moose platform reflected key tenets of the Progressive movement, calling for more extensive government antitrust action and for labor, social, government, and electoral reform.

Roosevelt was wounded in an assassination attempt while campaigning in Milwaukee, Wisconsin, in October, but he finished the campaign. In the general election Roosevelt received more than 4 million votes (27.4 percent of the popular vote) and carried six states. His percentage of the vote was the highest ever received by a third-party candidate in American history, but his candidacy split the Republican vote and enabled the Democrats' nominee, Woodrow Wilson, to win the election. The Progressive Party had minimal success at the state and local levels, winning thirteen House seats but electing no senators or governors.

Roosevelt declined the Progressive nomination in 1916 and endorsed the Republican candidate, Charles Evans Hughes. With the defection of its leader, the decline of the Progressive movement, and the lack of an effective party organization, the Bull Moose Party ceased to exist.

Progressive Party (La Follette) (1924)

Like the Bull Moose Party of Theodore Roosevelt, the Progressive Party that emerged in the mid-1920s was a reform effort led by a Republican. Wisconsin senator Robert M. La Follette led the new Progressive Party, a separate entity from the Bull Moosers, which, unlike the middle- and upper-class Roosevelt party of the previous decade, had its greatest appeal among farmers and organized labor.

The La Follette Progressive Party grew out of the Conference for Progressive Political Action (CPPA), a coalition of railway union leaders and a remnant of the Bull Moose effort that was formed in 1922. The Socialist Party joined the coalition the following year. Throughout 1923 the Socialists and labor unions argued over whether their coalition should form a third party, with the Socialists in favor and the labor unions against it. It was finally decided to run an independent presidential candidate, La Follette, in the 1924 election but not to field candidates at the state and local levels. La Follette was given the power to choose his running mate and selected Montana senator Burton K. Wheeler, a Democrat.

Opposition to corporate monopolies was the major issue of the La Follette campaign, although the party advocated various other reforms, particularly aimed at farmers and workers, which were proposed earlier by either the Populists or Bull Moosers. But the Progressive Party itself was a major issue in the 1924 campaign, as the Republicans attacked the alleged radicalism of the party.

Although La Follette had its endorsement, the American Federation of Labor (AFL) provided minimal support. The basic strength of the Progressives, like that of the Populists in the 1890s, derived from agrarian voters west of the Mississippi River. La Follette received 4,832,532 votes (16.6 percent of the popular vote) but carried just one state, his native Wisconsin. When La Follette died in 1925, the party collapsed as a national force. It was revived by La Follette's sons on a state-wide level in Wisconsin in the mid-1930s.

Robert M. La Follette. *Library of Congress*

Progressive Party (Wallace) (1948)

Henry A. Wallace's Progressive Party resulted from the dissatisfaction of liberal elements in the Democratic Party with the leadership of President Harry S. Truman, particularly in the realm of foreign policy. The Progressive Party was one of two bolting groups from the Democratic Party in 1948; conservative southern elements withdrew to form the States' Rights Party.

Henry Wallace, the founder of the Progressive Party, was secretary of agriculture, vice president, and finally secretary of commerce under President Franklin Roosevelt. He carried the reputation of one of the most liberal idealists in the Roosevelt administration. Fired from the Truman cabinet in 1946 after breaking with administration policy and publicly ad-

Henry Wallace. *Library of Congress*

vocating peaceful coexistence with the Soviet Union, Wallace began to consider the idea of a liberal third-party candidacy. Supported by the American Labor Party, the Progressive Citizens of America, and other progressive organizations in California and Illinois, Wallace announced his third-party candidacy in December 1947.

The Progressive Party was launched formally the following July at a convention in Philadelphia, which ratified the selection of Wallace for president and Sen. Glen H. Taylor, D-Idaho, as his running mate. The party adopted a platform that emphasized foreign policy—opposing the cold war anticommunism of the Truman administration and specifically urging abandonment of the Truman Doctrine and the Marshall Plan. These measures were designed to contain the spread of communism and bolster noncommunist nations. On domestic issues the Progressives stressed humanitarian concerns and equal rights for both sexes and all races.

Minority groups—women, youth, African Americans, Jews, Hispanic Americans—were active in the new party, but the openness of the Progressives brought Wallace a damaging endorsement from the Communist Party. Believing the two parties could work together, Wallace accepted the endorsement while characterizing his philosophy as "progressive capitalism."

In 1948 the Progressives appeared on the presidential ballot in forty-five states, but the Communist endorsement helped keep the party on the defensive the entire campaign. In the November election Wallace received only 1,157,326 votes (2.4 percent of the national popular vote), with nearly half of the votes from the state of New York. Not only were the

Progressives unable to carry a single state, but in spite of their defection from the Democratic Party, President Truman won reelection. The Progressives had poor results in the congressional races, failing to elect one representative or senator.

The Progressive Party's opposition to the Korean War in 1950 drove many moderate elements out of the party, including Henry Wallace. The party ran a national ticket in 1952 but received only 140,023 votes nationwide or 0.2 percent of the national popular vote. The party crumbled completely after the election.

Progressive Labor Party (1960–)

The Progressive Labor Party (PLP) emerged out of the Communist Party USA in the early 1960s. It was the first Maoist party in the United States, following the revolutionary philosophies of Joseph Stalin and Mao Zedong and adhering to Mao's dictum that "power emanates from the barrel of a gun." The PLP envisions Stalin's dictatorship as the ideal state and opposes democracy, elections, capitalism, religion, and freedom in any form.

The PLP took over the Students for a Democratic Society (SDS) in 1969, prompting the non–Progressive Labor people to walk out of SDS and leaving the organization as a shell of its former self. The SDS was an activist— its critics said radical—student organization that started in Michigan and drew many supporters on campuses nationwide, particularly during the Vietnam War years.

The PLP contends that experiments with socialism and communism failed in the former Soviet Union and in today's People's Republic of China, where, it says, capitalism has triumphed. The PLP's doctrine, proclaimed on its Web site, envisions the party leading an "armed struggle by masses of workers, soldiers, students and others, to destroy the dictatorship of the capitalist class and set up a dictatorship of the working class."

The PLP publishes a newspaper, *Challenge,* and a magazine, *Communist,* as well as leaflets on such topics as "The Imperialist War in the Mideast," "Smash Racist Police Terror," and "Fascism Grows in the Auto Industry." In strict adherence to its policy of "armed struggle," the party disavows electoral politics and has run almost no candidates for office during its history.

Prohibition Party (1869–   )

Prohibition and temperance movements sought to legislate an end to consumption of intoxicating beverages. Colonial and early national Americans preferred alcohol to impure water or milk and more expensive coffee or tea. By 1825 those over fifteen years of age drank an average of seven gallons of pure alcohol per year, diluted in cider, beer, wine, and distilled liquor; white males typically consumed substantially more, women much less, and black slaves very little. Physicians, Protestant ministers, and temperance advocates concerned about damage to health, morals, and industrial production urged voluntary abstinence from drinking. After achieving remarkable success, the temperance movement sought legal banishment of liquor. During the 1850s a dozen states—led by Maine in 1851—adopted alcohol bans.

After the Civil War, temperance crusaders created effective political pressure groups: the Prohibition Party in 1869, the Woman's Christian Temperance Union in 1874, and the Anti-Saloon League of America in 1895. Their campaigns won numerous statewide prohibition and local option laws, the latter giving individual communities the right to outlaw the sale of alcohol. In 1913 Congress banned shipment of liquor into any state that chose to bar it. Dissatisfied by uneven and sometimes short-lived state and local successes, goaded by rivalries between the Anti-Saloon League and competing temperance groups, and inspired by adoption of the first federal constitutional amendments in more than forty years (the income tax and direct Senate election amendments of 1913), reformers began calling for a total, permanent, nationwide solution to the liquor problem: a prohibition amendment to the Constitution.

National prohibition gathered support from evangelical Protestant denominations, feminists, nativists opposed to the recent flood of immigrants who drank, progressive social and political reformers, and industrial employers. Employing the unusual political tactic of pledging electoral support or punishment solely on the basis of a candidate's stand on the single issue of alcohol, proponents of Prohibition were able to get more and more supporters elected to Congress. U.S. entry into World War I against Germany added a final argument of patriotism, because the army needed the grain for bread and the troops needed to be sober to perform effectively. The Eighteenth (or Prohibition) Amendment was adopted with bipartisan backing in

Advocates against Prohibition present petitions to Congress.   *Library of Congress*

January 1919 and went into effect one year later; it operated with mixed success for fourteen years.

The Republicans, who were responsible for enforcement as the party in power throughout the 1920s, continued to defend Prohibition even as the Democrats' support was waning, especially in the urban North, as first Al Smith and later Franklin D. Roosevelt aligned with the repeal campaign. Differences regarding Prohibition were among the most clear-cut partisan divisions in the 1932 elections and helped account for the shift in the national political balance during the depths of the Great Depression. National Prohibition, widely viewed as a mistake, was repealed by the Twenty-first Amendment, which was ratified in December 1933.

The party remained after the repeal of Prohibition, however, becoming the longest running third party in American history in the twentieth century. The party has run a national ticket in every presidential election since 1872, but its candidates have never carried a single state. After the 1976 election, the Prohibition Party changed its name to the National Statesman Party, and its 1980 candidate registered using that party name. The 1984 candidate, Earl F. Dodge of Colorado, emphasized that his party—on the ballots once again as Prohibitionists—no longer focused on a single issue: the party backed religious liberty and an antiabortion amendment. Dodge ran again in 1988, 1992, 1996, and 2000. In 2000 the party could only muster 208 votes nationwide.

Reform Party (Independent Ross Perot) (1992–)

The Reform Party emerged almost full grown from Texas billionaire Ross Perot's independent self-financed presidential candidacy of 1992. That year Perot drew the highest vote share of any independent or third-party candidate in eighty years. Relying heavily on his wealth and on grass-roots volunteer efforts to get his name on the ballot in all fifty states and the District of Columbia, Perot received 19,741,657 votes or 18.9 percent of the nationwide vote. He did not win any sizable constituency or receive any electoral votes, but he drew a respectable 10 percent to 30 percent in popular voting across the nation.

Perot, who announced the possibility of his candidacy in February 1992, ran his early unofficial campaign mainly on one issue—eliminating the federal deficit. He had the luxury of funding his entire campaign, which included buying huge amounts of television time. Drawing on the disenchantment of voters, Perot and his folksy, no-nonsense approach to government reform struck a populist chord. But he also demonstrated his quirkiness by bizarrely withdrawing from the presidential race in mid-July and then reversing himself and reentering in October. He chose as his running mate retired admiral James B. Stockdale, who as a navy flier had been a prisoner during much of the Vietnam War.

United We Stand America (UWSA), formed from the ashes of Perot's candidacy, did not bill itself as an official political party. Promoting itself instead as a nonpartisan educational organization, UWSA called for a balanced budget, government reform, and health care reform. The group's leaders did not endorse candidates or offer them financial assistance.

Ross Perot. *File photo*

In 1993 Perot, rather than UWSA, commanded considerable attention on Capitol Hill, marshaling grass-roots support on congressional reform to unsuccessfully opposing the North American Free Trade Agreement (NAFTA). Democrats and Republicans were unable to co-opt his following as they had those of major third-party movements in the past. Perot continued to use his supporters' anger with government and the political process to sustain himself as an independent political force. In the fall of 1995 Perot created a full-fledged political party, the Reform Party, and ran as its nominee in a campaign financed with federal funds.

The Reform Party effort of 1996 qualified for federal funding and went along with the limitations that acceptance of the money entailed. By garnering more than 5 percent of the 1992 presidential vote, Perot's party qualified in 1996 for some $30 million, less than half the amount he spent from his own pocket four years earlier.

Perot was challenged for the Reform Party nomination by Richard D. Lamm, a former Democratic governor of Colorado who had shown a willingness to risk voter displeasure. Lamm had called, for example, for deep cuts in Medicare, the popular health care program for the elderly.

Perot defeated Lamm in an unusual two-stage procedure, with a preliminary vote after nominating speeches at a convention in Long Beach, California, followed by a mail and electronic vote with the winner announced a week later in Valley Forge, Pennsylvania. Ballots had been sent to 1.3 million voters who were registered party members or signers of its ballot access petitions. Less than 50,000 votes, though, were actually cast, with Perot a winner by a margin of nearly 2-to-1.

Perot again was on the general election ballot in all states. He chose as his running mate Pat Choate, a native Texan and economist who had coached Perot in his unsuccessful fight against NAFTA. The Reform Party also had congressional candidates in ten states.

Locked out of the presidential debates, Perot spent much of his campaign money on television "infomercials" espousing the party's principles. Besides a balanced budget these included higher ethical standards for the White House and Congress, campaign and election reforms, a new tax system, and lobbying restrictions.

Even with the restricted budget, Perot again placed third in the national election after the two major party candidates. However, his 8,085,402 votes, 8.4 percent of the total, came to less than half of his 1992 achievement of 18.9 percent, a third-party figure surpassed in the twentieth century only by former president Theodore Roosevelt and his Bull Moose candidacy of 1912. Perot had his best showing in Maine, where he received 14.2 percent of the vote. He won no electoral votes.

In 1998 the Reform Party scored a high-profile victory when former professional wrestler Jesse Ventura was elected governor of Minnesota running on the party label. Ventura's victory helped give the Reform Party the look of a growth stock, and several well-known personalities publicly considered running for the party's presidential nomination in 2000, including former Connecticut governor Lowell P. Weicker Jr. and financier Donald Trump. Ultimately, they did not run, although Patrick J. Buchanan did, bolting the Republican Party in October 1999.

Highly public party infighting followed, with Perot loyalists arrayed against Buchanan supporters. The latter claimed they offered the party energy and new blood; the former contended Buchanan was intent on a hostile takeover designed to give the Reform Party a socially conservative face.

Calling the party "dysfunctional," Ventura announced in February 2000 that he was leaving to become an independent. In June Perot publicly distanced himself from his creation by declining to run against Buchanan in the party's mail-in primary in July. But John Hagelin, the candidate of the Natural Law Party in 1992 and 1996, did enter.

The Reform Party's convention in Long Beach, California, in August, disintegrated into two competing conclaves: one favorable to Buchanan, the other, dominated by Perot loyalists, favorable to Hagelin. After Buchanan wrested control of the party and nomination, the Hagelin forces set up a splinter Reform Party. Hagelin chose Nat Goldhaber of California for the vice-presidential spot on his ticket. In September the splinter group joined in coalition with the Natural Law Party, Hagelin's old party.

Nevertheless, Buchanan retained control of the base party's apparatus, and a federal court awarded him full use of the $12.6 million in federal funds that Perot's 1996 showing had qualified the party's 2000 nominee to receive. Buchanan chose for his running mate Ezola Foster, a California teacher. The bipartisan Commission on Presidential Debates, however, denied Buchanan participation in the three presidential debates held in October. Buchanan support in the polls was under the 15 percent required to enter the debates.

The actual 2000 election results were a major disappointment to Reform Party supporters. Although commentators thought Buchanan's message would attract many social conservatives, the party garnered only 448,868 votes, just 0.43 percent of the total presidential vote. Some commentators, however, noted that Buchanan was on the ballot in four competitive states that were won by Democratic candidate Al Gore. They argued that the Reform vote in those states may have drawn off enough support from Republican George W. Bush to swing the states' thirty electoral votes into the Democratic column.

Republican Party (1854–)

The Republican Party, founded in 1854, dominated national politics from 1860 to the New Deal era and again from 1968 to the present. The party emerged in 1854–1856 out of a political frenzy, in all northern states, revolving around the expansion of slavery into the western territories. The new party was so named because "republicanism" was the core value of American politics, and it seemed to be mortally threatened by the expanding "slave power." The enemy was not so much the institution of slavery or the mistreatment of the slaves. Rather, it was the political-economic system that controlled the South, exerted disproportionate control over the national government, and threatened to seize power in the new territories.

Origins through Reconstruction

The party came into being in reaction to federal legislation allowing the new settlers of Kansas Territory to decide for themselves whether to adopt slavery or to continue the Compromise of 1820, which explicitly forbade slavery there. The new party lost on this issue, but in addition to bringing in most northern Whigs, it gained support from "Free Soil" northern Democrats who opposed the expansion of slavery. Only a handful of abolitionists joined. The Republicans adopted most of the modernization programs of the Whigs, favoring banks, tariffs, and internal improvements and adding, as well, a demand for a homestead law that would provide free farms to western settlers. In state after state, the Republicans outmaneuvered rival parties (the old Whigs, the Prohibitionists, and the Know Nothings), absorbing most of their supporters without accepting their doctrines.

The 1856 campaign, with strong pietistic, Protestant overtones, was a crusade for "Free Soil, Free Labor, Free Men, and Fremont!" John C. Fremont was defeated by a sharp countercrusade that warned against fanaticism and the imminent risk of civil war. By the late 1850s the new party dominated every northern state. It controlled enough electoral votes to win, despite its almost complete lack of support below the Mason-Dixon line. Leaders such as William H. Seward of New York and Salmon P. Chase of Ohio were passed over as presidential candidates in 1860 because they were too radical in their rhetoric and their states were safely in the Republican column. Abraham Lincoln was more moderate, and had more of an appeal in the closely divided western states of Illinois and Indiana. With only 40 percent of the popular vote, Lincoln swept the North and easily carried the electoral college. Interpreting the Republican victory as a signal of intense, permanent Yankee hostility, seven states of the Deep South seceded and formed their own confederation.

The Republicans had not expected secession and were baffled by it. The Lincoln administration, stiffened by the unionist pleas of conservative northern Democrats, rejected both the suggestion of abolitionists that the slaveholders be allowed to depart in peace and the insistence of Confederates that they had a right to revolution and self-governance.

Lincoln proved brilliantly successful in uniting all the factions of his party to fight for the Union. Most northern Democrats were likewise supportive until the fall of 1862, when Lincoln added the abolition of slavery as a war goal. All the state Republican parties accepted the antislavery goal except Kentucky. In Congress the party passed major legislation to promote rapid modernization, in-

Abraham Lincoln. *Library of Congress*

cluding measures for a national banking system, high tariffs, homestead laws, and aid to education and agriculture. How to deal with the ex-Confederates was a major issue; by 1864 radical Republicans controlled Congress and demanded more aggressive action against slavery and more vengeance toward the Confederates. Lincoln held them off, but just barely. His successor, Andrew Johnson, proved eager to reunite the nation, allowing the radicals to seize control of Congress, the party, and the army and nearly convict Johnson on a close impeachment vote.

Ulysses S. Grant was elected president in 1868 with strong support from radicals and the new Republican regimes in the South. He in turn vigorously supported radical Reconstruction programs in the South, the Fourteenth Amendment, and equal civil and voting rights for the freedmen.

Most of all, he was the hero of the war veterans, who gave him strong support. The party had become so large that factionalism was inevitable; it was hastened by Grant's tolerance of high levels of corruption. The Liberal Republicans split off in 1872 on the grounds that it was time to declare the war finished and bring the troops home from the occupied southern states.

Late Nineteenth Century

The depression of 1873 energized the Democrats. They won control of the House and formed "Redeemer" coalitions that recaptured control of each southern state, often using threats and violence. The Compromise of 1877 resolved the disputed election of 1876 by giving the White House to the Republicans and all of the southern states to the Democrats. The GOP, as it was now nicknamed, split into "Stalwart" and "Half-Breed" factions. In 1884, "Mugwump" reformers split off and helped elect Democrat Grover Cleveland.

In the North the Republican Party proved most attractive to men with an ambitious vision of a richer, more modern, and more complex society and economy. The leading modernizers were well-educated men from business, finance, and the professions. Commercial farmers, skilled mechanics, and office clerks largely supported the GOP, while unskilled workers and traditional farmers were solidly Democratic. The moral dimension of the party attracted pietistic Protestants, especially Methodists, Congregationalists, Presbyterians, Scandinavian Lutherans, and Quakers. By contrast, the high church or "liturgical" denominations (Roman Catholics, Mormons, German Lutherans, and Episcopalians) were offended by Republican crusaders who wanted to impose their own moral standards, especially through prohibition and control over public schools.

Millions of immigrants entered the political system after 1850 and usually started voting only a few years after arrival. The Catholics (Irish, German, and Dutch) became Democrats, but the Republicans won majorities among the Protestant British, German, Dutch, and Scandinavian newcomers and among German Jews. After 1890 new, much poorer ethnic groups arrived in large numbers—especially Italians, Poles, and Yiddish-speaking Jews. For the most part they did not become politically active until the 1920s. After 1876 southern voting was quite distinct from the rest of America—with very few white Republicans, apart from pockets of GOP strength

The Republican elephant made its first appearance in a Thomas Nast illustration for *Harper's Weekly* on November 7, 1874.   *Library of Congress*

in the Appalachian and Ozark Mountain districts. The party remained popular among black southerners, even as disenfranchisement minimized their political role. (They were allowed to select delegates to the Republican national convention.)

In the 1888 election, for the first time since 1872, the Republicans gained control of the White House and both houses of Congress. New procedural rules in the House gave the Republican leaders (especially Speaker Thomas Reed) the ability to pass major legislation. New spending bills, such as one that provided generous pensions to Civil War veterans, coupled with the new McKinley tariff, made the GOP the target of charges of "paternalism." Democrats ridiculed the "Billion Dollar Congress," to which Reed shot back, "It's a billion dollar country!"

At the grass roots, militant pietists overcame the advice of more tolerant professionals to endorse statewide prohibition. In the Midwest, reformers declared war on the large German community, trying to shut down their parochial schools as well as their saloons. The Republicans, relying too much on the old-stock coalition that had always dominated the party's voting base, were badly defeated in the 1890 off-year election and the 1892 presidential contest, won by Cleveland. Alarmed professionals thereupon reasserted control over the local organizations, leading to a sort of "bossism" that (after 1900) fueled the outrage of progressives. Meanwhile, a severe economic depression struck both rural and urban America in 1893—on Cleveland's watch. The depression, combined with violent nationwide coal and railway strikes and snarling factionalism inside the Democratic Party, led to a sweeping victory for the GOP in 1894.

The party seemed invincible in 1896, until the Democrats unexpectedly selected William Jennings Bryan as their presidential candidate. Bryan's hugely popular crusade against the gold standard, financiers, railroads, and industrialists—indeed, against the cities—created a crisis for Republican candidate William McKinley and his campaign manager, Mark Hanna. Because of civil service reforms, parties could no longer finance themselves internally. Hanna solved that problem by directly obtaining $3.5 million from large corporations threatened by Bryan. Over the next century, campaign finance would be hotly debated. McKinley promised prosperity for everyone and every group, with no governmental attacks on property or ethnic groups. The business community, factory workers, white-collar workers, and commercial farmers responded enthusiastically, becoming major components of the new Republican majority. As voter turnout soared to the 95 percent level throughout much of the North, Germans and other ethnic groups grew alarmed by Bryan's moralism and voted Republican.

Early Twentieth Century

Rejuvenated by their triumphs in 1894 and 1896 and by the glamour of a highly popular short war in 1898, against Spain over Cuba, the Philippines, and other Spanish possessions, the Republicans rolled to victory after victory. However, the party had again grown too large, and factionalism increasingly tore it apart.

The break within the party came in 1912 over the issue of progressivism. President William Howard Taft favored conservative reform controlled by the courts; former president Theodore Roosevelt went to the grass roots, attacking Taft, bosses, courts, big business, and the "malefactors of great wealth." Defeated at the convention, Roosevelt bolted and formed a third party. The vast majority of progressive politicians refused to follow Roosevelt's rash action, for it allowed the conservatives to seize control of the GOP; they kept it for the next thirty years. Roosevelt's quixotic crusade also allowed Democrat Woodrow Wilson to gain the White House with only 40 percent of the vote. But after Wilson's fragile coalition collapsed in 1920, the GOP won three consecutive presidential contests.

Herbert Hoover, elected in 1928, represented the quintessence of the modernizing engineer, bringing efficiency to government and the economy. His poor skills at negotiating with politicians hardly seemed to matter when the economy boomed in the 1920s and Democrats were in disarray. However, when the Great Depression hit in the 1930s, his political ineptitude compounded the party's weaknesses. For the next four decades, whenever Democrats were at a loss for words, they could always ridicule Hoover.

New Deal and Democratic Dominance

The Great Depression sidelined the GOP for decades. The old conservative formulas for prosperity had lost their magic. The Democrats, by contrast, built up majorities that depended on labor unions, big city machines, federal relief funds, and the mobilization of Catholics, Jews, and African Americans. However, middle-class hostility to new taxes, and fears about a repeat of the First World War, eventually led to a Republican rebound. Franklin Roosevelt's immense popularity gave him four consecutive victories, but by 1938 the GOP was doing quite well in off-year elections when FDR's magic was not at work.

In 1948 taxes were high, federal relief had ended, and big-city machines were collapsing, but union strength helped Harry S. Truman reassemble FDR's coalition for one last hurrah. The year 1948 proved to be the high-water mark of class polarization in American politics; afterward, the differences narrowed between the middle class and the working class.

The issues of Korea, communism, and corruption gave World War II hero Dwight D. Eisenhower a victory in 1952 for Republicans, along with narrow control of Congress. However, the GOP remained a minority party and was factionalized, with a northeastern liberal element basically favorable to the New Deal welfare state and the policy of containing communist expansion, versus midwestern conservatives who bitterly opposed New

Deal taxes, regulation, labor unions, and internationalism. Both factions used the issue of anticommunism and attacked the Democrats for harboring spies and allowing communist gains in China and Korea. New York governors Thomas E. Dewey and Nelson Rockefeller led the liberal wing, while Sens. Robert Taft of Ohio and Barry Goldwater of Arizona spoke for the conservatives. Eisenhower represented internationalism in foreign policy, and he sidetracked the isolationism represented by Taft and Hoover.

Richard Nixon, who was Eisenhower's vice president, was aligned with the eastern liberal GOP. Nominated in 1960 to succeed Eisenhower, he lost because the Democrats had a larger base of loyal supporters, especially among Catholics who turned out to support their candidate, John F. Kennedy. The defeat of yet another candidate sponsored by the eastern "establishment" opened the way for Goldwater's 1964 crusade against the New Deal and then-president Lyndon Johnson's Great Society programs. Goldwater permanently knocked out the eastern liberals, but in turn his crushing defeat as the GOP presidential candidate in 1964 retired many old-line conservatives. Goldwater in 1964 and independent George Wallace in 1968 took southern whites and many northern Catholics away from their Democratic roots, while at the same time the Democratic commitment to civil rights won over nine-tenths of all African American voters.

Republican Revival

President Johnson, who was Kennedy's vice president and succeeded him on Kennedy's assassination in 1963, won an overwhelming victory in 1964 and brought with him a large Democratic majority in Congress that enacted sweeping social programs that Johnson called the Great Society. However, support for these programs collapsed in the mid-1960s in the face of violence and protest over racial anger as the civil rights movement gained steam, the Vietnam War, generational conflicts, the perception of increased crime, burning inner cities growing in part from the assassination of important civil rights leaders, and charges that the federal government was badly out of control.

Nixon seized the moment and ran again, winning narrowly in 1968. As president he largely ignored his party—his 1972 reelection campaign was practically nonpartisan but wildly successful as he buried his Democratic opponent. But Nixon was not to serve out his second term. The Watergate scandal, which revealed White House and presidential involvement in criminal activities, forced him to resign from office in the face of certain congressional impeachment and removal from office. Nixon's self-destruction wreaked havoc in the 1974 election, in which Democrats swept to a massive victory in off-year contests, and set the stage for the Carter interregnum.

Georgia governor Jimmy Carter won the White House for the Democrats in 1976 but his presidency crashed even before it expired in 1980. Foreign affairs were unusually salient, as public opinion saw failure in policy toward the Soviet Union, Middle Eastern nations that forced an energy crises by withholding oil supplies, and Iranian revolutionaries that held Americans hostage for months. "Stagflation" in the economy meant a combination of high unemployment and high inflation. Most of all there was a sense of drift or, worse, of malaise. The country craved leadership.

Ronald Reagan answered that need. A former movie actor and Republican governor of California, Reagan had been a supporter of Goldwater and an articulate spokesman for the conservative views that the 1964 presidential candidate set in motion. Reagan led a political revolution in 1980,

President Ronald Reagan meets with Republican members of Congress in front of the White House in 1984. *National Republican Congressional Committee*

capitalizing on grievances and mobilizing an entirely new voting bloc, the religious right. Southern Baptists and other fundamentalists and evangelicals had been voting Democratic since the New Deal. Suddenly they began to react strongly against a perceived national tolerance of immorality (especially regarding abortion and homosexuality), rising crime, and America's apparent rejection of traditional family values. Reagan had vision and leadership qualities that many in the traditional political establishment did not initially understand. Reagan oversaw a massive military buildup, very large tax cuts, and—inadvertently—a massive increase in the national debt.

By 1984 inflation had declined significantly, unemployment had eased, profits were soaring, some changes had been made in the Social Security system, and Reagan carried forty-nine states in winning reelection. Most astonishing of all was Reagan's aggressive pursuit of cold war policy, followed closely by the collapse of the Soviet Union and the end of international communism in most nations. The best issue for the Democrats was the soaring national debt—long a conservative theme. For the first time since 1932, the GOP pulled abreast of the Democrats in terms of party identification on the part of voters. A greater number of higher-income people were voting Republican, which was not offset by the lower-income groups that had always been the mainstay of the Democratic Party. By the 1980s a gender gap was apparent, with men and housewives more Republican while single, divorced, and professional women tended to be Democratic. Groups that were part of the religious right helped deliver to the GOP the votes of their membership. Those gains were largely offset by the Democratic increases among holders of college and postgraduate degrees for the party's positions regarding multiculturalism and a tolerance of homosexuality and abortion.

George Herbert Walker Bush rode to the White House in 1988 on Reagan's popularity and could himself claim important victories in the cold war and in the Middle East, where the Persian Gulf War liberated Kuwait in 1991 after an invasion by neighboring Iraq. But Bush—so knowledgeable on international affairs—seemed unconcerned about taxes, deficits, and other domestic issues that bothered Americans far more. Most importantly, Bush was ambushed by the remnants of a nasty recession in 1990–1991 just as he was running for reelection in 1992, allowing Arkansas governor Bill Clinton to take back the White House for the Democrats.

The 1990s was a decade of travail for the Republican Party. It lost the 1992 and 1996 presidential elections to Clinton, the first time the GOP had lost successive White House elections since the Kennedy and Johnson wins in 1960 and 1964. Clinton proved a popular if controversial president, raising the specter that the generally Republican trend of recent decades had finally been broken. However, the GOP roared back in 1994, gaining control of Congress—both the House and Senate—for the first time since 1952 as well as control of governors' mansions in nearly all the major states. This remarkable achievement was engineered in important part by a backbencher Republican representative from Georgia, Newt Gingrich. As a result, he became House Speaker but then proceeded to all but self-destruct through an aggressive and ultimately futile combat with Clinton over programs and policies.

The rancorous leadership of Gingrich soured politics in Washington, and he was unable to deliver on most of his conservative program that he called the "Contract with America." The Republican condition worsened when the party attempted to impeach and remove Clinton from office over a

scandal that had its roots in a messy affair between Clinton and a young female intern in the White House that Clinton at first denied. The public, appalled at the scandal, never showed enthusiasm for removing Clinton and the Senate refused to convict the president after the House—in highly partisan proceedings—approved impeachment. This event, the Gingrich overreaching, and other missteps by Republicans gradually whittled down the Republican's control of Congress in elections after 1994.

Nevertheless, in the 2000 elections the Republican Party achieved a dream long thought impossible. In a contested election, former president Bush's son,

George W. Bush. *File photo*

George W. Bush, defeated Democrat Al Gore, a victory—although one of the most narrow in history—that revived the GOP dominance of national level politics that began with Richard Nixon in 1968. Equally important, the GOP retained control of Congress, giving it complete control of the federal government for the first time since 1953. To be sure, their margin in the House was further eroded and the margin in the Senate evaporated entirely with an exact tie of fifty Democrats and fifty Republicans. However, the GOP retained control since the new GOP vice president, as the Senate's presiding officer under the Constitution, could vote to break a tie vote.

Socialist Party (1901–)

The inception of the Socialist Party marked a unique, brief era of leftist organizational unity. Founded in 1901 by New York attorney Morris Hillquit and railroad worker and labor leader Eugene Debs, the Socialist Party brought together the Social Democratic Party; Social Laborites; Christian Socialists; a wing of the Socialist Labor Party; and followers of Henry George, Edward Bellamy, and assorted populist sympathizers. Rapid growth and early success continued through the 1912 presidential election, when Debs earned 6 percent of the votes cast and some twelve hundred Socialist Party candidates won state and local elections, including seventy-nine mayoral races.

Despite the party's continued strong showing in the 1916 and 1920 elections, World War I took a toll on the Socialist Party. Although party members were already persecuted for their opposition to the war, the Sedition Act of 1918 resulted in additional arrests and prevented the Socialist Party from using the mail to communicate with branches beyond its East Coast and Midwest bases. While many, including Debs, were being sent to prison for either their pacifist views or Sedition Act violations, the 1917 Bolshevik Revolution in Russia led by Vladimir Lenin further hastened the party's demise.

By 1919, Leninist sympathizers threatened the Socialist Party leadership. A schism ensued, resulting in the expulsion of radical party elements and the invalidation of the national executive committee elections. Thereafter, the Socialist Party and the Communist Party became two distinct organizations with decidedly different agendas. By breaking with its labor roots, the Socialist Party lost its legitimacy as an agent of radical social action. Debs's death in 1926 signaled the end of the worker-oriented party and the start of a more urban-middle-class-centered party under Norman Thomas's leadership. The Socialist Party, which had 9,500 members in 1929, experienced a revival between 1929 and 1934: party membership increased during the Great Depression to almost 17,000 in 1932, when Thomas polled almost 900,000 votes in the presidential election, and to 20,000 in 1934.

Many new members were young militants who increasingly disagreed with the party's old guard. Until Hillquit died in 1933, the old guard held their own, but they lost their grip thereafter. At

Eugene V. Debs. *Library of Congress*

the 1934 party convention in Detroit, the young militant wing, joined by Thomas and the Milwaukee mayor, Daniel W. Hoan, passed a new Socialist Party declaration of principles that the old guard believed encouraged too forcefully the nonelectoral seizure of power and sympathized too greatly with Soviet Russia. The old guard formally broke away in 1936 and formed the Social Democratic Federation (SDF). Party membership fell to 12,000 in 1936 and shrank to 6,500 the following year. More important, Thomas garnered only 187,000 votes during the 1936 presidential election and less than 100,000 in 1940.

From 1933 to 1940 the Socialist Party experienced further internal strains by criticizing President Franklin D. Roosevelt and the New Deal. Party members viewed New Deal programs as more sympathetic to corporate interests than to organized labor's concerns. Remaining party members split over wartime policy, with Thomas leading a pacifist faction; the party lost any influence it had as it was effectively co-opted by Roosevelt. Only in the cities of Bridgeport, Connecticut, and Milwaukee, Wisconsin, did the old Socialist Party maintain a real presence. However, Thomas continued to run as the Socialist presidential candidate through the 1948 election.

In the post–World War II era, all radicalism was suspect. Although the Socialists made inroads into the Congress of Industrial Organizations and helped organize Detroit autoworkers and southern sharecroppers, the party disintegrated as an organization. The party continued to field a presidential candidate until the 1960 election, when it failed to run a candidate. Radicals shifted their emphasis from organized labor to civil rights and, later, worked against the war in Vietnam.

In the early 1960s the Democratic Socialist Organizing Committee (DSOC), the New American Movement (NAM), and the Students for a Democratic Society (SDS) became the main organizational vehicles for the New Left. The SDS faded after Martin Luther King's assassination in 1968 and the Paris Peace Accords in 1973. Meanwhile NAM devoted its energies to feminism, gay rights, and local community organizing into the early 1980s.

The DSOC continued to operate in the old socialist manner as the left wing of the New Deal coalition—not as a separate political party as much as a socialist force within the Democratic Party and the labor movement. The DSOC was successful in attracting activists such as machinist union leader William Winpisinger, feminist Gloria Steinem, and gay rights activist Harry Britt. Bernard Sanders, member of Congress from Vermont who was elected in 1991, was the first self-avowed socialist elected to Congress in decades and perhaps the best known since Victor Berger served in the House of Representatives during the 1920s.

NAM and DSOC completed a formal merger in 1983 and emerged as the Democratic Socialists of America (DSA). The DSA brought together for the first time since World War I the disparate segments of leftist opinion, including the SDF and former socialists and communists. Although the American left was in disarray in the late 1960s and the administrations of Richard M. Nixon, Ronald Reagan, George Bush, and Bill Clinton were by and large conservative, a kind of socialist revival occurred at the end of the twentieth century. Although membership remained low, Socialist Party influences such as government-supported health care, minimum wage, and human rights were more apparent in the national political debate than at any time since the 1960s. In addition, more than one socialist faction has fielded a candidate in every presidential election since 1976.

Socialist Labor Party (1874–   )

The Socialist Labor Party, the first national socialist party in the United States, ranks second only to the Prohibitionists among third parties in longevity. Formed in 1874 by elements of the Socialist International in New York, it was first known as the Social Democratic Workingmen's Party. In 1877 the group adopted the name Socialist Labor Party. Throughout the 1880s the party worked in concert with other left-wing third parties, including the Greenbacks.

The Socialist Labor Party ran national tickets in every presidential election from 1892 through 1976. The party collected its highest proportion of the national vote in 1896, when its candidate received 36,356 votes (0.3 percent of the popular vote).

Led by the autocratic Daniel DeLeon (1852–1914), a former Columbia University law lecturer, the Socialist Labor Party became increasingly militant and made its best showing in local races in 1898. But DeLeon's insistence on rigid party discipline and his opposition to the organized labor movement created a feeling of alienation among many members. Moderate elements bolted from the party, eventually joining the Socialist Party of Eugene V. Debs, which formed in 1901.

The Socialist Labor Party continued as a small, tightly organized far-left group bound to DeLeon's uncompromising belief in revolution. As late as 1976 the party advocated direct worker action to take over control of production and claimed 5,000 members nationwide.

Socialist Workers Party (1938–   )

The Socialist Workers Party was formed in 1938 by followers of the Russian revolutionary Leon Trotsky. Originally a faction within the U.S. Communist Party, the Trotskyites were expelled in 1936 on instructions from

Soviet leader Joseph Stalin. A brief Trotskyite coalition with the Socialist Party ended in 1938 when the dissidents decided to organize independently as the Socialist Workers Party. Through its youth arm, the Young Socialist Alliance, the Socialist Workers Party was active in the anti–Vietnam War movement and contributed activists to civil rights protests.

Since 1948 the party has run a presidential candidate, but its entries have never received more than 0.1 percent of the popular vote. In 1992 presidential candidate James Warren was on the ballot in thirteen states and the District of Columbia and drew 23,096 votes nationwide. The party's 2000 candidate, James E. Harris Jr. of Georgia, received 7,378 votes.

Union Party (1936)

Advocating more radical economic measures in light of the Great Depression, several early supporters of President Franklin D. Roosevelt broke with him and ran their own ticket in 1936 under the Union Party label. Largely an outgrowth of the Rev. Charles E. Coughlin's National Union for Social Justice, the new party also had the support of Dr. Francis E. Townsend, leader of a movement for government-supported old-age pensions, and Gerald L. K. Smith, self-appointed heir of Louisiana senator Huey P. Long's share-the-wealth program.

Father Coughlin was the keystone of the Union Party and was instrumental in choosing its presidential ticket in June 1936—Rep. William Lemke, R-N.D., for president and Thomas O'Brien, a Massachusetts railroad union lawyer, for vice president. The new party did not hold a convention. The party's platform reportedly was written by Coughlin, Lemke, and O'Brien and was similar to the program espoused by Coughlin's National Union. Among the features of the Union Party platform were proposals for banking and currency reform, a guaranteed income for workers, restrictions on wealth, and an isolationist foreign policy.

Lacking organization and finances during the campaign, the party further suffered from the increasingly violent and often anti-Semitic tone of the oratory of both Coughlin and Smith.

The Union Party failed miserably in its primary goal of defeating Roosevelt. Roosevelt won a landslide victory and the Lemke ticket received only

892,267 votes (2 percent of the popular vote). The party standard-bearers were unable to carry a single state, and the Union Party's candidates for the House and Senate all were defeated. The party continued on a local level until it was finally dissolved in 1939.

U.S. Labor Party (Independent Lyndon LaRouche) (1973–)

Formed in 1973 as the political arm of the National Caucus of Labor Committees (NCLC), the U.S. Labor Party made its debut in national politics in 1976. The NCLC, a Marxist group, was organized in 1968 by splinters of the radical movements of the 1960s. New Yorker Lyndon LaRouche, the party's chairman and a self-taught economist who worked in the management and computer fields, became its 1976 presidential nominee and Wayne Evans, a Detroit steelworker, his running mate.

The party directed much of its fire at the Rockefeller family. It charged that banks controlled by the Rockefellers were strangling the U.S. and world economies. In an apocalyptic vein, the party predicted a world monetary collapse by election day and the destruction of the country by thermonuclear war by the summer of 1977.

LaRouche's party developed a reputation for harassment because of its shouted interruptions and demonstrations against its political foes, including the Communist Party and the United Auto Workers. It accused some left-wing organizations and individuals, such as linguist Noam Chomsky and Marcus Raskin and his Institute for Policy Studies, of conspiring with the Rockefellers and the Central Intelligence Agency.

During the 1976 campaign, LaRouche was more critical of challenger Jimmy Carter than President Gerald R. Ford. He depicted Ford as a well-meaning man out of his depth in the presidency, but Carter as a pawn of nuclear war advocates and a disgracefully unqualified presidential candidate. LaRouche captured only 40,043 votes, less than 0.1 percent of the national vote. He was on the ballot in twenty-three states and the District of Columbia.

Although the U.S. Labor Party did not run a presidential candidate in the 1980 election, LaRouche ran a strident campaign—as a Democrat. By this time, LaRouche's politics had shifted to the right, and his speeches were fraught with warnings of conspiracy.

He continued his crusade in 1984 but as an "independent Democrat," dismissing Democratic presidential nominee Walter F. Mondale as an "agent of Soviet influence." LaRouche received 78,807 votes, or 0.1 percent of the vote, in the fall election.

In 1988 LaRouche again attempted to run as a Democrat but, failing the nomination, garnered 25,562 votes under the banner of the National Economic Recovery Party. On December 16, 1988, LaRouche and six of his associates were convicted on forty-seven counts of mail fraud and conspiracy to commit mail fraud. LaRouche was sentenced to fifteen years in prison.

In 1992 the unflagging LaRouche ran again for president from his jail cell. As a convicted felon, he no longer had the right to vote himself. LaRouche ran as an independent although his name appeared on several state ballots under various party names, including Economic Recovery. His supporters, experienced in winning ballot access, placed him on the ballot in seventeen states and the District of Columbia. He received 26,333 votes nationwide.

In 1996 LaRouche's name disappeared from the general election ballot, although he continued to be a quadrennial entry in the Democratic primaries. LaRouche ran in the party's primaries in every election from 1980 through 2000, with his best showing in 1996 when President Bill Clinton had no major opposition for renomination. That year, LaRouche drew nearly 600,000 Democratic primary votes (5.4 percent of the party's total primary ballots). In 2000 LaRouche received only 3,743 votes in the Democratic primaries.

U.S. Taxpayers Party and Constitution Party (1992–)

Making its second appearance in a presidential election, the U.S. Taxpayers Party was on the ballot in thirty-nine states in 1996. Its nominee, Howard Phillips of Virginia, drew 184,658 votes or more than four times his 1992 total of 43,434. Of the eighteen minor parties receiving at least 750 votes in 1996, the Taxpayers Party received the fourth highest total. In 2000

Phillips—running under the banner of several party labels—was on the ballot in 41 states. He won 98,004 votes, the sixth highest total of all presidential candidates in 2000.

Phillips, longtime chairman of the Conservative Caucus, founded the party to counter what he perceived to be a left-of-center movement by the Republican Party under George Herbert Walker Bush. Failing to recruit rightist icons such as Pat Buchanan, Oliver North, or Jesse Helms to be the party's nominee, Phillips ran himself as its standard-bearer. In addition to taxes the party opposed welfare, abortion and affirmative action.

Phillips was nominated to run for president again in 2000, by which time the U.S. Taxpayers had changed its name to the Constitution Party, to more broadly reflect its conservative agenda. Phillips, though, was willing to step aside at several stages of the campaign when the prospect of the party nominating a more prominent politician was possible. First, it was New Hampshire senator Robert C. Smith, a short-lived independent who returned to the Republican Party on the eve of the third party's convention in September 1999. Second, was Republican presidential contender Alan Keyes, who indicated in the spring of 2000 that he might bolt to the Constitution Party if the GOP weakened the antiabortion plank in the party's platform. It did not, and Keyes stayed in the Republican Party.

Whig Party (1834–1856)

Whigs were nineteenth-century modernizers who saw President Andrew Jackson (1829–1837) as a dangerous man with a reactionary opposition to the forces of social, economic, and moral change. As Jackson purged his opponents, vetoed internal improvements, and killed the Bank of the United States, alarmed local elites fought back.

The Whigs, led by Henry Clay, celebrated Clay's vision of the "American System." They demanded government support for a more modern, market-oriented economy, in which skill, expertise, and bank credit would count for more than physical strength or land ownership. They also sought to promote industrialization through high tariffs, a business-oriented money supply based on a national bank, and a vigorous program of government-funded "internal improvements," especially expansion of the road and canal

Henry Clay. *Library of Congress*

systems. To modernize the inner American, the Whigs helped create public schools, private colleges, charities, and cultural institutions.

The Democrats, by contrast, harkened to the Jeffersonian ideal of an equalitarian agricultural society, insisting that traditional farm life bred republican simplicity, whereas modernization threatened to create a politically powerful caste of rich aristocrats who might subvert democracy. In general, the Democrats enacted their policies at the national level; the Whigs succeeded in passing modernization projects in most states.

Although the Whigs won votes in every socioeconomic class, including the poorest, they appealed especially to more prosperous Americans. The Democrats likewise won support up and down the scale, but they often sharpened their appeals to the lower half by ridiculing the aristocratic pretensions of the Whigs. Most bankers, storekeepers, factory owners, master mechanics, clerks, and professionals favored the Whigs. Moreover, commercially oriented farmers in the North voted Whig, as did most large-scale planters in the South.

In general, the commercial and manufacturing towns and cities were heavily Whig, save for Democratic wards filled with recent Irish Catholic and German immigrants. Waves of Protestant religious revivals in the 1830s injected a moralistic element into the Whig ranks. Nonreligious individuals who found themselves the targets of moral reform, such as calls for prohibition, denounced the Whigs as Puritans and sought refuge in the Democratic Party. Rejecting the automatic party loyalty that was the hallmark of the tight Democratic Party organization, the Whigs suffered from factionalism. Yet the party's superb network of newspapers provided an internal information system.

Whigs clashed with Democrats throughout what historians term the "Second American Party System." When they controlled the Senate, Whigs passed a censure motion in 1834 denouncing Jackson's arrogant assumption of executive power in the face of the true will of the people as represented by Congress. Backing Henry Clay in 1832 and a medley of candidates in 1836, the opposition finally coalesced in 1840 behind a popular general, William Henry Harrison, and proved that the national Whig Party could win. Moreover, in the 1840s Whigs won 49 percent of gubernatorial elections, with strong bases in the manufacturing Northeast and in the border states. Yet the party revealed limited staying power. Whigs were ready to enact their programs in 1841, but Harrison died and was succeeded by John Tyler, an old-line Democrat who never believed in Whiggery and was, in fact, disowned by the party while he was president. Factionalism ruined the party's program and helped defeat Henry Clay, the Whig presidential candidate, in 1844. In 1848 opportunity beckoned as the Democrats split. By ignoring Clay and nominating a famous war hero, Gen. Zachary Taylor, the Whigs papered over their deepening splits on slavery, and they won. The trend, however, was for the Democratic vote to grow faster and for the Whigs to lose more and more marginal states and districts. After the close 1844 contest, the Democratic advantage widened and the Whigs could win the White House only if the Democrats split.

The Whigs were unable to deal with the slavery issue after 1850. Almost all of their southern leaders owned slaves. The northeastern Whigs, led by Daniel Webster, represented businessmen who loved the national flag and a national market but cared little about slavery one way or another. Many Whig voters in the North, however, felt slavery was incompatible with a free labor–free market economy, and no one discovered a compromise that would keep the party united. Furthermore, the burgeoning economy made full-time careers in business or law much more attractive than politics for ambitious young Whigs. For example, the party leader in Illinois, Abraham Lincoln, simply abandoned politics for several years after 1849. When new issues of nativism, prohibition, and antislavery burst on the scene in the mid-1850s, no one looked to the fast-disintegrating Whig Party for answers. In the North most ex-Whigs joined the new Republican Party, and in the South they flocked to a new, short-lived "American" (Know Nothing) Party. During the Lincoln administration (1861–1865), ex-Whigs enacted much of the "American System"; in the long run, America adopted Whiggish economic policies coupled with a Democratic strong presidency.

Workers World Party (1959–)

With the Hungarian citizen revolt and other developments in eastern Europe providing some impetus, the Workers World Party in 1959 split off from the Socialist Workers Party. The party theoretically supports worker uprisings in all parts of the world. Yet it backed the communist governments that put down rebellions in Hungary during the 1950s, Czechoslovakia in the 1960s, and Poland in the 1980s. Workers World is an activist revolutionary group that, until 1980, concentrated its efforts on specific issues, such as the antiwar and civil rights demonstrations during the 1960s and 1970s. The party has an active youth organization, Youth Against War and Fascism.

In 1980 party leaders saw an opportunity, created by the weakness of the U.S. economy and the related high unemployment, to interest voters in its revolutionary ideas. That year it placed Deirdre Griswold, the editor of the party's newspaper and one of its founding members, on the presidential ballot in ten states. Together with her running mate Larry Holmes, a twenty-seven-year-old black activist, Griswold received 13,300 votes. In 1984 Holmes ran as the presidential candidate, getting on the ballot in eight states and receiving 15,329 votes. In 1988 Holmes ran with Gloria La Riva, and they garnered 7,846 votes. La Riva ran as the presidential candidate in 1992 and was on the ballot only in New Mexico, where she received 181 votes.

The Workers World Party dramatically improved its electoral fortunes in 1996. Its candidate, Monica Moorehead of New Jersey, was on the ballot in twelve states and received 29,082 votes. But in 2000 Moorehead won only 4,795 votes in three states.

part III

campaigns
and elections

Campaigning

A political candidate's success in winning an election depends largely on his or her effectiveness in campaigning—the process of seeking votes through a wide variety of means. These may range from door-to-door neighborhood visits to gigantic outdoor rallies; from simple lawn signs to elaborate and costly television barrages.

Stages of Campaigning

Whether for local office, such as the city council, or national office, such as Congress or even the presidency, all political campaigns go through the same stages. First is the exploratory stage, in which the candidate sizes up the competition and assesses the chances of winning. Sometimes the candidate will form an exploratory committee or hire a polling organization to help make the decision.

If the decision is to run, the candidate must file with the appropriate elections authority and perhaps pay a filing fee. To get on the ballot, many jurisdictions require the submission of petitions signed by a specified number of qualified voters. Candidates for the presidency and Congress must file with the Federal Election Commission (FEC) and report regularly on receipts and spending.

Another campaign stage is the formation of an organization, usually made up mostly of volunteers. For all but the least competitive races, a candidate needs help—to raise money, devise strategy, gain media attention, operate phone banks, and do all manner of things to try to win the nomi-

As this pastiche of buttons shows, campaigns, even prior to the media age, were conducted through simple images and slogans. *Fred Sons, Congressional Quarterly*

nation and the election. Today, most nominations are made in primary elections or caucuses. Candidates who clear that first hurdle are likely to keep and augment the same organization for the general election campaign.

Modern elections are expensive, particularly for television advertising. In the 1996 election, television spots were the largest single expense for President Bill Clinton and challenger Sen. Robert J. Dole of Kansas. Between them they spent $113 million on television ads, dwarfing their next-highest combined expense, $32 million for nonmedia campaigning. For most other candidates, local and state, television advertising is also the largest expense. It is the medium by which most candidates reach the voters in the early twenty-first century.

To raise sometimes massive funds in conformance with federal or state campaign finance laws, the candidate may form a separate organization called a political action committee (PAC). Under the Federal Election Campaign Acts (FECA) of 1972 and 1976, political parties may also accept money for party-building activities. The use of this so-called soft money to skirt FECA spending limits for presidential candidates exposed a significant and controversial loophole in existing campaign reform laws. Presidential candidates who accept public funding must abide by spending limits. Congressional campaigns are not publicly funded and therefore are not subject to spending limits under the Supreme Court's *Buckley v. Valeo* decision (1976), which in effect said that such limits inhibit free speech.

Evolution of Campaigning

The use (or misuse) of money has been a hallmark of campaigns since the earliest days of the Republic. Some candidates, including George Washington, reportedly rewarded their supporters with free whiskey. With the growth of government and the "spoils system," politicians held out the promise of jobs as an enticement for votes. Later reforms in campaign finance and the civil service system outlawed some of the more blatant vote-inducing practices, but one of the most prevalent—negative campaigning—remains a characteristic of many U.S. political contests. Some nineteenth-century campaign rhetoric—focusing on an opponent's physical appearance, for example—makes today's "attack ads" seem mild.

Supporters of President John Quincy Adams in 1828 dredged up thirty-five-year-old allegations that challenger Andrew Jackson and Rachel Robards had married before her divorce became final (they had remarried in 1794). Jackson won, but Rachel died of a heart attack before his inauguration, a death Jackson attributed partly to her distress over the attacks on her morality. In their famed 1858 debates over the national issue of slavery, Senate candidates Stephen Douglas and Abraham Lincoln pandered to racial fears and assailed each other with insults. But instead of being "turned off" by the slurs, the large crowds cheered and jeered in delight.

Sometimes a derogatory political taunt can backfire, as happened to opponents of Grover Cleveland's presidential candidacy in 1884. They chanted, "Ma! Ma! Where's my Pa?" because Cleveland had fathered an illegitimate son, whom he continued to support. After Cleveland won, his supporters gloated, "Gone to the White House, ha, ha, ha!"

Captioned "Another Voice for Cleveland," this 1884 cartoon played on Grover Cleveland's admission that he had fathered an illegitimate son. *Library of Congress*

The use of the term "campaign" in U.S. politics dates to the early nineteenth century. John Quincy Adams used it in 1816, referring to one of his political efforts. But early presidential candidates, including Adams in his 1824 and 1828 campaigns, considered it unseemly to solicit votes directly from the people. Believing the office should seek the candidate, they left it largely to their supporters to publicize their qualifications and positions on issues, in hopes of obtaining the electoral vote majority needed for election.

The popular vote was less important in early U.S. elections than it is today. State legislatures chose electors in many cases, and the right to vote was extended only gradually to all adult citizens. South Carolina in 1868 was the last state to choose presidential electors by popular vote. Black males did not gain the vote in all states until ratification of the Fifteenth Amendment in 1870, and by 1900 the South had disfranchised most of them. They did not regain the vote in substantial numbers until passage of the Voting Rights Act of 1965. Women did not gain voting rights in all states until ratification of the Nineteenth Amendment in 1920. Popular election of U.S. senators became mandatory with the Seventeenth Amendment in 1913.

As the nation inched closer to universal suffrage (at least for males), it became essential for candidates to gain exposure to large numbers of voters. To that end, supporters held parades and rallies to whip up enthusiasm for their causes and leaders. Among the most colorful paraders were cape-wearing young men belonging to the Wide Awake Society, a Republican marching club. The "Wide Awakes" carried lanterns, sang songs, and performed intricate maneuvers as they marched for Abraham Lincoln in 1860. Almost half a million "Wide Awakes" helped make Lincoln the first Republican president.

In the late nineteenth century, large barbecues or picnics became common as events where politicians could mingle with the voters, "pressing the flesh" (shaking hands), and perhaps addressing the crowd from the bandstand. In the twenty-first century, such gatherings remain popular at the local level.

The practice of presidential aspirants traveling extensively to appeal for votes began in 1896 when William Jennings Bryan covered eighteen thousand miles by train to make six hundred speeches. Nevertheless, Republican William McKinley defeated Bryan with a front-porch campaign in Canton, Ohio. The term "whistle stop," however, did not come into popular usage until President Harry S. Truman popularized it with his cross-country train treks in 1948. Truman scored an upset victory over New York governor Thomas E. Dewey.

Truman's fiery speeches also gave rise to a slogan—"Give 'em Hell, Harry!"—that became permanently identified with his campaign. Other candidates have tried to find catchy phrases to use on campaign buttons, which first appeared in 1896, and on more recent inventions such as bumper stickers and television spot ads. The first buttons featured McKinley's likeness and his "Full Dinner Pail" slogan.

Most slogans are positive, such as "I Like Ike" for Dwight D. Eisenhower, or "Tippecanoe and Tyler, Too," for the 1840 ticket of William Henry Harrison, hero of the 1811 Battle of Tippecanoe, and John Tyler. But others are negative, such as "Dump the Hump," used against presidential nominee Hubert H. Humphrey in 1968, and "If Tydings Wins, You Lose," used by gun owners to defeat Sen. Joseph Tydings of Maryland in 1970.

Although President Herbert Hoover denied that he ever promised Americans "a Chicken in Every Pot, a Car in Every Garage," food has long been associated with appeals for votes, especially from ethnic groups. In New York City, with its large Jewish population, candidates pose for pictures while eating kosher Coney Island hot dogs. In a Polish community, the favored sausage may be kielbasa. In Chinatown, candidates may opt for chopsticks and egg rolls. As African Americans and Hispanics have grown in number, so have the pictures of politicians devouring stereotypical ribs or tortillas.

But ethnic campaigning is not confined to food. To court the Irish vote, candidates don green and strut in St. Patrick's Day parades on March 17. In October they try to be seen at Columbus Day festivities in Italian areas. The wise candidate tailors his or her campaign to the characteristics of the constituency at stake.

The high cost of political advertising on television leaves candidates little money to spend on campaign buttons, billboards, and other traditional artifacts of campaigning. Modern campaigns often hand out buttons only in return for donations, and the buttons' scarcity adds to their value as collectors' items. Nevertheless, candidates and their supporters usually manage to buy relatively inexpensive printed material such as bumper stickers, posters, and lawn signs on stakes. When several competitive races are being fought, suburban lawns may sprout a forest of cardboard messages vying for the voters'

President Gerald R. Ford, campaigning in San Antonio for reelection in 1976, bites into a tamale with the husk on and seems to convey to his bemused Hispanic audience that he does not know what he did wrong.

Gerald R. Ford Library

eyes and attention. The objective is to build support for the candidates through name recognition that may translate into votes on election day.

Music, too, may be important to a campaign. The anti-Cleveland chant in 1884 was set to music and widely distributed as a ditty. During the Great Depression, "Happy Days Are Here Again!" became the theme song of Democrats and their 1932 presidential candidate, Franklin D. Roosevelt. Republicans happily sang Irving Berlin's "I Like Ike" for their war hero nominee, Eisenhower, in the 1950s. And after the nomination of Clinton in 1992, the Democratic convention hall rocked to Fleetwood Mac's "Don't Stop Thinking About Tomorrow."

Campaigning takes many other forms of electioneering. There is no one sure way to campaign. What works for one candidate may do nothing for another; or it might do the candidate more harm than good. Most candidates make promises to the voters, sometimes effectively. Eisenhower kept his 1952 pledge to go to Korea to seek an end to the war there. But Walter Mondale's admission that he or Ronald Reagan would have to raise taxes if elected in 1984 proved detrimental to Mondale's already weak campaign against the popular Reagan.

After losing the Republican presidential nomination to George W. Bush in 2000, Arizona senator John McCain recanted his campaign pledge to let the people of South Carolina decide whether to let the Confederate flag continue flying over the statehouse in defiance of African Americans offended by the flag. Calling for the flag's removal, McCain admitted he had compromised his principles for fear of losing the South Carolina primary. He lost anyway to Bush, who had taken the same leave-it-to-the-people stand.

The first face-to-face debate between presidential nominees took place in 1960 between John F. Kennedy and Richard Nixon. Since then, televised candidate debates have become commonplace in state and local races, as well as those for president and vice president. In 1998 the Cable-Satellite Public Affairs Network (C-SPAN) broadcast 103 congressional and gubernatorial candidate debates, many of which were also covered by the commercial and public networks.

Televised debates at all levels also figured prominently in the 2000 primary elections. Both major party front-runners, Republican George W. Bush and Democrat Al Gore, debated their presidential primary opponents. By May 13 each had secured his party's nomination—the earliest ever for candidates who faced significant opposition for the White House nomination.

Besides debates, standard forms of modern electioneering include stump speeches, greeting voters at factory gates, direct mail, obtaining endorsements from newspapers and community leaders, operating phone banks, and appearing on radio and television talk shows. Use of the Internet also has become a standard campaign procedure. In the 2000 elections, most major candidates had campaign Web sites.

Candidate-Centered Campaigns

Most political campaigns today are candidate-centered as opposed to party-centered. Far-reaching changes in election procedures and communications technology since the early twentieth century have freed candidates from much of their former dependency on political party organizations for money and other necessities of an effective campaign. Through telephones, radio, television, and the Internet, candidates may now pitch their appeals directly to the electorate. They gain nomination by winning party primaries and caucuses, rather than by being hand-picked by the Democratic or Republican Parties, which have dominated the American two-party system since the mid-nineteenth century. In a primary or caucus the candidates compete, in effect, for the party's endorsement. Only a few states permit a formal preprimary endorsement, which indicates on the ballot the candidate favored by the party leadership.

Although the primary system has empowered rank-and-file voters, it has also contributed to the long duration and skyrocketing cost of political campaigns. The successful candidate must campaign extensively to win the nomination, then campaign again to defeat the opposing party's nominee in the general election. Both campaigns can be expensive. In early 2000 Bush raised a record $70 million for his campaign and reportedly spent most of it just in winning the Republican nomination to oppose Gore.

A decline in party identification among voters also has contributed to the trend toward candidate-centered campaigns. Since the 1970s, when the major parties (especially the Democrats) changed their rules to strengthen the primary system and give more representation to women and racial minorities, more voters began to think of themselves as independents rather than as Democrats, Republicans, or third-party members. A 1995 Gallup poll showed 36 percent of voters identified themselves as independents, compared with about 32 percent for each of the two major parties. Similarly, studies detect a rise in ticket splitting and a decline in voting the straight party ticket.

Faced with this situation, candidates try to focus the campaign on their positive attributes, including personality, physical appearance, education, experience, and views on issues of concern to the constituencies they want to represent. In most cases the candidate will not run away from the party but will merely say little about it in campaign speeches or advertising. Where the party or its philosophy is deemed a liability, the candidate may try to disassociate the campaign from the national party or some of its most prominent members. In the 1980s, for example, when the term "liberal" was widely shunned as "the L-word," Democratic candidates in some states preferred not to be linked with Sen. Edward M. Kennedy of Massachusetts or others closely associated with liberal causes.

For offices where candidates run as a pair, as for president and vice president, or governor and lieutenant governor in some states, the top candidate may try to find a running mate who balances the ticket geographically, philosophically, or in some other way. In 2000, for example, Bush chose former defense secretary Richard Cheney to compensate for Bush's lack of experience in foreign affairs. And although most nominees strive for a geographic balance, Clinton of Arkansas chose Gore of Tennessee as vice president in 1992, making it the first successful all-southern ticket since Andrew

Jackson of Tennessee and John C. Calhoun of South Carolina won in 1828. With Gore, Clinton won with a largely candidate-centered campaign.

Candidate-centered campaigns rely more on the news and advertising media than on the party to get their messages to the voters. And with the rise of the Internet they are becoming even less dependent on the print and broadcast media. Campaign Web sites, besides disseminating the candidate's position on issues, help collect the e-mail addresses of swing voters as well as likely supporters. These addresses may be used in turn for candidate appeals for money or for volunteers to make phone calls or do other work for the campaign. The collected names and addresses can be stored for future campaigns as well as the one at hand. In this way, said political scientist Michael Cornfield, a specialist in political Internet usage, the candidates are "building digital political machines" with a potential for continuous two-way correspondence between the politician and the voters.

Candidate-centered campaigning is more personal than party-centered campaigning and therefore is more likely to be negative, attacking the opponent's character and qualifications instead of emphasizing the attacker's own fitness for the office being sought. Consequently, it is not surprising that recent elections have seen a rise in negative campaigning, despite the public's distaste for it as shown in numerous polls. A classic example of negative political advertising was the use of the "Willie Horton" ad in 1988 by supporters of presidential candidate George Herbert Walker Bush. The controversial television spot sought to portray Bush's opponent, Massachusetts governor Michael S. Dukakis, as soft on crime because he had signed a prisoner furlough law. William R. Horton Jr., a convicted murderer, had raped a woman while on furlough from a Massachusetts prison. In the 1990s a new type of attack ad became prevalent, partly through the use of "soft money" given to parties supposedly for party-building activities. Such ads circumvented federal and state contribution limits because they did not use the candidate's name even though clearly targeted at a particular candidate.

Political Action Committees

Political action committees, or PACs, have been part of the American political system since the 1940s, but only in the 1970s did they become a major factor in political campaigns. PACs are organizations that raise and distribute campaign contributions to candidates for the presidency, Congress, and other offices.

Political action committees fall into two main categories. Some are affiliated with specific economic interests such as businesses, professional associations, and labor unions. Others are independent organizations devoted to advancing the political beliefs of their members, usually a single issue such as reproductive rights or gun control. Even some members of Congress have PACs.

As the giving arms of special interests, PACs serve as a megaphone for a group of individuals. Rather than one thousand people giving $5 apiece, a PAC can write a $5,000 check on behalf of all of those individuals. To qualify as a "multicandidate committee," its legal name, a PAC must raise money from at least fifty persons and contribute to at least five candidates. At the beginning of 2001, the maximum contribution was $5,000 per candidate per campaign, with the primary and general elections counted separately. A candidate could raise $100,000 from just ten PACs, each giving the maximum for the primary and general elections. Otherwise, it would take fifty persons giving the maximum $1,000 for the primary and $1,000 for the general election to reach that threshold. The PAC itself could accept no more than $5,000 from a particular individual for each campaign, and it must regularly report its contributions and expenditures to the Federal Election Commission.

Critics call PACs the "cash constituents of Congress," interests that may have no presence in a member's district but still can command the attention of the lawmaker or a top aide by virtue of their campaign contributions. Lawmakers and PAC directors admit that the contributions buy access. An industry's PAC donations tend to rise or fall depending on whether important issues are pending before Congress.

PACs date back to 1943 when the Congress of Industrial Organizations (CIO), banned from using union dues to aid favored candidates, set up a fund called the Political Action Committee to collect voluntary contributions from its members. The CIO later merged with the American Federation of Labor, and today the AFL-CIO's PAC is one of the largest in the country.

In 1971 Congress passed legislation codifying earlier bans on union and corporate contributions, allowing those groups instead to pay the costs of running PACs and soliciting the voluntary donations needed to fill the committee's coffers. As a result, the number of PACs skyrocketed, from 608 in 1974 to 4,268 in 1988. At the end of 1999, 3,835 PACs were registered with the Federal Election Commission.

Although PACs originally were considered a reform, some lawmakers trying to overhaul the campaign finance laws tried to ban PACs in 1996. Their colleagues, however, refused to go along. Led by Republican senator John McCain of Arizona and Democratic senator Russell Feingold of Wisconsin, the reformers turned their attention away from PACs after the 1996 elections and instead launched an effort to ban "soft money," the unregulated contributions to political parties from corporations and unions that are banned from giving directly to campaigns.

Because incumbents usually win, PACs tend to favor incumbents over challengers—one reason it is difficult for insurgent candidates to raise enough money to compete. During the 1998 elections, PACs gave 78 percent of their money to incumbents. PACs play another important role in

Sen. John McCain of Arizona (left) and Sen. Russell Feingold of Wisconsin discuss their campaign finance bill in March 2001. *Scott J. Ferrell, Congressional Quarterly*

helping incumbents: many give early in the election cycle, allowing a lawmaker to amass a large campaign bank account and dissuade potentially strong challengers from entering the race.

PACs usually direct their contributions to the lawmakers who oversee their interests. The Senate and House banking committees are considered plum fundraising assignments because they attract contributions from Wall Street and the financial community. Defense PACs tend to support members of the House and Senate panels that oversee the Pentagon budget. Lawmakers who switch committees find that their mix of PAC contributions changes to reflect their new assignments. Donations by advocacy groups such as the National Rifle Association tend to be more ideological in nature, favoring challengers who agree with them on the issues, rather than incumbents who disagree with them but are more likely to win in November.

Many members of Congress also have set up their own political action committees. These "leadership PACs" allow lawmakers to raise additional funds from special interests—money that is then used to help threatened incumbents and strong challengers win election. Later, lawmakers hoping to move up the leadership ladder can ask the colleagues they helped at election time to return the favor. Although most lawmakers who have leadership PACs use the money they raise to make contributions to other candidates, some use these accounts to defray expenses such as travel or attending the national political conventions.

Watershed Elections

Five presidential contests stand out as "watershed elections," or crucial turning points in American political history. They are the elections of 1800, 1828, 1860, 1896, and 1932. Each led to a long-lasting shift in party power and a fundamental change in national policy. Each also led to the election of a president generally considered to be "great" or "near great," including two of the nation's three greatest presidents: Abraham Lincoln and Franklin D. Roosevelt.

In 1800 Thomas Jefferson defeated the incumbent John Adams for the presidency. This was the first time in the history of the modern world that an incumbent national executive was "overthrown" by a peaceful revolution at the ballot box. Jefferson's ascension to office confirmed the success of the American political system created by the Constitution of 1787. The election also signaled the emergence of the most important nonconstitutional aspect of American politics, the political party. Finally, the election set the stage for twenty-eight years of domination of American politics by the Democratic-Republican Party, as Jefferson's followers called themselves.

With the effective demise of the Federalist Party as a national force by 1816, the Democratic-Republican Party of Thomas Jefferson evolved into an amorphous organization that incorporated virtually all political viewpoints. The inherent instability of a one-party system became apparent in 1824 when four candidates competed for the presidency, with no one getting a majority of the popular or electoral vote. Andrew Jackson led in both categories, but the House of Representatives chose John Quincy Adams, the heir apparent to President James Monroe. In 1828 Jackson and Adams squared off directly, leading to a huge victory for Jackson and the emergence of a new Democratic Party. The nationalist wing of the old Democratic-Republican Party—led by men like Henry Clay, Daniel Webster, and John Quincy Adams—eventually coalesced into a new party, the Whigs. Jackson's victory set the stage for his party to dominate American politics until 1860. The party abandoned the nationalism of Madison and Monroe, with Jackson vetoing a recharter of the Bank of the United States, ending federal support for internal improvements, and deferring to state demands for the removal of Indians in the east. Jackson also instituted an aggressively proslavery domestic policy, using the Fugitive Slave Law of 1793 as a litmus test for judicial appointments, while creating an aggressive foreign policy that led, after his presidency, to the annexation of Texas and war with Mexico.

By the 1850s the sectional pressures caused by slavery undermined the Jacksonian coalition. The Democratic Party's repeal of the ban on slavery in the trans-Mississippi West to force slavery into Kansas led to a huge northern backlash and the creation of a new party, the Republicans. In 1860 Lincoln carried every non-slave state, and with it the election. By the time of his inauguration seven slave states had seceded from the Union, and four years of horribly costly and bloody civil war followed, ending with the elimination of slavery in the United States, a reunification of the states, and the assassination of Lincoln shortly after he began his second term in office. Lincoln's party dominated politics for the next two decades, controlling the

The 1896 presidential campaign of William McKinley (center), conducted from the front porch of his Ohio home, resulted in a watershed victory for the Republican Party. *Library of Congress*

White House, one or both houses of Congress, and the courts. The party favored high tariffs, federal support for railroads, federal protections for the recently emancipated slaves, and suppression of Mormons in the West.

Democrats made a comeback in 1884, taking the White House for the first time since Lincoln's election, and they recaptured it in 1892, along with both houses of Congress. In 1896 the Democrats nominated the radical midwestern populist William Jennings Bryan. The Democrats offered a sharp contrast to the Republicans, demanding lower tariffs, railroad regulations, banking reform, and inflationary policies based on increased production of silver and higher farm prices. The Republicans responded with a highly organized, well financed national campaign that raised $4 million and sent out more than 250,000 pieces of literature. The campaign appealed to traditional Republicans, new captains of industry, and, most important, to urban workers and some new immigrants, who were convinced that Bryan's agrarian populism was not in their best interest. Bryan carried twenty-two states to McKinley's twenty-three, but the Republican had a decisive majority in both the electoral and popular vote and was the first president since Ulysses S. Grant to win more than 50 percent of the popular vote. He was also the first president since Grant to win more than 60 percent of the electoral vote. McKinley's election set the stage for Republican dominance of Congress and the presidency for sixteen years, and then for another twelve after Woodrow Wilson's two terms.

The collapse of the American economy following the stock market crash of 1929 set the stage for the most successful political realignment in American history. In 1932, running against Herbert Hoover's failure to come to terms with the Great Depression on either a policy or a psychological level, Franklin D. Roosevelt carried forty-two states, with 472 electoral votes to Hoover's 59. In the 1934 off-year elections, the Democrats increased their majority in the House and Senate, setting the stage for a massive landslide victory in 1936, with FDR carrying forty-six of forty-eight states and 61 percent of the popular vote. The FDR victory in 1932 led to Democratic domination of Congress for most of the next sixty years, as well as Democratic control of the White House for twenty-eight of the next thirty-six years. The "Roosevelt coalition" of urban workers, midwestern and southern farmers, Catholics, Jews, eastern and southern European immigrants and their children, Asian Americans, southern whites, northern blacks, and

Franklin D. Roosevelt, seen here in the back seat of a car surrounded by supporters in 1932, made an indelible mark on the nation. *Franklin D. Roosevelt Library*

intellectuals seemed invincible until the Vietnam War and the demise of Jim Crow in the South tore it apart in the late 1960s.

From 1968 to the end of the century the parties were more evenly divided. Five Republican presidential victories were balanced by three Democratic victories. Although Congress remained in Democratic control for much of this period, Republicans regained control of both houses in the mid-1990s, even while a Democrat sat in the White House.

The election of 2000 demonstrated how closely split the county had become. Republican presidential candidate George W. Bush won the electoral vote and hence the presidency, but he lost the popular vote to Democratic candidate Al Gore. Congress, although still in Republican hands, was nearly as evenly divided between the two parties. Should the Republican Party hold on to the White House and Congress for a few terms, it will be possible to see the election of Richard M. Nixon in 1968, or Ronald Reagan in 1980, as watersheds that altered the trajectory of politics. On the other hand, if Democrats regain control of Congress and regain the White House in the first part of the twenty-first century, scholars may look back on Bill Clinton's 1992 victory as a watershed that defeated a sitting president and paved the way for a new Democratic coalition of industrial workers, blacks, Hispanics, Jews, Asian Americans, new economy "techies," and women of all ethnic backgrounds.

Landslide Elections

Presidential elections are often close, and many presidents have won with less than 50 percent of the popular vote. On occasion, however, the winner takes 55 or even 60 percent of the popular vote and 80 or even 90 percent of the electoral college vote. Because the winner of a state's popular vote—no matter how small the margin—takes that state's entire electoral vote, the two counts do not necessarily track closely. Rather, a candidate who wins a great many states by narrow margins might win with a large majority in the electoral college.

Through 1820, electors were chosen through other means than popular election. In those nine campaigns, four candidates took more than 90 percent of the electoral college vote: George Washington in both of his elections, Thomas Jefferson when he won reelection in 1804, and James Monroe when he was reelected in 1820. Washington, the only president ever to receive a unanimous vote in the electoral college, accomplished the feat both times. Monroe won every state in 1820, but his final tally was 231 to 1; one elector refused to vote for him, so that Washington would remain the only president to have the honor of being unanimously elected.

Between 1824 and 1996 the nation had forty-four presidential elections. In six elections (14 percent) after 1820, the winner took 90 percent of the electoral college vote. Only four times (9 percent of the time), all in the twentieth century, did the winner get as much as 60 percent of the popular vote.

Those four popular landslide victories are instructive. Rather than signaling a long-term transformation in Americans' voting behavior, they were likely to be soon reversed. The Republican candidate, Warren G. Harding, won in a popular landslide in 1920, yet in 1936 a Democrat, Franklin D. Roosevelt, won reelection with a similar majority. In 1964 Lyndon B. Johnson, a Democrat, won by the largest popular percentage ever recorded in a U.S. presidential election, but, challenged within his own party four years later, he withdrew from the race rather than seek reelection. Republican Richard M. Nixon won the presidency that year, and in 1972 he won his bid for reelection in a landslide, but he resigned from office in disgrace less than two years later.

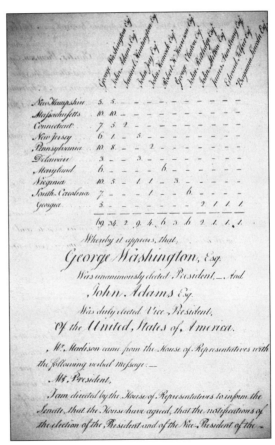

Page 7 of the *Senate Journal,* April 6, 1789, showing the electoral vote in the first presidential election, which awarded George Washington a unanimous vote.
National Archives

Landslide victories in the popular count are not necessarily reflected in the electoral count, and vice versa. Three of the twentieth century's four winners of landslide victories in the popular election also won 90 percent of the electoral college count. Harding's margin in the electoral college was well under 80 percent, however. More notable are Ronald Reagan's two victories. In 1980 he took a bare majority, 50.7 percent, of the popular vote, yet he won by narrow majorities in so many states that commentators have often spoken of his landslide victory, which he did in fact win in the electoral college. Four years later, his winning percentage of the popular vote, though in the high fifties, did not meet the 60 percent threshold, yet he won in the electoral college by an even wider margin than four years earlier, 525 to 13, the fifth widest margin ever, after those of Washington, Monroe, and Franklin Roosevelt.

By definition, a candidate who takes 60 percent of the popular vote beats his nearest competitor by at least 20 percentage points. In the history of American presidential sweepstakes, the widest margin ever recorded came

President Lyndon B. Johnson's 61.1 percent of the popular vote in 1964 is the record for the highest margin in U.S. presidential elections. *Lyndon Baines Johnson Library*

in 1920, when Harding won by 26 points. In addition to the four landslide victors, Theodore Roosevelt won by more than 20 points in 1904.

If one relaxes the requirements and sets the threshold for a landslide victory at 55 percent in the popular vote or 80 percent of the electoral college, far more candidates have won by landslide victories—so many as to dilute the meaning of the term. Fourteen of the forty-four winners from 1824 to 1996 (32 percent) took at least 55 percent of the popular vote, and nineteen (43 percent) took at least 80 percent in the electoral college.

Andrew Jackson, the only president to meet the 55 percent standard before the Civil War, won both of his terms with at least that amount, and he took 80 percent of the electoral college vote in his reelection victory in 1832. Franklin Pierce won in 1852 with only 50.9 percent of the popular vote, but his electoral college count exceeded 80 percent. In 1864, with eleven states out of the Union, Abraham Lincoln met the 55 percent popular standard as well as the higher 90 percent electoral college figure. In 1872 Ulysses S. Grant won with at least 55 percent of the popular vote and 80 percent of the electoral count. No other president of the nineteenth century reached either the 55 percent or the 80 percent threshold figures.

During the twentieth century, winners almost routinely met the lower 55 percent or 80 percent thresholds, if not both. In fact, a majority of winners from 1904 through 1984 accomplished the feat. During those twenty-one campaigns, only seven candidates failed to meet at least one of the two easier standards in winning the presidency—William Howard Taft in 1908, Woodrow Wilson in 1916, Calvin Coolidge in 1924, Harry S. Truman in 1948, John F. Kennedy in 1960, Richard M. Nixon in 1968, and Jimmy Carter in 1976. Every winner from 1928 through 1956 won in a landslide according to one of the looser definitions. Franklin Roosevelt won all four times with at least 80 percent of the electoral college count. Dwight D. Eisenhower met both the 55 percent and 80 percent figures in 1952 and again in 1956. After the Reagan years the dominant twentieth-century pattern receded, but it will likely return.

In the history of the republic—or at least since 1820—four presidents have won with 60 percent of the popular vote: two Democrats and two Republicans. Franklin Roosevelt did it once in his four campaigns, and Nixon did it once in his three. What are considered watershed elections, however, were not typically won by landslides. Jefferson narrowly won the "Revolution of 1800," though his victory four years later came by a landslide. Jackson won the election of 1828 by a hefty popular majority, but not 60 percent. Lincoln attracted the support of far less than half the voters in his victory in the four-way campaign of 1860. Franklin Roosevelt's win in 1936 met the 60 percent and 90 percent figures, but his victory four years earlier is better characterized as a watershed election.

Campaign Finance

The issue of campaign finance has been fodder for critics who charge that American politicians are overly influenced by special interest groups, but reform efforts have failed to stem the tide of money from groups and individuals with a major stake in the outcome of legislation or an executive decision.

Congress passed the first campaign finance overhaul measure in 1867, when the naval appropriations bill that year contained a provision preventing federal employees from soliciting contributions from Navy Yard workers. The issue first made headlines at the beginning of the twentieth century, when President Theodore Roosevelt was found to have benefited by large corporate contributions to his 1904 campaign. In response, Roosevelt called for campaign finance reform in both his 1905 and 1906 State of the Union addresses.

The resulting legislation, passed in 1907, was known as the Tillman Act and banned corporations and national banks from contributing to federal campaigns. Four decades later, Congress applied the same ban to contributions from labor unions; the prohibition was part of the Taft-Hartley Act of 1947. (During World War II, southern Democrats had teamed with Republicans to outlaw labor donations, but the 1943 bill, adopted over President Franklin D. Roosevelt's veto, expired at the end of the war.)

At the close of the twentieth century, campaign finance again became a major issue. The Democratic National Committee returned millions of dollars in questionable contributions in 1996, much of it from foreign sources, and both parties were accused of getting around federal spending limits by running advertisements in support of their presidential nominees. The Republican-controlled Congress held hearings into alleged Democratic abuses, but lawmakers failed to pass any new campaign finance legislation.

Despite Congress's inaction—or perhaps because of it—campaign finance is an issue that will not go away. In 2000 both Republican John McCain and Democrat Bill Bradley made overhauling the campaign finance laws a key element of their presidential campaigns. Although neither gained his party's nomination, the candidates who defeated them—Texas governor George W. Bush on the Republican side and Vice President Al Gore on the Democratic side—called for changes in the way campaigns are financed.

Today's campaign finance system is largely a product of the post-Watergate reforms enacted in 1974. The Watergate scandal, which brought down President Richard Nixon, included six-figure donations to the presidential campaign from individuals and corporations with issues pending before the White House. Congress since then has rebuffed almost yearly efforts to impose new rules on fund raising and spending. The laws are enforced by a six-member Federal Election Commission (FEC), which was created in 1974. Three of the six members are Republicans and three are Democrats, with four votes needed to approve a course of action. Critics say this bipartisan split makes the FEC a weak and ineffective watchdog. And the FEC is so understaffed that it often does not investigate potential violations of laws until years later, too late to prevent candidates from abusing the regulations during a campaign.

Candidates raise most of their money from three sources: their own pockets, individual contributors, and political action committees (PACs). Corporations and unions cannot give directly to federal campaigns. At the beginning of 2001, individuals could give no more than $1,000 per election or $2,000 per election cycle (primary and general election) to one candidate. Political action committees could give $5,000 per election or $10,000 per cycle.

Presidential candidates can get money from a fourth source: the U.S. taxpayer. The account is funded through a $3 checkoff on income tax returns. If a presidential candidate agrees to limit his or her spending while seeking the nomination and raises at least $100,000 in contributions of no more than $250 each, the federal government will match the first $250 of each individual contribution. Since the system went into effect for the first post-Watergate presidential election in 1976, only three candidates—Republicans John Connally in 1980, Steve Forbes in 1996 and 2000, and George W. Bush in 2000—have refused the federal funds and therefore were not bound by spending limits for the primary campaigns.

Once the Democrats and Republicans choose their nominees, the entire cost of the full campaign is covered by taxpayers. The nominees agree to spend only what the federal government provides and to refrain from raising any more money for their campaigns. No major-party candidate yet has refused federal funding for the general election.

No federal funds are provided for congressional campaigns, and efforts to provide taxpayer funding of House and Senate races have failed in the face of Republican opposition. Nor are there any limits on how much a congressional candidate can spend; the Supreme Court struck down restrictions on spending in *Buckley v. Valeo* (1976). In that landmark case the Court upheld contribution limits but struck down restrictions on spending, calling them a violation of the First Amendment. That Court decision also struck down limits on how much money candidates could pour into their own races. Some proponents of campaign finance reform have proposed amending the U.S. Constitution to overturn the decision and allow Congress to limit campaign spending and thus the need to raise so much money from special interests.

Political Action Committees

Political action committees, or PACs, are the giving arms of special interests. The first PAC was formed in the 1940s by the Congress of Industrial Organizations, the labor federation that later merged with the American Federation of Labor to become the AFL-CIO.

But PACs did not come into their own as a major financing force until the 1970s. In 1971 President Nixon signed legislation allowing unions and corporations, otherwise banned from giving directly to campaigns, to pay the expenses of PACs that would be funded with voluntary contributions from employees, officers, union workers, or members of organizations. The number of PACs skyrocketed as a result, from 608 at the end of 1974 to 4,268 at the end of 1988. The growth of PACs—and the perception of a growing influence on the political process—led to unsuccessful efforts to ban them.

Besides corporations and unions, ideological organizations also have formed their own PACs, such as the National Rifle Association, which backs gun owners' rights, or the pro-Israel National PAC.

Corporate PACs traditionally favor incumbents, most of whom win reelection time after time. The extent to which these PACs favor current officeholders was illustrated starkly when the Republicans took control of the House in 1995. During the 1993–1994 election cycle, Democrats, who had a majority of the House, took in 54 percent of the corporate PAC money. But after the GOP gained control, corporate PACs gave the Republicans 70 percent of their contributions in 1995–1996.

In recent years, members of Congress and other public officials have founded their own PACs, known as leadership PACs. These organizations offer special interests another way to contribute to powerful lawmakers. At the beginning of 2001, after giving $10,000 to a candidate's reelection campaign, a special interest PAC could give another $5,000 to that candidate's leadership PAC.

Most lawmakers use these PACs to make donations to candidates of their own political party. This financial assistance helps them earn the gratitude of incumbents and newly minted lawmakers, who may be asked at a later date to support their patron's attempt to win a leadership role in the party conference.

Soft Money

Although corporations have been banned from contributing to federal campaigns since 1907 and unions have been blocked since 1947, both groups still contribute millions of dollars each year to help elect favored candidates. They do so thanks to a loophole known as "soft money," which is not regulated by federal election laws and therefore cannot go directly to the candidates; rather, it goes to the political parties. The parties cannot spend the money on activities that urge a vote for or against a particular candidate, which is known as "express advocacy."

Soft money is a relatively recent phenomenon. In 1979 Congress voted to allow the political parties to raise these unregulated contributions for party-building activities such as voter registration and get-out-the-vote drives. However, the political parties began using the money to air what are known as "issue advertisements." This practice came to a head during the 1996 presidential elections, when both parties ran advertisements in support of their nominees. Indeed, FEC auditors said that the political party advertisements were nothing more than campaign commercials and recommended that both campaigns repay millions of dollars in federal funds for exceeding spending limits. The six-member commission rejected its auditors' recommendations.

Both political parties continue to raise record amounts of soft money, despite efforts in Congress to ban it. In both 1998 and 1999, the House passed a ban on soft money, but Senate Republicans successfully blocked the legislation. Even members of Congress have begun to raise soft money for their leadership PACs. Some have set up PACs in the state of Virginia, which does not limit the size of campaign contributions to candidates or PACs. Others do not even disclose their donors, and because the money is not used to directly elect a federal candidate, the FEC does not regulate those committees. Besides the candidates and the parties, a host of interest groups—including antiabortion forces, term limits supporters, gun rights advocates, unions, and environmental groups—have run their own advertisements for or against candidates.

If their advertisements urge viewers to vote for or against a particular candidate (express advocacy), the organizations must disclose their spending to the FEC. More frequently, however, the organizations run advertisements that mention a particular candidate but do not urge a vote for or against that person. This is called "issue advocacy," and the courts have

Protesters from the National Campaign Finance Reform Coalition shout at people entering a Republican fundraising event in Washington, D.C.   *R. Michael Jenkins, Congressional Quarterly*

ruled that the FEC cannot regulate this First Amendment exercise of free speech. As a result, millions of dollars worth of commercials are being broadcast, oftentimes without anyone knowing who is funding the effort. Because they are not considered campaign advertisements, the commercials can be funded out of union dues or corporate treasuries. Efforts to curb such advertisements, or at least require that their source be disclosed, have run into opposition from some lawmakers who claim that the proposals violate the First Amendment.

Modern Reform Efforts

Modern efforts to overhaul the campaign finance system have their roots in the election of President John F. Kennedy in 1960. Stung by allegations that his family's wealth bought his narrow victory, Kennedy formed a campaign finance commission in 1961. The panel recommended placing limits on the size of contributions and disclosing campaign contributors. In 1964 Kennedy's successor, Lyndon B. Johnson, hosted $1,000-a-plate "President's Club" dinners, but the Democratic National Committee declined to release the names of the donors. To avoid the appearance of anonymous big donors buying a candidate, Congress passed legislation providing for public financing of presidential campaigns through an income tax checkoff, but the program was suspended until rules could be developed to govern the distribution of the money.

Congress did vote in 1970 to impose limits on how much candidates for president, vice president, senator, representative, governor, and lieutenant governor could spend on broadcast advertisements, but President Nixon vetoed the measure. Two years later, however, Nixon signed legislation that limited how much money candidates could contribute to their own campaigns and how much money they could spend on advertising. The bill also authorized the establishment of political action committees.

In 1974, in the wake of Watergate, President Gerald Ford signed legislation imposing new restrictions on campaign fund raising. The bill limited campaign contributions to $1,000 per individual per election, set spending limits for federal campaigns while repealing the restrictions on media expenditures, imposed restrictions on how much money candidates could give to their own campaigns, set up the current system of public financing for presidential elections, imposed new reporting requirements for contributions and expenditures, and established the FEC. The Supreme Court two years later declared unconstitutional the spending limits as well as the restrictions on how much candidates could spend on their own campaigns.

In the wake of the Supreme Court decision, congressional Democrats tried to draft legislation that would provide public financing of campaigns if candidates voluntarily agreed to limit their spending, but the proposals repeatedly ran into opposition from Republicans. The only time Congress managed to pass a bill, offering Senate candidates taxpayer-financed vouchers to buy television time and House candidates federal matching funds, President George Herbert Walker Bush vetoed it.

During the second half of the 1990s, McCain and Democratic senator Russell D. Feingold of Wisconsin and Reps. Christopher Shays, R-Conn., and Martin Meehan, D-Mass., proposed bipartisan campaign finance overhaul legislation. Their initial legislation would have banned PACs and offered financial incentives to candidates to voluntarily limit their spending. A later version of the legislation simply would have banned soft money. But a majority of Senate Republicans, claiming that further restrictions of campaign contributions would violate the First Amendment right to free speech, but also wishing to preserve their party's traditional edge in raising money, were able to block the legislation from reaching the Senate floor for a vote.

With the Senate evenly divided between the two parties at the start of 2001, McCain and Feingold had enough votes to bring their ban on soft money to the Senate floor. After weeks of spirited debate and votes on amendments and alternative measures, the bill passed the Senate in April 2001. One new provision of the bill would raise the direct contribution limit of individuals to candidates from $1,000 to $2,000 per election. The final shape and fate of the bill remained uncertain after its historic passage in the Senate, however, as the bill moved on to face fierce scrutiny in the House. President George W. Bush also declined to say in what form a campaign finance reform bill had to be for him to sign it into law.

Presidential Primaries

The quadrennial political process of electing a president has two distinct parts—the nominating process and the general election. Yet while the latter has been generally static in form—a one-day nationwide vote on the first

Tuesday after the first Monday in November—the former is constantly evolving.

The changes in the nominating process over the course of the nation's history have been dramatic—from congressional caucuses in the early nineteenth century, through the heyday of the national conventions over the next century and a half, to the present nominating system, where conventions merely ratify the choices made months earlier in the election year by Democratic and Republican primary voters.

Nominations are now decided in the presidential primaries. And they have been since the Democrats' tumultuous convention in Chicago in 1968 encouraged both parties, but the Democrats in particular, to look for ways to open the nominating process to greater grass-roots participation.

The principal way to more voter involvement has been through the proliferation of presidential primaries. While a product of the Progressive era in the early twentieth century, primaries were few and far between until the late 1960s. But after that, they quickly mushroomed in number—from fifteen in 1968, to thirty-six in 1980, to more than forty in 1996.

As the number of primaries grew, power in the nominating process quickly shifted from party kingmakers at the national conventions to voters in the primary states. Gone were the days when candidates could win their party's nomination without entering the primaries. No nominee of either major party has done so since Democrat Hubert H. Humphrey in 1968. Gone too were the days when candidates could win their party's nomination without first proving broad-based popularity among millions of voters. Since Democrat George McGovern in 1972, every major-party nominee has first been their party's highest vote-getter in the primaries. In the process, the once climactic conventions have become little more than giant pep rallies, ratifying the choices of Democratic and Republican primary voters.

"Front-Loaded" Process

As the number of primaries has grown, nominations have been settled earlier and earlier as more and more states have moved their primaries forward to dates near the beginning of the election year in a bid to heighten their influence (a process that has become known as "front-loading.")

In 1968 only one presidential primary (New Hampshire's) was held before the end of March. In 1980 ten states held primaries so early. By 1988 the number surpassed twenty, and in 2000, more than half the country held primary elections before the end of March.

The result has been an increasingly truncated nominating process that has followed a clear pattern. Early votes in Iowa and New Hampshire have winnowed the field to a handful of candidates. Then, after a short period of unpredictability, one candidate has scored a knockout in the glut of March primaries, with their victory ratified by a string of essentially meaningless primary votes over the spring months.

That is what happened in the campaign for the Republican nomination in 2000. Sen. John McCain of Arizona routed the Republican front-runner, Gov. George W. Bush of Texas, in New Hampshire, and battled him ballot for ballot in the array of Republican primaries scattered across the rest of February. But once the calendar flipped to March, Bush's superior organization and resources kicked in. On March 7 alone, eleven primaries were held from Maine to California. Bush triumphed convincingly in most of them—including the featured events in California, New York, and Ohio—driving McCain from the race and essentially wrapping up the nomination.

The Democratic presidential contest ended at the same time, as Vice President Al Gore defeated former Sen. Bill Bradley of New Jersey in all eleven of the day's Democratic primaries. Roughly five months remained before both parties' national conventions, but the nominations for both parties were settled. Cut out of any meaningful role in the year's nominating process were Florida, Illinois, New Jersey, North Carolina, Pennsylvania, Wisconsin, and more than a dozen other states, which held their primaries after the competitive stage of the primary season had ended.

The last time that either party had an elongated tug-of-war for its nomination was 1984, when former vice president Walter F. Mondale and Sen. Gary Hart of Colorado battled into the final week of Democratic primaries before Mondale won the final delegates needed to nail down his nomination. Neither party has had a nominating contest that was even vaguely competitive at the time of its national convention since the 1976 Republican race between President Gerald R. Ford and former governor Ronald Reagan of California.

Reversal of Fortune

When they were regularly winning the White House in the 1970s and 1980s, Republicans showed little interest in tinkering with the nominating process; they were happy to leave that as a concern of the Democrats. But once the GOP began to lose presidential elections in the 1990s, many Republicans began to decry the "front-loaded" primary calendar that produced nominees within a few weeks of voting.

At their convention in San Diego in 1996, Republicans approved a rules change designed to help spread out the calendar. States were offered bonus delegates the later they held their primary or caucus. It did not get many takers, though, in 2000.

But in the wake of that year's Bush-McCain contest, a party commission headed by former Tennessee senator and national GOP chairman Bill Brock recommended that the primary calendar be dramatically overhauled, so that small states would vote first in 2004 and large states would vote last.

States were to be grouped into four "pods" of roughly equal number, with each pod voting over the course of a month. The initial calendar called for voting from March to June, but in the course of discussion the calendar was moved up a month to start in February and end in May. Still, the fourth pod was to be comprised of the largest states, holding roughly half the delegates. The idea was to slow the rush to judgment evident in the "front-loaded" primary system by making it mathematically impossible for a candidate to amass a majority of delegates before most, if not all, of the states had voted.

The idea, dubbed the "Delaware Plan" because of its state of origin, was controversial, particularly among the larger states, who feared a loss of influence if they were required to vote en masse at the end of the primary season. The "Delaware Plan," though, did win the approval of the rules committee of the Republican National Committee (RNC) in May 2000 and the full RNC itself on the eve of the party's convention that summer.

But the plan was defeated in the convention rules committee July 28, after the Bush campaign shifted from a position of neutrality to opposition. Several reasons were cited for the eleventh-hour change of heart, including complaints from the big states over their potential loss of influence, the lack of an agreement with the Democrats over a common course of action, and a loss of control by the states over their primary or caucus dates if the "Delaware Plan" were imposed. But it was also obvious that the Bush campaign wanted a harmonious convention without any contested issues on the floor.

Change Certain in Future

Even if the "Delaware Plan" had been approved by the Republican convention, it still would have faced an uncertain future. Earlier in 2000, the rules committee of the Democratic Party had expressed support for the status quo and urged Republicans to embrace the Democratic primary calendar, which allowed Iowa and New Hampshire to vote first but prohibited other states from voting before the first Tuesday in March. Meanwhile, the nation's secretaries of state recommended a different solution, a system of regional primaries, whose order would be rotated every four years. Yet with neither of the major parties rallying behind it, the secretaries' plan had little chance of being embraced.

Still, even without the Democrats or Republicans opting for bold changes, the nominating process is by nature evolutionary. Every four years at least a few states move their primary or caucus date, creating a new calendar. And nearly every four years, at least one of the parties makes a change in its rules that proves significant. In 2000 Republicans added four delegates to each state's total in 2004 and created automatic delegate seats for the members of the RNC.

An Evolutionary Process

During the early years of the nation, presidential nominations were decided by party caucuses in Congress (derided by their critics as "King Caucus"). At the dawn of the Jacksonian era in the 1830s, though, the nominating role shifted to national conventions, a broader-based venue where party leaders from around the country held sway.

In the early twentieth century, presidential primaries appeared on the scene, adding a new element of grass-roots democracy and voter input. But for the next half century, the primaries were relatively few in number and played a limited advisory role. Nominations continued to be settled in the party conventions.

After World War II American society became more mobile and media-oriented, and once-powerful party organizations began to lose their clout. An increasing number of presidential aspirants saw the primaries as a way to generate popular support that might overcome the resistance of party leaders. Both Republican Dwight D. Eisenhower in 1952 and Democrat

John F. Kennedy in 1960 scored a string of primary victories that demonstrated their vote-getting appeal and made their nominations possible.

Yet the conventions continued to reign supreme through the 1960s, although 1968 proved to be a watershed year in the evolution of the nominating process. Sens. Eugene McCarthy of Minnesota and Robert F. Kennedy of New York used the handful of Democratic primaries that spring to protest the war in Vietnam, together taking more than two-thirds of the party's primary vote and driving President Lyndon B. Johnson from the race.

History might have been different if Kennedy had not been assassinated after his victory in the California primary that June. But without Kennedy on the scene, the party's embattled leadership was able to maintain a tenuous control of the convention that August in Chicago, nominating Vice President Humphrey, who had not competed in a single primary state.

But Humphrey's nomination came at a price. For the first time in several generations, the legitimacy of the convention itself was thrown into question. And as an outgrowth, a series of Democratic rules review commissions began to overhaul the presidential nominating process to encourage much greater grass-roots participation.

Change Comes Quickly

The immediate result was a dramatic increase in presidential primaries that enhanced the chances of long-shot outsiders, such as George McGovern and Jimmy Carter, who captured the Democratic nomination in 1972 and 1976, respectively.

Democrat Hubert H. Humphrey in 1968 was the last candidate to win a major party's presidential nomination without entering the primaries.
File photo

In the 1970s, the primary calendar started slowly, giving little-known candidates the time to raise money and momentum after doing well in the early rounds. Most of the primaries then were held in May and June.

But the layout of the nominating process has been less favorable to dark horses since then. In the 1980s Democrats reinserted party and elected officials into the process, creating a new category of automatic delegate seats for them that have come to be known as "superdelegates." And states began to move forward on the calendar in a bid to increase their influence, heightening the need for candidates to be well organized and well funded at the beginning of the primary season.

Democrats sought to put a brake on the calendar sprawl toward the beginning of the election year by instituting the "window," which prohibited any of the party's primaries or caucuses from being held before early March, with the exception of Iowa, New Hampshire, and for a while, Maine.

With the creation of that early March firewall, many states parked their primary in March—gradually at first, but then in tidal wave proportions in 1988, with the creation of a full-scale primary vote across the South on the second Tuesday in March that came to be known as "Super Tuesday."

The event did not have the effect that its Democratic sponsors had hoped for, in terms of steering the nomination toward a centrist son of the South, such as Sen. Al Gore of Tennessee. In the early 1990s, the early March southern primary lost some of its members.

But the concept of early regional primaries took hold elsewhere. In 1996 all of New England except New Hampshire voted on the first Tuesday in March. Six southern states, led by Texas and Florida, voted on the second Tuesday. Four states in the industrial Midwest—Illinois, Michigan, Ohio, and Wisconsin—voted on the third Tuesday in March. And California anchored a three-state western primary on the fourth Tuesday.

In 2000 the bulk of the New England states continued to vote on the first Tuesday in March, and much of the South on the second Tuesday. But the big story was the dramatic movement toward a broad-based, coast-to-coast vote on the first Tuesday in March. The day's primaries and caucuses involved states with nearly 40 percent of the nation's population, including three of the seven most populous states—California, New York, and Ohio.

Current Arrangement

Even though much of the primary calendar has changed dramatically over the last few decades, the accepted starting points have remained Iowa and New Hampshire (even though other states have occasionally voted before them).

Both states have made their early events into cottage industries, but the candidates and the media have helped make them so. More than ever, Iowa and New Hampshire are about the only places left where candidates have some control over their destinies. They can woo voters one-on-one, whether in bowling alleys, coffee shops, or the frequent gatherings in neighborhood living rooms.

For if there is one thing that has become certain in recent years, once the New Hampshire primary is over and candidates must compete in several states simultaneously, there is a frenetic burst of tarmac-to-tarmac campaigning heavily dependent on media advertising.

With one exception, every presidential nominee since 1976 has won either Iowa or New Hampshire, and finished no lower than third in the other. The exception was Bill Clinton in 1992, who did not seriously contest Iowa in deference to the home-state appeal of Sen. Tom Harkin and finished second in New Hampshire behind former Senator Paul E. Tsongas of Massachusetts.

Iowa and New Hampshire illustrate the two different types of delegate-selection processes that states have to choose from. Iowa is a caucus; New Hampshire is a primary. Primaries require voters only to cast a ballot, an exercise that usually takes just a few minutes. The deliberative nature of a neighborhood caucus, though, often requires the commitment of an afternoon or evening.

A Small Slice of the Electorate

Voter turnout is usually much higher in a primary than a caucus, but even in primaries the turnout is much lower than a general election. In New Hampshire, for instance, where interest in the presidential primary is probably greater than any other state, nearly 400,000 voters turned out in February 2000 for the presidential primary.

The disparity is much greater in many other states. Roughly 35 million votes were cast in all the presidential primaries in 2000. Meanwhile, turnout in the handful of states that held caucuses was no more than several hundred thousand more voters. By comparison, 96 million voters turned out for the 1996 general election.

Rules governing voter participation play a role in the comparatively low turnouts for the nominating process. Every primary is not as open as a general election, where any registered voter can participate. A number of states limit participation to registered Democratic and Republican voters.

Some others allow independents to participate, but list them on the voting rolls afterward as members of the party in which they cast their primary ballot.

Still, the vast majority of registered voters across the country can participate in a presidential primary or caucus if they want. The fact that more do not has generated the conventional wisdom that the nominating process is dominated by ideological activists—liberals on the Democratic side, conservatives on the Republican.

That is debatable in the primaries, where the winners in recent years have been from the mainstreams of both parties. An ideological bent is usually more evident in the low-turnout world of the caucuses, where a small cadre of dedicated voters can significantly affect the outcome.

When religious broadcaster Pat Robertson tried for the Republican presidential nomination in 1988, for instance, he won first-round caucus voting in three states and finished second in three others, including Iowa. But Robertson did not come close that year to winning a presidential primary.

Clues to the Fall

It has been a matter of debate within the political community whether the current primary-dominated nominating process is better than the old system, in which party leaders controlled the selection process.

But it is a fact that the increased number of primaries helps provide valuable clues about the vote-getting potential of candidates in the general election. Nominees who have exhibited broad-based appeal among the diverse array of primary voters in the winter and spring have gone on to be quite competitive in the fall, while those nominees who have struggled through the primaries showing limited appeal among one or two of their party's major constituency groups have usually been buried under landslides in November.

A less reliable indicator of what will happen in the fall is the number of votes cast in each party's primaries. In every year from 1956 through 1992, more ballots were cast in Democratic than Republican primaries. In part, it was due to the simple fact that through much of this period, Democrats outnumbered Republicans.

But it also reflected the fact that the Democratic primaries drew more voter interest because they often exhibited more conflict between competing constituencies within the party. That kind of political drama and angst was good for primary turnout, but not for the party's chances in the fall elections, as Republicans won most of the presidential contests in this period.

Types of Primaries and Procedures

In many respects, the presidential nominating process is like a modern-day Alice in Wonderland. Its basic dynamics do not always appear very logical. Primaries and caucuses are strewn across the calendar from January to June, culminating with party conventions in the summer. A nomination is won by a candidate attaining a majority of delegates, an honor that is formally bestowed at the conventions but for years has informally occurred much earlier during the primary season.

Size is less important in determining a state's importance in the nominating process than its tradition and place on the calendar (early is best). Hence, the quadrennial starring role for Iowa and New Hampshire, and the bit parts frequently assigned California and New York.

States have different ground rules in the nominating process. Some have caucuses, many more have primaries. Most primaries allocate a state's delegates, but some are nonbinding "beauty contests," with the delegates elected independently of the preference vote for presidential candidates.

Rules on voter participation vary from state to state. Some states hold "closed" contests, which are open only to a party's registered voters. Some hold "semi-open" events, which allow independent voters to participate along with registered members of the party. About half the states have "open" primaries or caucuses, in which any registered voter can participate. (The bulk of these states do not have party registration to begin with.)

The parties themselves also have different playing fields. Since 1980, Democrats have not allowed any states except Iowa, New Hampshire, and sometimes Maine to hold a primary or caucus before early March. Republicans have had no such restriction, and in some years a state or two on the GOP side has voted in advance of Iowa and New Hampshire.

Since 1984, Democrats have reserved between 10 and 20 percent of their delegate seats for high-level party and elected officials (such as Democratic governors, members of Congress, and members of the party's national committee). Often called "superdelegates," these automatic delegates do not have to declare a presidential preference. (Republicans did not have "superdelegates" until the 2000 GOP convention approved automatic delegate seats for RNC members in 2004.) Since 1992, Democrats have required states to distribute delegates among their candidates in proportion to their vote, statewide and in congressional districts, with 15 percent required to win a share.

Republicans, in contrast, allow a variety of delegate allocation methods, including proportional representation, statewide winner-take-all (in which the candidate winning the most votes statewide wins all the delegates), congressional district and statewide winner-take-all (in which the high vote-getter in a district wins that district's delegates and the high vote-getter statewide wins all the at-large delegates), or some combination of the three. Still another method is the selection of individual delegates in a "loophole," or direct election, primary. And in Republican caucus states, delegates often run as individuals and frequently are not officially allocated to any candidate.

How delegates are actually elected can vary from state to state. Most primary states hold presidential preference votes, in which voters choose among the candidates who have qualified for the ballot in their states. Although preference votes may be binding or nonbinding, in most states the vote is binding on the delegates, who are elected in the primary itself or chosen outside of it by a caucus process, by a state committee, or by the candidates who have qualified to win delegates.

For those primaries in which the preference vote is binding upon delegates, state laws may vary as to the number of ballots through which delegates at the convention must remain committed. Delegates may be bound for as short as one ballot or as long as a candidate remains in the race. National Democratic rules were changed in 1980 to bind delegates for one ballot unless released by the candidate they were elected to support. The rule, though, became a flash point of controversy between the front-runner, President Jimmy Carter, and his major challenger, Sen. Edward M. Kennedy of Massachusetts. The Carter forces prevailed in having the rule sustained at the 1980 convention, but it was subsequently dropped during the quadrennial review of party rules after the election.

Until 1980 the Republicans had a rule requiring delegates bound to a specific candidate by state law in primary states to vote for that candidate at the convention regardless of their personal presidential preferences. That rule was repealed at the party's July 1980 convention.

Legacy of the Progressive Era

Yet, entrenched as they now are in the electoral process, primaries are still relatively recent replacements for the old smoke-filled rooms where party bosses once dictated the choice of presidential nominees. Presidential primaries originated as an outgrowth of the Progressive movement in the early twentieth century. Progressives, populists, and reformers in general were fighting state and municipal corruption. They objected to the links between political bosses and big business and advocated returning the government to the people.

Part of this "return to the people" was a turn away from what were looked upon as boss-dominated conventions. It was only a matter of time before the primary idea spread from state and local elections to presidential contests. Because there was no provision for a nationwide primary, state primaries were initiated to choose delegates to the national party conventions (delegate-selection primaries) and to register voters' preferences on their parties' eventual presidential nominees (preference primaries).

Florida enacted the first presidential primary law in 1901. The law gave party officials an option of holding a party primary to choose any party candidate for public office, as well as delegates to the national conventions. However, there was no provision for placing names of presidential candidates on the ballot—either in the form of a preference vote or with information indicating the preference of the candidates for convention delegates.

Wisconsin's Progressive Republican politician, Gov. Robert M. La Follette, gave a major boost to the presidential primary following the 1904 Republican National Convention. It was at that convention that the credentials of La Follette's Progressive delegation were rejected and a regular Republican delegation from Wisconsin was seated. Angered by what he considered his unfair treatment, La Follette returned to his home state and began pushing for a presidential primary law. The result was the Wisconsin law of 1905 mandating the direct election of national convention delegates. The law, however, did not include a provision for indicating the delegates' presidential preference.

Pennsylvania followed Wisconsin in 1906 with a statute providing that each candidate for delegate to a national convention could have printed beside his name on the official primary ballot the name of the presidential candidate he would support at the convention. However, no member of either party exercised this option in the 1908 primary.

La Follette's sponsorship of the delegate-selection primary helped make the concept a part of the Progressive political program. The growth of the Progressive movement rapidly resulted in the enactment of presidential primary laws in other states.

The next step in presidential primaries—the preferential vote for president—took place in Oregon. There, in 1910, Sen. Jonathan Bourne, a Progressive Republican colleague of La Follette (then a senator), sponsored a referendum to establish a presidential preference primary, with delegates legally bound to support the primary winner. By 1912, with Oregon in the lead, fully a dozen states had enacted presidential primary laws that provided for either direct election of delegates, a preferential vote, or both. The number had expanded to twenty-six states by 1916.

Primaries and Conventions

The first major test of the impact of presidential primary laws—in 1912—demonstrated that victories in the primaries did not ensure a candidate's nomination. Former president Theodore Roosevelt, campaigning in twelve Republican primaries, won nine of them, including Ohio, the home state of incumbent Republican president William Howard Taft. Roosevelt lost to Taft by a narrow margin in Massachusetts and to La Follette in North Dakota and Wisconsin.

Despite this impressive string of primary victories, the convention rejected Roosevelt in favor of Taft. Taft supporters dominated the Republican National Committee, which ran the convention, and the convention's credentials committee, which ruled on contested delegates. Moreover, Taft was backed by many state organizations, especially in the South, where most delegates were chosen by caucuses or conventions dominated by party leaders.

On the Democratic side, the convention more closely reflected the primary results. Gov. Woodrow Wilson of New Jersey and Speaker of the House Champ Clark of Missouri were closely matched in total primary votes, with Wilson only 29,632 votes ahead of Clark. Wilson emerged with the nomination after a long convention struggle with Clark.

Likewise, in 1916, Democratic primary results foreshadowed the winner of the nomination, although Wilson, who was then the incumbent, had no major opposition for renomination. But once again, Republican presidential primaries had little impact upon the nominating process at the convention. The eventual nominee, Supreme Court Justice Charles Evans Hughes, had won only two primaries.

In 1920 presidential primaries did not play a major role in determining the winner of either party's nomination. James M. Cox, the eventual Democratic nominee, ran in only one primary, in his home state of Ohio. Most of the Democratic primaries featured favorite-son candidates, unpledged delegate slates, or write-in votes. And at the convention Democrats took forty-four ballots to settle on Cox.

Similarly, the main entrants in the Republican presidential primaries that year failed to capture their party's nomination. Sen. Warren G. Harding of Ohio, the compromise choice, won the primary in his home state but lost badly in Indiana and garnered only a handful of votes elsewhere. The three primary leaders—Sen. Hiram Johnson of California, Gen. Leonard Wood of New Hampshire, and Gov. Frank O. Lowden of Illinois—lost out in the end.

After the first wave of enthusiasm for presidential primaries, interest in them waned. By 1935, eight states had repealed their presidential primary laws. The diminution of reform zeal during the 1920s, the preoccupation of the country with the Great Depression in the 1930s, and war in the 1940s appeared to have been leading factors in this decline. Also, party leaders were not enthusiastic about primaries; the cost of conducting them was relatively high, for both the candidates and the states. Many presidential candidates ignored the primaries, and voter participation often was low.

But after World War II, interest picked up again. Some politicians with presidential ambitions, knowing the party leadership was not enthusiastic about their candidacies, entered the primaries to try to generate a bandwagon effect. In 1948 Harold Stassen, Republican governor of Minnesota from 1939 to 1943, entered presidential primaries in opposition to the Republican organization and made some headway before losing in Oregon to

Gov. Thomas E. Dewey of New York. And in 1952 Sen. Estes Kefauver, D-Tenn., riding a wave of public recognition as head of the Senate Organized Crime Investigating Committee, challenged Democratic Party leaders by winning several primaries, including an upset of President Harry S. Truman in New Hampshire. The Eisenhower-Taft struggle for the Republican Party nomination that year also stimulated interest in the primaries.

In 1960 Sen. John F. Kennedy of Massachusetts challenged Sen. Hubert Humphrey of Minnesota in two primaries: Wisconsin, which bordered on Humphrey's home state, and West Virginia, a labor state with few Catholic voters. (Kennedy was Roman Catholic, and some questioned whether voters would elect a Catholic president.) After Kennedy won both primaries, Humphrey withdrew from the race. The efforts of party leaders to draft an alternative to Kennedy came to be viewed as undemocratic by rank-and-file voters. The primary now significantly challenged approval by party leaders as the preferred route to the nomination.

Similarly, Sen. Barry M. Goldwater, R-Ariz., in 1964, former vice president Richard Nixon in 1968, and Sen. George S. McGovern, D-S.D., in 1972, were able to use the primaries to show their vote-getting and organizational abilities on the way to becoming their party's presidential nominees.

The Democrats Begin to Tinker

Despite the growing importance of primaries, party leaders until 1968 maintained some control of the nominating process. With only a handful of the fifteen to twenty primaries regularly contested, candidates could count on a short primary season. They began in New Hampshire in March, then tested their appeal during the spring in Wisconsin, Nebraska, Oregon, and California before resuming their courtship of party leaders. In 1968—admittedly an unusual year, with incumbent Democratic president Lyndon B. Johnson suddenly withdrawing from his race for reelection, and the leading Democratic candidate (Sen. Robert F. Kennedy of New York) assassinated a few weeks before the convention—Vice President Humphrey was able to gain the party's nomination without entering a single primary.

But after 1968, the Democrats began tinkering with the nominating rules, in an effort to reduce the alienation of liberals and minorities from the political system and to allow the people to choose their own leaders. Victors in 1968, and four of the five presidential elections that followed, the Republicans were slow to make any changes in their rules. This era of grass-roots control produced for the Democrats presidential candidates such as McGovern, a liberal from South Dakota who lost in a landslide to Nixon in 1972, and Jimmy Carter, a former governor of Georgia, who beat incumbent President Gerald R. Ford in 1976 but lost to Ronald Reagan in 1980.

With a then-record high of thirty-seven primaries held in 1980 (including the District of Columbia and Puerto Rico), the opportunity for mass participation in the nominating process was greater than ever before. President Carter and Republican nominee Reagan were the clear winners of the long 1980 primary season. Although Carter received a bare majority of the cumulative Democratic primary vote, he amassed a plurality of more than 2.5 million votes over his major rival, Sen. Edward M. Kennedy of Massachusetts. With no opposition in the late primary contests, Reagan emerged as a more one-sided choice of GOP primary voters. He finished nearly 4.8 million votes ahead of his closest competitor, George Herbert Walker Bush.

Disheartened by Carter's massive defeat in 1980, the Democrats revised their nominating rules for the 1984 election. The party created a new bloc of so-called "superdelegates"—that is, delegate seats were reserved for party leaders who were not formally committed to any presidential candidate. This reform had two main goals. First, Democratic leaders wanted to ensure that the party's elected officials would participate in the convention. Second, they wanted to ensure that these uncommitted party leaders could play a major role in selecting the presidential nominee if no candidate was a clear front-runner.

While the reforms of the 1970s were designed to give more influence to grass-roots activists and less to party regulars, this revision was intended to bring about a deliberative process in which experienced party leaders could help select a consensus Democratic nominee with a strong chance to win the presidency.

The Democrats' new rules had some expected, as well as unexpected, results. For the first time since 1968, the number of primaries declined and the number of caucuses increased. The Democrats held only thirty primaries in 1984 (including the District of Columbia and Puerto Rico). Yet, like McGovern in 1972 and Carter in 1976, Colorado Senator Gary Hart used the primaries to pull ahead (temporarily) of former vice president Walter F.

Mondale, an early front-runner whose strongest ties were to the party leadership and its traditional core elements. In 1984 the presence of superdelegates was important because about four out of five backed Mondale. (But Mondale did wind up with more primary votes than Hart.)

A few critics regarded the seating of superdelegates as undemocratic, and there were calls for reducing their numbers. Yet to those most influential within the party, the superdelegates had served their purpose. The Democratic National Committee (DNC) set aside additional seats for party leaders, increasing the number of superdelegates from 14 percent of the delegates in 1984 to 18 percent in 1996. All members of the DNC were guaranteed convention seats, as were all Democratic governors and members of Congress.

The Republican Party did not guarantee delegate seats to its leaders until the 2000 convention voted to make members of the RNC automatic "superdelegates" at the party's convention in 2004. Republicans had not acted before that, in part because their rules permit less rigid pledging of delegates, which generally has led to substantial participation by Republican leaders, despite the absence of such guarantees.

Regional Primaries and Super Tuesday

In addition to the Democrats' internal party concerns with the nominating process, other critics often cited the length of the primary season (nearly twice as long as the general election campaign), the expense, the physical strain on the candidates and the variations and complexities of state laws as problems of presidential primaries.

To deal with these problems, several states in 1974 and 1975 discussed the feasibility of creating regional primaries, in which individual states within a geographical region would hold their primaries on the same day. Supporters of the concept believed it would reduce candidate expenses and strain and would permit concentration on regional issues.

The idea achieved some limited success in 1976 when three western states (Idaho, Nevada, and Oregon) and three southern states (Arkansas, Kentucky, and Tennessee)—decided to organize regional primaries in each of their areas. However, the two groups chose May 25 to hold their primaries, thus defeating one of the main purposes of the plan by forcing candidates to shuttle across the country to cover both areas.

Attempts also were made in New England to construct a regional primary. But New Hampshire would not participate because its law required the state to hold its primary at least one week before any other state. Hesitancy by the other New England state legislatures defeated the idea. Only Vermont joined Massachusetts, on March 2, in holding a simultaneous presidential primary, although New Hampshire voted only one week earlier.

In 1980 and 1984, limited regional primaries were held again in several areas of the country. Probably the most noteworthy was the trio of southern states (Alabama, Florida, and Georgia) that voted on the second Tuesday in March—first, in 1980; then again in 1984. It became the basis for "Super Tuesday," which became a full-blown southern-oriented regional primary in 1988.

But the biggest change was that more and more states, hoping to increase their impact on the presidential campaign, decided to hold their primaries early. When South Dakota announced that it would hold its presidential primary in 1988 on February 23, New Hampshire moved its date to February 16.

Sixteen states—a dozen from the South—held primaries on Super Tuesday, March 8, 1988. The long-held goal of many southern political leaders to hold an early regional primary was finally realized. Most of the GOP primaries were winner-take-all, and when Vice President George Bush swept every Republican primary on Super Tuesday, he effectively locked up the GOP nomination. His major opponent, Sen. Robert Dole of Kansas, withdrew by the end of the month. For the Democrats, Massachusetts Gov. Michael S. Dukakis also fared well on Super Tuesday. But the Rev. Jesse Jackson—the first serious black candidate for a major-party presidential nomination—kept the contest going into June.

'March Madness'

In 1992 Super Tuesday had become part of a general rush among states to hold their primaries as early as possible. Dubbed "March Madness," the early clustering of primaries—seventeen states held primaries in February or March—was viewed with dismay by some political analysts. They said it could lead to nominees being locked in before most voters knew what was happening, resulting in less informed and deliberative voting in the general election.

Republican presidential candidates face off in debate before the 1996 primaries. Left to right: Alan Keyes, Morry Taylor, Steve Forbes, Robert Dornan, Bob Dole, Richard Lugar, Lamar Alexander, and Pat Buchanan. *Reuters*

As winner in the eight Super Tuesday primaries (six of which were again in the South) on March 10, 1992, President Bush was well on his way to renomination on the GOP side. Although he lost the two New England primaries (Massachusetts and Rhode Island) that day, Bill Clinton by winning all six southern primaries (Florida, Louisiana, Mississippi, Oklahoma, Tennessee, and Texas) established himself as the Democratic front-runner. Most of his competitors had dropped out of the race by the end of the following week. Former governor Jerry Brown of California held out until the Democratic convention, but Brown was never able to establish any sort of momentum to overtake Clinton.

In 1996 the process was even more heavily weighted in favor of early primaries, as more than two-thirds of them were held before the end of March. The idea of regional primaries also came the closest to fruition in 1996. "Junior Tuesday Week" (March 2–7) featured primary voting in ten states (five of which were in New England); Super Tuesday (March 12) had seven primaries (six of which were in the South); and "Big Ten" Tuesday (March 19) had four primaries in important midwestern states. By the time California (which had moved its primary forward in the hope of increasing its sway on the nominating process) had its primary on March 26 (along with two other western states—Nevada and Washington), Dole had all but clinched the Republican nomination.

2000 Outcome

In 2000 there was not only a glut of early primaries, but also a large concentration on a single day, the first Tuesday in March (March 7). The clustering on this date was not coincidental. It was the earliest date allowed by Democratic rules for states other than Iowa and New Hampshire to hold their primary or caucus. Eleven states scheduled primaries on March 7, 2000, creating a de facto national primary that became variously known as "Titanic Tuesday" or the new "Super Tuesday," although the large southern-oriented vote of the same name remained on the second Tuesday in March.

Political analysts predicted the huge volume of early primaries would result in both parties' nominations being decided by the ides of March. And they were right. George W. Bush and John McCain battled almost evenly through the seven states that held Republican primaries in February—Bush winning four, McCain, three. But once the calendar turned to March, Bush's superior organization and financial resources proved decisive as he dominated the vote March 7 and drove McCain from the race.

With Democratic rules preventing a wholesale movement of states into February, the early Democratic calendar was quite different from the Republican one. The Democratic campaign essentially went "dark" from the early February voting in New Hampshire until the huge array of primaries on March 7.

But the result was the same on the Democratic side as it was on the Republican, an early knockout by the front-runner. Vice President Al Gore was closely contested by his major challenger, former Senator Bill Bradley of New Jersey, in raising funds and drawing media attention during the long stretch before the primaries. But once the balloting began, Bradley proved no match for Gore. The vice president won the late January caucuses in Iowa decisively, the New Hampshire primary narrowly, and swept all the Democratic primaries and caucuses March 7, driving Bradley to the sidelines. Only half the states had voted by then, but the Democratic and Republican races were over.

Nominating Conventions

Although the presidential nominating convention has been a target of criticism throughout its existence, it has survived to become a traditional fixture of American politics. The convention owes its longevity and general acceptance in large part to the multiplicity of functions that the convention uniquely combines.

The convention is a nominating body that the Democrats, Republicans, and most of the principal third parties have used since the early 1830s to choose their candidates for president and vice president. The convention also produces a platform containing the party's positions on issues of the campaign. Convention delegates form the supreme governing body of the party and as such they make major decisions on party affairs. Between conventions such decisions are made by the national committee with the guidance of the party chair.

The convention provides a forum for compromise among the diverse elements within a party, allowing the discussion and often the satisfactory solution of differing points of view. As the ultimate campaign rally, the convention also gathers together thousands of party leaders and rank-and-file members from across the country in an atmosphere that varies widely, sometimes encouraging sober discussion but often resembling a carnival. But even though the process has drawn heavy criticism, the convention has endured because it successfully performs a variety of actions.

The convention is an outgrowth of the American political experience. Nowhere is it mentioned in the Constitution nor has the authority of the convention ever been a subject of congressional legislation. Rather, the convention has evolved along with the presidential selection process. The convention has been the accepted nominating method of the major political parties since the election of 1832, but internal changes within the convention system have been massive since the early, formative years.

Convention Sites

Before the Civil War, conventions frequently were held in small buildings, even churches, and attracted only several hundred delegates and a minimum of spectators. Transportation and communications were slow, so most conventions were held in the late spring in a city with a central geographical location. Baltimore, Maryland, was the most popular convention city in this initial period, playing host to the first six Democratic conventions (1832 through 1852), two Whig conventions, one National Republican convention, and the 1831 Anti-Masonic gathering—America's first national nominating convention. With the nation's westward expansion, the heartland city of Chicago emerged as the most frequent convention center. Since its first one in 1860, Chicago has been the site of twenty-five major party conventions (fourteen Republican, eleven Democratic). The Democrats held their national convention in Chicago as recently as 1996. In 2000 Republicans held their national convention in Philadelphia, which has hosted eight conventions. Democrats chose that year to meet in Los Angeles—the second time that the California city hosted a national party convention.

Locating and Financing Conventions

Since 1976, presidential elections have been publicly funded. Early on, the newly created Federal Election Commission (FEC) ruled that host-city contributions to conventions are allowable, enabling the parties to far exceed the technical limit on convention spending. In 1988, for example, the FEC allotted the two major parties $9.2 million each in public funds for their conventions. The money came from an optional checkoff for publicly financing presidential campaigns on federal income tax forms. (Congress raised the original $1 checkoff to $3 per taxpayer beginning in 1993.) In 1988 the Republicans, however, spent a total of $18 million on their New Orleans convention, while the Democrats spent $22.5 million in Atlanta. To attract the Democratic convention, Atlanta levied a special tax on hotel guests, which enabled the host committee to offer a package of $5 million in borrowed money. For both conventions, General Motors (with FEC permission) provided fleets of cars at an estimated cost of $350,000.

In 1992 the Democrats spent a record $38.6 million on their New York City meeting, according to political scientist Herbert E. Alexander. For the 1996 conventions, the FEC allotted the two major parties $12.4 million each in public funds, but the total spending for both parties, according to Alexander, was at least twice that amount. In 2000 the federal money given each of the two major parties for their conventions reached $13.5 million. The Reform Party was given $2.5 million.

Major outlays typically go for construction, administration, office space, convention committees, and police and fire protection. Besides adequate

hotel and convention hall facilities, safety of the delegates and other attend-
ees is increasingly a major consideration in selection of a national party
convention site. The island location of Miami Beach, for example, made it
easier to contain protest demonstrators and reportedly was a factor in its
selection by the Republicans in 1968 and by both parties in 1972.

For the party that controls the White House, often the overriding factor
in site selection is the president's personal preference—as in the GOP's decision to meet in 1992 in President George Herbert Walker Bush's adopted
home city of Houston, or the Democrats' decision to meet in Atlantic City
in 1964, because President Lyndon Johnson wanted a site within helicopter
distance of Washington and convenient to New York City.

The national committees of the two parties select the sites about one year
before the conventions are to take place.

Call of the Convention

The second major step in the quadrennial convention process follows several months after the site selection with the announcement of the convention call, the establishment of the three major convention committees—credentials, rules, and platform (resolutions)—the appointment of convention
officers, and finally the holding of the convention itself. While these basic
steps have undergone little change during the past 170 years, there have
been major alterations within the nominating convention system.

The call to the convention sets the date and site of the meeting and is issued early in each election year, if not before. The call to the first Democratic convention, held in 1832, was issued by the New Hampshire Legislature. Early Whig conventions were called by party members in Congress.
With the establishment of national committees later in the nineteenth century, the function of issuing the convention call fell to these new party organizations. Each national committee currently has the responsibility for allocating delegates to each state.

Delegate Selection

Both parties have modified the method of allocating delegates to the individual states and territories. From the beginning of the convention system
in the nineteenth century, both the Democrats and Republicans distributed
votes to the states based on their electoral college strength.

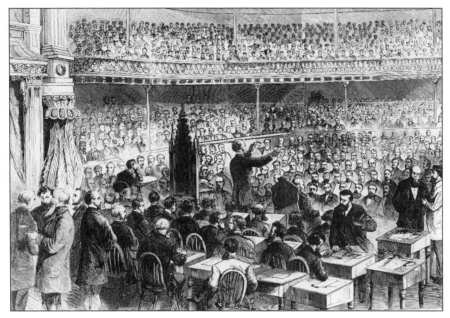

A scene from the 1868 Republican convention that nominated Ulysses S. Grant for president.
Library of Congress

The first major deviation from this procedure was made by the Republicans after their divisive 1912 convention, in which President William Howard Taft won renomination over former President Theodore Roosevelt. Taft's nomination was due largely to almost solid support from the South—a region vastly overrepresented in relation to its number of Republican voters. Before their 1916 convention the Republicans reduced the allocation of votes to the southern states. At their 1924 convention the Republicans applied the first bonus system, by which states were awarded extra votes for supporting the Republican presidential candidate in the previous election. The concept of bonus votes, applied as a reward to the states for supporting the party ticket, has been used and expanded by both parties since that time.

The Democrats first used a bonus system in 1944, completing a compromise arrangement with southern states for abolishing the party's controversial two-thirds nominating rule. Since then both parties have used various delegate-allocation formulas. At their 1972 convention the Republicans revised the formula and added more than 900 new delegate slots for

1976, increasing the size of the convention by two-thirds. The Ripon Society, an organization of liberal Republicans, sued to have the new rules overturned. They argued that, because of the extra delegates awarded to states that voted Republican in the previous presidential election, small southern and western states were favored at the expense of the more populous but less Republican eastern states. The challenge failed when the Supreme Court in February 1976 refused to hear the case and thus let stand a U.S. Court of Appeals decision upholding the rules.

Only 116 delegates from thirteen states attended the initial national nominating convention held by the Anti-Masons in 1831, but with the addition of more states and the adoption of increasingly complex voting-allocation formulas by the major parties, the size of conventions spiraled. The 1976 Republican convention had 2,259 delegates, while the Democrats in the same year had 3,075 delegates casting 3,008 votes. (The number of delegate votes was smaller than the number of delegates because Democratic Party rules provide for fractional voting.)

The expanded size of modern conventions in part reflected their democratization, with less command by a few party leaders and dramatic growth among youth, women, and minority delegations. Increased representation for such groups was one of the major reasons given by the Republicans for the huge increase in delegate strength authorized by the 1972 convention (and effective for the 1976 gathering).

The Democrats adopted new rules in June 1978, expanding the number of delegates by 10 percent to provide extra representation for state and local officials. The new Democratic rules also required that women account for at least 50 percent of the delegates beginning with the 1980 convention. That party's national convention continued to grow throughout the next decade—from 3,331 delegate votes in 1980 to 4,339 in 2000. An Associated Press (AP) survey in 2000 found that nearly one-half of the Democratic delegates were women, and fully one-quarter were from minority groups.

In contrast, 2,066 delegates attended the 2000 Republican convention in Philadelphia. Unlike the Democrats, the Republican Party had no rules mandating the makeup of its convention delegates. Barely one-third of the convention delegates were women, according to the AP, and less than 10 percent were from minority groups.

With the increased size of conventions has come a formalization in the method of delegate selection, which at first was often haphazard and informal. At the Democratic convention in 1835, for example, Maryland had 188 delegates to cast the state's ten votes. In contrast, Tennessee's fifteen votes were cast by a traveling businessman who happened to be in the convention city at the time. While the number of delegates and the number of votes allocated tended to be equal or nearly so later in the nineteenth century, a few party bosses frequently exercised domination of national conventions.

Two basic methods of delegate selection were employed in the nineteenth century and continued to be used into the twentieth: the caucus method, by which delegates were chosen by meetings at the local or state level, and the appointment method, by which delegates were appointed by the governor or a powerful state leader.

Presidential Primaries

A revolutionary new mechanism for delegate selection emerged during the early 1900s: the presidential primary election in which the voters directly elected convention delegates.

Initiated in Florida at the turn of the century, the presidential primary by 1912 was used by thirteen states. In his first annual message to Congress the following year, President Woodrow Wilson advocated the establishment of a national primary to select presidential candidates: "I feel confident that I do not misinterpret the wishes or the expectations of the country when I urge the prompt enactment of legislation which will provide for primary elections throughout the country at which the voters of several parties may choose their nominees for the presidency without the intervention of nominating conventions." Wilson went on to suggest the retention of conventions for the purpose of declaring the results of the primaries and formulating the parties' platforms.

Before any action was taken on Wilson's proposal, the progressive spirit that spurred the growth of presidential primaries died out. Not until the late 1960s and early 1970s, when widespread pressures for change touched both parties but especially the Democratic, was there a rapid growth in presidential primaries. In the mid-1980s some states reverted to the caucus method of delegate selection, but their revival soon abated. A record forty-four primaries were held in 2000, including those in the District of Columbia and Puerto Rico.

In many states participation in the presidential primary is restricted to voters belonging to the party holding the primary. In some states, however, participation by voters outside the party is allowed by state-mandated open primaries, usually with the caveat, though, that the party in which they cast a primary ballot is publicly recorded.

Democratic Rules in the 1980s and 1990s

In June 1982 the Democratic National Committee (DNC) adopted several changes in the presidential nominating process recommended by the party's Commission on Presidential Nominations, chaired by Gov. James B. Hunt Jr. of North Carolina. The Hunt Commission, as it came to be known, suggested revisions to increase the power of party regulars and give the convention more freedom to act on its own. It was the fourth time in twelve years that the Democrats, struggling to repair their nominating process without repudiating earlier reforms, had rewritten their party rules.

One major change in the Democrats' rules was the creation of a new group of "superdelegates," party and elected officials who would go to the 1984 convention uncommitted and would cast about 14 percent of the ballots. The DNC also adopted a Hunt Commission proposal to weaken the rule binding delegates to vote for their original presidential preference on the first convention ballot. But the new rule also allowed a presidential candidate to replace any disloyal delegate with a more faithful one.

One of the most significant revisions was the Democrats' decision to relax proportional representation at the convention and end the ban on the "loophole" primary-winner-take-all by district. Proportional representation is the distribution of delegates among candidates to reflect their share of the primary or caucus vote, both statewide and in congressional districts. Mandated by party rules in 1980, it was blamed by some Democrats for the protracted primary fight between President Jimmy Carter and Sen. Edward M. Kennedy of Massachusetts. Because candidates needed only about 20 percent of the vote in most places to qualify for a share of the delegates, Kennedy was able to remain in contention. But while the system kept Kennedy going, it did nothing to help his chances of winning the nomination.

Although the Democrats' 1984 rules permitted states to retain proportional representation, they also allowed states to take advantage of two op-tions that could help a front-running candidate build the momentum to wrap up the nomination early in the year.

One was a winner-take-more system. States could elect to keep proportional representation but adopt a winner bonus plan that would award the top vote-getter in each district one extra delegate.

The other option was a return to the loophole primary, which party rules outlawed in 1980 (with exemptions allowing Illinois and West Virginia to retain their loophole voting systems). In the loophole states, voters balloted directly for delegates, with each delegate candidate identified by presidential preference. Sometimes several presidential contenders would win at least a fraction of the delegates in a given district, but the most common result is a sweep by the presidential front-runner, even if he has less than an absolute majority. Loophole primaries aid the building of a consensus behind the front-runner, while still giving other candidates a chance to inject themselves back into the race by winning a major loophole state decisively.

The DNC retained the delegate-selection season adopted in 1978, a three-month period stretching from the second Tuesday in March to the second Tuesday in June. But, in an effort to reduce the growing influence of early states in the nominating process, the Democrats required Iowa and New Hampshire to move their highly publicized elections to late winter. Party rules maintained the privileged status of Iowa and New Hampshire before other states but mandated that their initial nominating rounds be held only eight days apart in 1984. Five weeks had intervened between the Iowa caucuses and New Hampshire primary in 1980.

The DNC also retained rules requiring primary states to set candidate filing deadlines thirty to ninety days before the election and limiting participation in the delegate selection process to Democrats only. This last rule eliminated cross-over primaries where voters could participate in the Democratic primary without designating their party affiliation. African Americans and Hispanics won continued endorsement of affirmative action in the new party rules. Women gained renewed support for the equal division rule, which required state delegations at the national convention to be divided equally between men and women.

The Democratic Party's 1988 presidential nominating process remained basically the same as that used in 1984. The rules adopted by the national committee included only minor modifications suggested by the party's rules review panel, the Fairness Commission.

The bloc of uncommitted party and elected officials (superdelegates) was expanded slightly to 16 percent and rearranged to reserve more convention seats for members of Congress, governors, and the DNC; the rules restricting participation in Democratic primaries and caucuses to Democrats only was relaxed so the open primaries in Wisconsin and Montana could be conducted with the approval of the national party; and the share of the vote a candidate needed to win in a primary or caucus to qualify for delegates was lowered from the 20 percent level used in most places in 1984 to 15 percent.

Only the rule regarding the 15 percent "threshold" spawned much debate during the rules-writing process, and though the discussion of the issue seldom was acrimonious, it did reveal a yawning chasm in the party on what the proper role of the national convention should be.

Most party leaders, including DNC Chairman Paul G. Kirk Jr., wanted a threshold of at least 15 percent because they thought it would help steadily shrink the field of presidential candidates during the primary and caucus season and ensure that the convention would be a "ratifying" body that confirmed the choice of the party's voters.

But civil rights leader and presidential candidate Jesse L. Jackson saw it differently, as did a cadre of liberal activists. They wanted a convention that was more "deliberative," and they complained that getting one was virtually impossible under the system as it existed because it discriminated against long-shot candidates and produced an artificial consensus behind one candidate.

Most Democratic leaders were satisfied with the way the nominating process operated in 1984, and they felt it would be a disaster for the party to go through a free-wheeling, multiballot convention. Not since 1952—at the beginning of the television age—has a national party taken more than one ballot to nominate its presidential candidate.

At the DNC meeting where the new rules were approved, some African American committee members joined with a few white liberal activists in proposing to eliminate the 15 percent threshold altogether. The proposal was rejected by voice vote. A second proposal to lower the threshold to 10 percent was defeated 178 to 92.

In 1990 the DNC made two basic changes that directly affected the delegate-selection process for the 1992 convention. One change moved forward the officially sanctioned start of the presidential primary season by one week, from the second Tuesday in March to the first. This was an invitation to California to move its 1992 primary from June to March 3. (California declined in 1992, but in 1996 moved its primary from June to late March. This was part of a desire by both parties in 1992 to speed up the nominating contest and settle it by April or early May, so that united parties could organize their conventions with eyes focused on the November election.) The second change banned winner-reward systems, which gave extra delegates to the winner of a primary or caucus. Fifteen states had used some form of winner-reward system in 1988.

Modern conventions have turned into carefully choreographed events that focus on party-building speeches. *Library of Congress*

The Democrats required all states in 1992 and thereafter to divide their publicly elected delegates proportionally among candidates who drew at least 15 percent of the primary or caucus vote.

The Democratic Party also continued to steadily increase the number of superdelegates, expanding their number to 802 for the 2000 convention (or 18 percent of the 4,339 delegate votes).

Republican Primary Rules

The Republican Party, wrote political scientist Nelson W. Polsby, "in many respects remains unreformed." Virtually anything has been permitted in the nominating process so long as it was not baldly discriminatory. And that has been the way GOP leaders have wanted it—at least until the past few years.

While the Democratic Party has a tightly crafted, nationalized set of rules that govern its nominating process, Republicans historically have shunned control by a central authority. The individual GOP state parties have been given wide latitude to determine how their delegates are selected, with guidelines from the national party kept to a minimum.

The result has been a nominating procedure with a simplicity and continuity that the Democrats lack. A more homogeneous party than the Democrats, the Republicans until the late 1990s had not felt the pressure for rules reform that had engulfed the Democrats as long as the GOP was winning presidential elections. No major rules changes were made by the Republicans between 1974 and 1996.

For the year 2000, though, the Republicans instituted bonus delegates for those states that chose their delegates to the national convention after the middle of March. The quickness of the 1996 decision convinced many party leaders that a longer selection process would be more desirable.

At the 2000 GOP convention, the party voted to eliminate the bonus delegates but added automatic "superdelegate" seats for Republican National Committee members at the 2004 convention as well as increasing the base delegate vote total of every state.

Yet even in earlier years when Republicans had a laissez faire approach to their nominating process, they were not able to operate totally in their own world. Campaign finance laws and the rising influence of mass media affected Republicans as well as Democrats. In states where legislatures accommodated the Democrats and created a presidential primary, the Republicans were dragged along.

The Republican Party held twenty primaries in 1972, but during the next twenty-four years the number of primaries has steadily increased. In 2000 the party held a record forty-four primaries, including those in the District of Columbia and Puerto Rico (the Democrats' record was forty primaries in 1992). Primaries helped to select roughly 85 percent of delegates to the GOP convention in 2000.

An attempt to lengthen the primary season by adopting the controversial "Delaware Plan"—which would put the smallest states first in the nominating season—was scuttled by the party in favor of having a harmonious convention.

Credentials Disputes

Before the opening of a convention the national committee compiles a temporary roll of delegates. The roll is referred to the convention's credentials committee, which holds hearings on the challenges and makes recommendations to the convention, the final arbiter of all disputes.

Some of the most bitter convention battles have concerned the seating of contested delegations. In the twentieth century most of the heated credentials fights have concerned delegations from the South. In the Republican Party the challenges focused on the power of the Republican state organizations to dictate the selection of delegates.

The issue was hottest in 1912 and 1952, when the party throughout most of the South was a skeletal structure whose power was restricted largely to selection of convention delegates. Within the Democratic Party the question of southern credentials emerged after World War II on the volatile issues of civil rights and party loyalty. The following are notable credentials fights at Republican and Democratic conventions:

- **1848, Democratic.** Two rival New York state factions, known as the Barnburners and the Hunkers, sent separate delegations. By a vote of 126 to 125, the convention decided to seat both delegations and split New York's vote between them. This compromise suited neither faction: the Barnburners bolted the convention; the Hunkers remained but refused to vote.

- **1860, Democratic.** Dissatisfaction with the slavery plank in the party platform spurred a walkout by several dozen southern delegates from the Charleston convention. When the tumultuous convention reconvened in Baltimore six weeks later, a credentials controversy developed on the status of the bolting delegates. The majority report of the credentials committee recommended that the delegates in question, except those from Alabama and Louisiana, be reseated. The minority report recommended that a larger majority of the withdrawing Charleston delegates be allowed to return. The minority report was defeated, 150 to 100½, prompting a walkout by the majority of delegates from nine states.

- **1880, Republican.** Factions for and against the candidacy of former president Ulysses S. Grant clashed on the credentials of the Illinois delegation. By a margin of 387 to 353, the convention rejected a minority report that proposed seating pro-Grant delegates elected at the state convention over other delegates elected at a congressional district caucus. Three other votes were taken on disputed credentials from different Illinois districts, but all were decided in favor of the anti-Grant forces by a similar margin. The votes indicated the weakness of the Grant candidacy. The nomination went to a dark-horse candidate, Rep. James A. Garfield of Ohio, on the thirty-sixth ballot.

- **1912, Republican.** The furious struggle between President William Howard Taft and Theodore Roosevelt for the presidential nomination centered on credentials. The Roosevelt forces brought seventy-two delegate challenges to the floor of the convention, but the test of strength between the two candidates came on a procedural motion. By a vote of 567 to 507, the convention tabled a motion presented by the Roosevelt forces barring any of the delegates under challenge from voting on any of the credentials contests. This procedural vote clearly indicated Taft's control of the convention. All the credentials cases were settled in favor of the Taft delegates, and the presidential nomination ultimately went to the incumbent president.

- **1932, Democratic.** Two delegations favorable to the front-runner for the presidential nomination, Franklin D. Roosevelt, came under challenge. However, in a show of strength, the Roosevelt forces won both contests: seating a Louisiana delegation headed by Sen. Huey P. Long by a vote of 638¾ to 514¼ and a Roosevelt delegation from Minnesota by an even wider margin, 658¼ to 492¾. Roosevelt won the nomination on the fourth ballot.

- **1952, Democratic.** The refusal of three southern states—Louisiana, South Carolina, and Virginia—to agree to a party loyalty pledge brought their credentials into question. The Virginia delegation argued that the problem prompting the loyalty pledge was covered by state law. By a vote of 650½ to 518, the convention approved the seating of the Virginia delegation. After Louisiana and South Carolina took positions similar to that of Virginia, they were seated by a voice vote.

- **1952, Republican.** Sixty-eight delegates from three southern states (Georgia, Louisiana, and Texas) were the focal point of the fight for the presidential nomination between Gen. Dwight D. Eisenhower and Sen. Robert A. Taft of Ohio. The national committee, controlled by forces favorable to Taft, had voted to seat delegations from these three states that were friendly to the Ohio senator. But by a vote of 607 to 531 the convention seated the Georgia delegation favorable to Eisenhower. It seated the Eisenhower delegates from Louisiana and Texas without roll calls. The general went on to win the presidential nomination on the first ballot.

- **1968, Democratic.** A struggle between the anti–Vietnam War forces, led by Sen. Eugene J. McCarthy of Minnesota, and the party regulars, headed by Vice President Hubert H. Humphrey, dominated the seventeen cases considered by the credentials committee. Three of the cases, involving the Texas, Georgia, and Alabama delegations, required roll calls on the convention floor. All were won by the Humphrey forces. By a vote of 1,368¼ to 956¾, the regular Texas delegation headed by Gov. John B. Connally was seated. A minority report to seat the entire Georgia delegation led by black leader Julian Bond was defeated, 1,415.45 to 1,043.55. And a minority report to seat a McCarthy-backed, largely black delegation from Alabama was also rejected, 1,607 to 880¾. Humphrey, having shown his strength during the credentials contests, went on to win an easy first ballot nomination.

- **1972, Democratic.** There were numerous credentials challenges at the 1972 Democratic convention, but, unlike those at its immediate predecessors, the challenges involved delegations from across the nation and focused on violations of the party's newly adopted guidelines. These challenges tested the strength of South Dakota senator George McGovern's delegation against party regulars. Key challenges brought to the convention floor concerned the South Carolina, California, and Illinois delegations. The South Carolina challenge was brought by the National Women's Political Caucus in response to alleged underrepresentation of women in the delegation. Although the caucus' position was supposedly supported by the McGovern camp, votes were withheld to avoid jeopardizing McGovern's chances of winning the important California contest. The caucus' challenge lost 1,555.75 to 1,429.05. The California challenge was of crucial importance to McGovern, since it involved 151 delegates initially won by the South Dakota senator in the state's winner-take-all primary, but stripped from him by the credentials committee. By a vote of 1,618.28 to 1,238.22, McGovern regained the contested delegates, thereby nailing down his nomination. With victory in hand, the dominant McGovern camp sought a compromise on the Illinois case, which pitted a delegation headed by Chicago's powerful mayor Richard Daley against an insurgent delegation composed of party reformers. Compromise was un-

Riots over the Vietnam War erupt outside the 1968 Democratic convention in Chicago.   *File photo*

attainable and with the bulk of McGovern delegates voting for the reformers, a minority report to seat the Daley delegates was rejected.

After their 1952 credentials battle, the Republicans established a contest
committee within the national committee to review credentials challenges
before the convention. After their divisive 1968 convention the Democrats
also created a formal credentials procedure to review all challenges before
the opening of the convention.

Equally important to the settlement of credentials challenges are the rules
under which the convention operates. The Republican Party adopts a completely new set of rules at every convention. Although large portions of the
existing rules are enacted each time, general revision is always possible.

After its 1968 convention the Democratic Party set out to reform itself
and the convention system. The Commission on Rules and the Commission
on Party Structure and Delegate Selection, both created by the 1968 convention, proposed many changes that were accepted by the national committee. As a result, a formal set of rules was adopted for the first time at the
party's 1972 convention.

Controversial Rules

Although it did not have a formal set of rules before 1972, the Democratic Party had long operated with two controversial rules never used by the Republicans: the unit rule and the two-thirds nominating rule. The unit rule enabled the majority of a delegation, if authorized by its state party, to cast the entire vote of the delegation for one candidate or position. In use since the earliest Democratic conventions, the unit rule was abolished by the 1968 convention.

From their first convention in 1832 until the 1936 convention, the Democrats employed the two-thirds nominating rule, which required any candidate for president or vice president to win not just a simple majority but a two-thirds majority. Two presidential candidates—Martin Van Buren in 1844 and Champ Clark in 1912—received majorities in convention balloting but failed to attain the two-thirds requirement. On the first ballot in 1844 Van Buren received 146 of the 266 convention votes, 54.9 percent of the total. His total fell under a simple majority on succeeding roll calls and on the ninth ballot the nomination went to a dark-horse candidate, former governor James K. Polk of Tennessee.

In 1912 from the tenth through the sixteenth ballots Clark recorded a simple majority. He reached his peak on the tenth ballot, receiving 556 of the 1,094 convention votes, 50.8 percent of the total. The nomination, however, ultimately went to New Jersey governor Woodrow Wilson, who was selected on the forty-sixth ballot.

In its century of use the two-thirds rule frequently produced protracted, multiballot conventions, often giving the Democrats a degree of turbulence the Republicans, requiring only a simple majority, did not have. Between 1832 and 1932, seven Democratic conventions took more than ten ballots to select a presidential candidate. In contrast, in their entire convention history, the Republicans have had just one convention that required more than ten ballots to select a presidential candidate.

Viewed as a boon to the South since it allowed that region a virtual veto power over any possible nominee, the two-thirds rule was abolished at the Democrats' 1936 convention with the stipulation that the South would receive an increased vote allocation at later conventions.

Another controversy that surfaced during the 1980 Democratic Party convention concerned a rule that bound delegates to vote on the first ballot for the candidates under whose banner they had been elected. Supporters of Sen.

Ted Kennedy had devoted their energy to prying the nomination from incumbent President Carter by defeating that rule. But the final tally showed 1,936.42 delegates favoring the binding rule and 1,390.58 opposing it. Passage of the binding rule ensured Carter's renomination, and shortly after the vote Kennedy announced that his name would not be placed in nomination.

Convention Officers

Credentials, rules, and platform are three of the major convention committees.

Within the Republican Party, though, the committee on permanent organization ratifies the slate of convention officials. In the Democratic Party, this function is performed by the rules committee.

In both the Democratic and Republican parties, the presiding officer during the bulk of the convention is the permanent chairman. For much of the postwar period, the position has gone to the party's leader in the House of Representatives, particularly at the GOP convention.

However, this loose precedent was broken in the Democratic Party by a rule adopted at the 1972 convention requiring that the presiding officer position alternate every four years between the sexes.

Party Platforms

The adoption of a party platform is one of the principal functions of a convention. The platform committee is charged with the responsibility of writing a party platform to be presented to the convention for its approval.

The main challenge before the platform committee has traditionally been to write a platform all party candidates can use in their campaigns. For this reason, platforms often fit the description given them by Wendell L. Willkie, Republican presidential candidate in 1940: "fusions of ambiguity."

Despite the best efforts of platform-builders to resolve their differences in the comparative privacy of the committee room, they sometimes encounter so controversial a subject that it cannot be compromised. Under these conditions dissident committee members often submit a minority report to the convention floor. Open floor fights are not unusual and, like credentials battles, often reflect the strength of the various candidates.

When the party has an incumbent president, the platform often is drafted in the White House or at least has the approval of the president. Rarely does a party adopt a platform that is critical of an incumbent president of the

The effects of a Tariff exclusively for Revenue as laid down in the Democratic Plat_ form and which the Democratic Congressmen tried to enact last winter at Washington.

The effects of Protection to American Industries as guaranteed by the Republican Party and Platform.

Democratic Free Trade Means low wages, children in rags and ignorance

Republican Protection Means good wages, happy homes and education for your children

If you are satisfied with this picture vote for Cleveland and Hendricks.

If you prefer this picture vote for Blaine and Logan.

This Republican poster depicts the difference between the 1884 GOP platform and the Democratic one. High tariffs supported working families because they kept products made by cheap foreign labor out of the country. With such protection, the factories hum (compare smokestacks), food is on the table, and mom does not yell at the kids. *Library of Congress*

same party. When Democratic delegates at their 1896 convention, inspired by William Jennings Bryan's "Cross of Gold" speech, repudiated President Grover Cleveland and his support for a gold standard for hard currency, and nominated Bryan for president on a "free silver" platform, they signaled a major sea change in American politics. A similar change took place in 1948, when Democratic delegates led by Mayor Hubert Humphrey of Minneapolis overturned a recommendation by the platform committee and precipitated a walkout of southern delegates by adopting a strong civil rights plank. Although overridden, President Harry S. Truman accepted the Humphrey plank—and won with it.

The following are major platform fights that have occurred at Republican and Democratic conventions:

- **1860, Democratic.** A minority report on the slavery plank, stating that the decision on allowing slavery in the territories should be left to the

Supreme Court, was approved, 165 to 138. The majority report (favored by the South) declared that no government—local, state, or federal—could outlaw slavery in the territories. The acceptance of the minority report precipitated a walkout by several dozen southern delegates and the eventual sectional split in the party.

- **1896, Democratic.** The monetary plank of the platform committee, favoring free and unlimited coinage of silver at a ratio of 16 to 1 with gold, was accepted by the convention, which defeated a proposed gold plank, 626 to 303. During debate William Jennings Bryan made his famous "Cross of Gold" speech supporting the platform committee plank, bringing him to the attention of the convention and resulting in his nomination for president.

- **1908, Republican.** A minority report, proposing a substitute platform, was presented by Sen. Robert M. La Follette of Wisconsin. Minority proposals included increased antitrust activities, enactment of a law requiring publication of campaign expenditures, and popular election of senators. All the proposed planks were defeated by wide margins; the closest vote, on direct election of senators, was 114 for, 866 against.

- **1924, Democratic.** A minority plank was presented that condemned the activities of the Ku Klux Klan, then enjoying a resurgence in the South and some states in the Midwest. The plank was defeated $542\frac{7}{20}$ to $54\frac{3}{20}$, the closest vote in Democratic convention history.

- **1932, Republican.** A minority plank favoring repeal of the Eighteenth Amendment (Prohibition) in favor of a state-option arrangement was defeated, $690\frac{19}{36}$ to $460\frac{2}{3}$.

- **1948, Democratic.** An amendment to the platform, strengthening the civil rights plank by guaranteeing full and equal political participation, equal employment opportunity, personal security, and equal treatment in the military service, was accepted, $651\frac{1}{2}$ to $582\frac{1}{2}$.

- **1964, Republican.** An amendment offered by Sen. Hugh Scott of Pennsylvania to strengthen the civil rights plank by including voting guarantees in state as well as in federal elections and by eliminating job bias was defeated, 897 to 409.

- **1968, Democratic.** A minority report on Vietnam called for cessation of the bombing of North Vietnam, halting of offensive and search-and-destroy missions by American combat units, a negotiated withdrawal of American troops, and establishment of a coalition government in South Vietnam. It was defeated, 1,567¾ to 1,041¼.

- **1972, Democratic.** By a vote of 1,852.86 to 999.34, the convention rejected a minority report proposing a government-guaranteed annual income of $6,500 for a family of four. By a vote of 1,572.80 to 1,101.37, a women's rights plank supporting abortion rights was defeated.

- **1980, Democratic.** The platform battle, one of the longest in party history, pitted President Jimmy Carter against his persistent rival, Sen. Edward M. Kennedy of Massachusetts. Stretching over seventeen hours, the debate focused on Kennedy's economics plank, which finally was defeated by a voice vote. Yet Carter was forced to concede on so many specific points, including Kennedy's $12 billion antirecession jobs program, that the final document bore little resemblance to the draft initially drawn up by Carter's operatives.

- **1992, Democratic.** A tax fairness plank offered by former senator Paul E. Tsongas of Massachusetts was defeated by a vote of 2,287 to 953. The plank called for a delay in any middle-class tax cut and tax credit for families with children until the deficit was under control.

The first platform was adopted by the Democrats in 1840. It was a short document, fewer than 1,000 words. Since then the platforms with few exceptions have grown longer and longer, covering more issues and appealing to more and more interest groups. One of the exceptions to the growth trend was the 4,500-word Democratic platform of 1988—about one-tenth the length of the 1984 platform. But by 2000 the Democrats' platform had grown again, to more than 50,000 words, compared with about 33,000 words in its Republican counterpart.

Third Parties: Radical Ideas

Throughout American history, many daring and controversial political platforms adopted by third parties have been rejected as too radical by the major parties. Yet many of these proposals later have won popular acceptance and have made their way into the major party platforms—and into law. Ideas such as the abolition of slavery, prohibition, the graduated income tax, the popular election of senators, women's suffrage, minimum wages, Social Security, and the eighteen-year-old vote were advocated by Populists, Progressives, and other third parties long before they were finally accepted by the nation as a whole.

The radical third parties and their platforms have been anathema to the established wisdom of the day, denounced as impractical, dangerous, destructive of moral virtues, and even traitorous. They have been anti-establishment and more far-reaching in their proposed solutions to problems than the major parties have dared to be.

Major Parties: Broader Appeal

In contrast with the third parties, Democrats and Republicans traditionally have been much more cautious against adopting radical platform planks. Trying to appeal to a broad range of voters, the two major parties have tended to compromise differences or to reject controversial platform planks.

The Democratic Party has been more ready than the Republicans to adopt once-radical ideas, but there is usually a considerable time lag between their origin in third parties and their eventual adoption in Democratic platforms. For example, while the Democrats by 1912 had adopted many of the Populist planks of the 1890s, the Bull Moose Progressives of that year already were way ahead of them in proposals for social legislation. Not until 1932 were many of the 1912 Progressive planks adopted by the Democrats.

Similarly, it was not until the 1960s that Democratic platforms incorporated many of the more far-reaching proposals originally put forward by the Progressive Party in 1948.

Filling Vacancies

Starting with the Democratic convention of 1848, and the Republican Party's first national organizing meeting in 1856, both major parties have elected national committees to run the day-to-day business of the parties between conventions.

Since their beginning, one of the most important functions of national committees has been to replace a candidate who dies or resigns after the convention adjourns, or after election day but before the electors cast their votes for president and vice president. This replacement power was assumed informally, but without controversy, at first. It was granted by several national conventions during the Progressive era (1900–1912), and was made part of both parties' permanent standing rules by the 1920s.

There have been four such vacancies:

- In 1860 the Democratic designee for vice president, Sen. Benjamin Fitzpatrick of Alabama, declined the nomination after the ruinously chaotic Baltimore convention of that year finally adjourned. The national committee then nominated former governor Herschel V. Johnson of Georgia as Sen. Stephen A. Douglas's running mate.

- In 1872 the Democratic nominee for president, Horace Greeley, founder of the *New York Tribune*, died shortly after election day. (Incumbent Republican President Ulysses S. Grant had won the election.) Greeley's dispirited party's national committee declined to select a replacement candidate, and the Democratic electors voted for four different candidates.

- In 1912 Vice President James S. Sherman of New York died in office the week before election day. The Republican convention of that year had authorized the national committee to fill vacancies, and the committee quickly replaced Sherman. His name remained on state ballots as President William Howard Taft's running mate, but the eight Republican electors voted, as recommended by the committee, for the replacement candidate, Nicholas Murray Butler of New York, president of Columbia University.

- In 1972 the Democratic nominee for vice president, Sen. Thomas Eagleton of Missouri, resigned his candidacy after the convention adjourned. The nominee for president, Sen. George McGovern, recommended R. Sargent Shriver of Illinois, former head of the Peace Corps, as his replacement running mate, and Shriver was selected by a special meeting of an expanded national committee.

Communications and the Media

Major changes in the national nominating convention have resulted from the massive advances in transportation and communications technologies during the twentieth century.

A scene from the 1992 Democratic convention in New York City that nominated Bill Clinton for president.   *R. Michael Jenkins, Congressional Quarterly*

The revolution in transportation has affected the scheduling of conventions. In the nineteenth century, conventions were sometimes held a year or more before the election and at the latest were completed by late spring of the election year. With the ability of people to assemble quickly, conventions in recent years have been held later in the election year, usually in July or August. Advances in transportation also have affected site location. Geographic centrality is no longer a primary consideration in the selection of a convention city.

Radio coverage of conventions began in 1924; television coverage sixteen years later. One of the first changes inspired by the media age was the termination of the custom that a presidential candidate not appear at the convention but accept his nomination in a ceremony several weeks later. Franklin D. Roosevelt was the first major party candidate to break this tradition when in 1932 he delivered his acceptance speech in person before the Democratic convention. Twelve years later, Thomas E. Dewey became the first Republican nominee to give his acceptance speech to the convention. Since then, the final activity of every Democratic and Republican convention has been the delivery of the acceptance speech by the presidential nominee.

Party leaders have also, in recent years, streamlined the schedule, with the assumption that the interest level of most of the viewing public for politics is limited. The result has been shorter speeches and generally fewer roll calls than at those conventions in the pretelevision era. And at both conventions in 2000, the address of the vice-presidential candidate was delivered on the night before that of the presidential nominee.

Party leaders desire to put on a good show for the viewing public with the hope of winning votes for their party in November. The convention is a showcase, designed to present the party as both a model of democracy and an efficient, harmonious body. The schedule of convention activities is drawn up with an eye on the peak evening television viewing hours. There is an attempt to put the party's major selling points—the highly partisan keynote speech, the nominating ballots, and the candidates' acceptance speeches—on in prime time. (The effort to put acceptance speeches on in prime time has been especially strong since 1972, when Democratic nominee George S. McGovern was forced to wait until the wee hours of the morning to make his speech.) Conversely, party leaders try to keep evidence of bitter party factionalism—such as explosive credentials and platform battles—out of the peak viewing period.

Both the Republicans and Democrats went to extraordinary lengths to turn their 2000 conventions into a tightly scripted, visually appealing television shows. But it seems that the harder the political parties try to win over American audiences, the less they have to show for their efforts. Many TV viewers voted with their remote controls—tuning out the 2000 conventions. By and large, ratings for the three major networks' broadcasts of the conventions have been on a steady decline for the past two decades.

In the media age the appearance of fairness is important, and in a sense this need to look fair and open has assisted the movement for party reform. Some influential party leaders, skeptical of reform of the convention, have found resistance difficult in the glare of television.

Before the revolution in the means of transportation and communication, conventions met in relative anonymity. Today conventions are held in all the privacy of a fishbowl, with every action and every rumor closely scrutinized. They have become media events and as such are targets for political demonstrations that can be not only an embarrassment to the party but a security problem as well.

In spite of its difficulties, the convention system has survived. As the nation has developed during the past century and a half, the convention has evolved as well, changing its form but retaining its variety of functions. Criticism has been leveled at the convention, but no substitute has yet been offered that would nominate a presidential ticket, adopt a party platform, act as the supreme governing body of the party, and serve as a massive campaign rally and propaganda forum. In addition to these functions, a convention is a place where compromise can take place—compromise often mandatory in a major political party that combines varying viewpoints.

appendix

U.S. Presidents and Vice Presidents

President and political party	Born	Died	Age at inauguration	Native of	Elected from	Term of service	Vice president
George Washington (F)	1732	1799	57	Va.	Va.	April 30, 1789–March 4, 1793	John Adams
George Washington (F)			61			March 4, 1793–March 4, 1797	John Adams
John Adams (F)	1735	1826	61	Mass.	Mass.	March 4, 1797–March 4, 1801	Thomas Jefferson
Thomas Jefferson (DR)	1743	1826	57	Va.	Va.	March 4, 1801–March 4, 1805	Aaron Burr
Thomas Jefferson (DR)			61			March 4, 1805–March 4, 1809	George Clinton
James Madison (DR)	1751	1836	57	Va.	Va.	March 4, 1809–March 4, 1813	George Clinton
James Madison (DR)			61			March 4, 1813–March 4, 1817	Elbridge Gerry
James Monroe (DR)	1758	1831	58	Va.	Va.	March 4, 1817–March 4, 1821	Daniel D. Tompkins
James Monroe (DR)			62			March 4, 1821–March 4, 1825	Daniel D. Tompkins
John Q. Adams (DR)	1767	1848	57	Mass.	Mass.	March 4, 1825–March 4, 1829	John C. Calhoun
Andrew Jackson (D)	1767	1845	61	S.C.	Tenn.	March 4, 1829–March 4, 1833	John C. Calhoun
Andrew Jackson (D)			65			March 4, 1833–March 4, 1837	Martin Van Buren
Martin Van Buren (D)	1782	1862	54	N.Y.	N.Y.	March 4, 1837–March 4, 1841	Richard M. Johnson
William H. Harrison (W)	1773	1841	68	Va.	Ohio	March 4, 1841–April 4, 1841	John Tyler
John Tyler (W)	1790	1862	51	Va.	Va.	April 6, 1841–March 4, 1845	
James K. Polk (D)	1795	1849	49	N.C.	Tenn.	March 4, 1845–March 4, 1849	George M. Dallas
Zachary Taylor (W)	1784	1850	64	Va.	La.	March 4, 1849–July 9, 1850	Millard Fillmore
Millard Fillmore (W)	1800	1874	50	N.Y.	N.Y.	July 10, 1850–March 4, 1853	
Franklin Pierce (D)	1804	1869	48	N.H.	N.H.	March 4, 1853–March 4, 1857	William R. King
James Buchanan (D)	1791	1868	65	Pa.	Pa.	March 4, 1857–March 4, 1861	John C. Breckinridge
Abraham Lincoln (R)	1809	1865	52	Ky.	Ill.	March 4, 1861–March 4, 1865	Hannibal Hamlin
Abraham Lincoln (R)			56			March 4, 1865–April 15, 1865	Andrew Johnson
Andrew Johnson (R)	1808	1875	56	N.C.	Tenn.	April 15, 1865–March 4, 1869	
Ulysses S. Grant (R)	1822	1885	46	Ohio	Ill.	March 4, 1869–March 4, 1873	Schuyler Colfax
Ulysses S. Grant (R)			50			March 4, 1873–March 4, 1877	Henry Wilson
Rutherford B. Hayes (R)	1822	1893	54	Ohio	Ohio	March 4, 1877–March 4, 1881	William A. Wheeler
James A. Garfield (R)	1831	1881	49	Ohio	Ohio	March 4, 1881–Sept. 19, 1881	Chester A. Arthur
Chester A. Arthur (R)	1830	1886	50	Vt.	N.Y.	Sept. 20, 1881–March 4, 1885	
Grover Cleveland (D)	1837	1908	47	N.J.	N.Y.	March 4, 1885–March 4, 1889	Thomas A. Hendricks
Benjamin Harrison (R)	1833	1901	55	Ohio	Ind.	March 4, 1889–March 4, 1893	Levi P. Morton
Grover Cleveland (D)	1837	1908	55	N.J.	N.Y.	March 4, 1893–March 4, 1897	Adlai E. Stevenson

(continued)

U.S. Presidents and Vice Presidents (continued)

President and political party	Born	Died	Age at inauguration	Native of	Elected from	Term of service	Vice president
William McKinley (R)	1843	1901	54	Ohio	Ohio	March 4, 1897–March 4, 1901	Garret A. Hobart
William McKinley (R)			58			March 4, 1901–Sept. 14, 1901	Theodore Roosevelt
Theodore Roosevelt (R)	1858	1919	42	N.Y.	N.Y.	Sept. 14, 1901–March 4, 1905	
Theodore Roosevelt (R)			46			March 4, 1905–March 4, 1909	Charles W. Fairbanks
William H. Taft (R)	1857	1930	51	Ohio	Ohio	March 4, 1909–March 4, 1913	James S. Sherman
Woodrow Wilson (D)	1856	1924	56	Va.	N.J.	March 4, 1913–March 4, 1917	Thomas R. Marshall
Woodrow Wilson (D)			60			March 4, 1917–March 4, 1921	Thomas R. Marshall
Warren G. Harding (R)	1865	1923	55	Ohio	Ohio	March 4, 1921–Aug. 2, 1923	Calvin Coolidge
Calvin Coolidge (R)	1872	1933	51	Vt.	Mass.	Aug. 3, 1923–March 4, 1925	
Calvin Coolidge (R)			52			March 4, 1925–March 4, 1929	Charles G. Dawes
Herbert Hoover (R)	1874	1964	54	Iowa	Calif.	March 4, 1929–March 4, 1933	Charles Curtis
Franklin D. Roosevelt (D)	1882	1945	51	N.Y.	N.Y.	March 4, 1933–Jan. 20, 1937	John N. Garner
Franklin D. Roosevelt (D)			55			Jan. 20, 1937–Jan. 20, 1941	John N. Garner
Franklin D. Roosevelt (D)			59			Jan. 20, 1941–Jan. 20, 1945	Henry A. Wallace
Franklin D. Roosevelt (D)			63			Jan. 20, 1945–April 12, 1945	Harry S. Truman
Harry S. Truman (D)	1884	1972	60	Mo.	Mo.	April 12, 1945–Jan. 20, 1949	
Harry S. Truman (D)			64			Jan. 20, 1949–Jan. 20, 1953	Alben W. Barkley
Dwight D. Eisenhower (R)	1890	1969	62	Texas	N.Y.	Jan. 20, 1953–Jan. 20, 1957	Richard Nixon
Dwight D. Eisenhower (R)			66		Pa.	Jan. 20, 1957–Jan. 20, 1961	Richard Nixon
John F. Kennedy (D)	1917	1963	43	Mass.	Mass.	Jan. 20, 1961–Nov. 22, 1963	Lyndon B. Johnson
Lyndon B. Johnson (D)	1908	1973	55	Texas	Texas	Nov. 22, 1963–Jan. 20, 1965	
Lyndon B. Johnson (D)			56			Jan. 20, 1965–Jan. 20, 1969	Hubert H. Humphrey
Richard Nixon (R)	1913	1994	56	Calif.	N.Y.	Jan. 20, 1969–Jan. 20, 1973	Spiro T. Agnew
Richard Nixon (R)			60		Calif.	Jan. 20, 1973–Aug. 9, 1974	Spiro T. Agnew
Gerald R. Ford
Gerald R. Ford (R)	1913		61	Neb.	Mich.	Aug. 9, 1974–Jan. 20, 1977	Nelson A. Rockefeller
Jimmy Carter (D)	1924		52	Ga.	Ga.	Jan. 20, 1977–Jan. 20, 1981	Walter F. Mondale
Ronald Reagan (R)	1911		69	Ill.	Calif.	Jan. 20, 1981–Jan. 20, 1985	George Bush
Ronald Reagan (R)			73			Jan. 20, 1985–Jan. 20, 1989	George Bush
George Bush (R)	1924		64	Mass.	Texas	Jan. 20, 1989–Jan. 20, 1993	Dan Quayle
Bill Clinton (D)	1946		46	Ark.	Ark.	Jan. 20, 1993–Jan. 20, 1997	Albert Gore Jr.
Bill Clinton (D)			50			Jan. 20, 1997–Jan. 20, 2001	Albert Gore Jr.
George W. Bush (R)	1946		54	Conn.	Texas	Jan. 20, 2001–	Richard Cheney

Note: D—Democrat; DR—Democratic-Republican; F—Federalist; R—Republican; W—Whig.

Political Party Affiliations in Congress and the Presidency, 1789–2003

Year	Congress	House		Senate		President
		Majority party	Principal minority party	Majority party	Principal minority party	
1789–1791	1st	AD-38	Op-26	AD-17	Op-9	F (Washington)
1791–1793	2nd	F-37	DR-33	F-16	DR-13	F (Washington)
1793–1795	3rd	DR-57	F-48	F-17	DR-13	F (Washington)
1795–1797	4th	F-54	DR-52	F-19	DR-13	F (Washington)
1797–1799	5th	F-58	DR-48	F-20	DR-12	F (J. Adams)
1799–1801	6th	F-64	DR-42	F-19	DR-13	F (J. Adams)
1801–1803	7th	DR-69	F-36	DR-18	F-13	DR (Jefferson)
1803–1805	8th	DR-102	F-39	DR-25	F-9	DR (Jefferson)
1805–1807	9th	DR-116	F-25	DR-27	F-7	DR (Jefferson)
1807–1809	10th	DR-118	F-24	DR-28	F-6	DR (Jefferson)
1809–1811	11th	DR-94	F-48	DR-28	F-6	DR (Madison)
1811–1813	12th	DR-108	F-36	DR-30	F-6	DR (Madison)
1813–1815	13th	DR-112	F-68	DR-27	F-9	DR (Madison)
1815–1817	14th	DR-117	F-65	DR-25	F-11	DR (Madison)
1817–1819	15th	DR-141	F-42	DR-34	F-10	DR (Monroe)
1819–1821	16th	DR-156	F-27	DR-35	F-7	DR (Monroe)
1821–1823	17th	DR-158	F-25	DR-44	F-4	DR (Monroe)
1823–1825	18th	DR-187	F-26	DR-44	F-4	DR (Monroe)
1825–1827	19th	AD-105	J-97	AD-26	J-20	DR (J.Q. Adams)
1827–1829	20th	J-119	AD-94	J-28	AD-20	DR (J.Q. Adams)
1829–1831	21st	D-139	NR-74	D-26	NR-22	DR (Jackson)
1831–1833	22nd	D-141	NR-58	D-25	NR-21	D (Jackson)
1833–1835	23rd	D-147	AM-53	D-20	NR-20	D (Jackson)
1835–1837	24th	D-145	W-98	D-27	W-25	D (Jackson)
1837–1839	25th	D-108	W-107	D-30	W-18	D (Van Buren)
1839–1841	26th	D-124	W-118	D-28	W-22	D (Van Buren)
1841–1843	27th	W-133	D-102	W-28	D-22	W (W. Harrison)
						W (Tyler)
1843–1845	28th	D-142	W-79	W-28	D-25	W (Tyler)
1845–1847	29th	D-143	W-77	D-31	W-25	D (Polk)
1847–1849	30th	W-115	D-108	D-36	W-21	D (Polk)
1849–1851	31st	D-112	W-109	D-35	W-25	W (Taylor)
						W (Fillmore)
1851–1853	32nd	D-140	W-88	D-35	W-24	W (Fillmore)
1853–1855	33rd	D-159	W-71	D-38	W-22	D (Pierce)
1855–1857	34th	R-108	D-83	D-40	R-15	D (Pierce)
1857–1859	35th	D-118	R-92	D-36	R-20	D (Buchanan)
1859–1861	36th	R-114	D-92	D-36	R-26	D (Buchanan)
1861–1863	37th	R-105	D-43	R-31	D-10	R (Lincoln)
1863–1865	38th	R-102	D-75	R-36	D-9	R (Lincoln)
1865–1867	39th	U-149	D-42	U-42	D-10	R (Lincoln)
						R (A. Johnson)

(continued)

Political Party Affiliations in Congress and the Presidency, 1789–2003 *(continued)*

Year	Congress	House		Senate		President
		Majority party	Principal minority party	Majority party	Principal minority party	
1867–1869	40th	R-143	D-49	R-42	D-11	R (A. Johnson)
1869–1871	41st	R-149	D-63	R-56	D-11	R (Grant)
1871–1873	42nd	R-134	D-104	R-52	D-17	R (Grant)
1873–1875	43rd	R-194	D-92	R-49	D-19	R (Grant)
1875–1877	44th	D-169	R-109	R-45	D-29	R (Grant)
1877–1879	45th	D-153	R-140	R-39	D-36	R (Hayes)
1879–1881	46th	D-149	R-130	D-42	R-33	R (Hayes)
1881–1883	47th	R-147	D-135	R-37	D-37	R (Garfield)
						R (Arthur)
1883–1885	48th	D-197	R-118	R-38	D-36	R (Arthur)
1885–1887	49th	D-183	R-140	R-43	D-34	D (Cleveland)
1887–1889	50th	D-169	R-152	R-39	D-37	D (Cleveland)
1889–1891	51st	R-166	D-159	R-39	D-37	R (B. Harrison)
1891–1893	52nd	D-235	R-88	R-47	D-39	R (B. Harrison)
1893–1895	53rd	D-218	R-127	D-44	R-38	D (Cleveland)
1895–1897	54th	R-244	D-105	R-43	D-39	D (Cleveland)
1897–1899	55th	R-204	D-113	R-47	D-34	R (McKinley)
1899–1901	56th	R-185	D-163	R-53	D-26	R (McKinley)
1901–1903	57th	R-197	D-151	R-55	D-31	R (McKinley)
						R (T. Roosevelt)
1903–1905	58th	R-208	D-178	R-57	D-33	R (T. Roosevelt)
1905–1907	59th	R-250	D-136	R-57	D-33	R (T. Roosevelt)
1907–1909	60th	R-222	D-164	R-61	D-31	R (T. Roosevelt)
1909–1911	61st	R-219	D-172	R-61	D-32	R (Taft)
1911–1913	62nd	D-228	R-161	R-51	D-41	R (Taft)
1913–1915	63rd	D-291	R-127	D-51	R-44	D (Wilson)
1915–1917	64th	D-230	R-196	D-56	R-40	D (Wilson)
1917–1919	65th	D-216	R-210	D-53	R-42	D (Wilson)
1919–1921	66th	R-240	D-190	R-49	D-47	D (Wilson)
1921–1923	67th	R-301	D-131	R-59	D-37	R (Harding)
1923–1925	68th	R-225	D-205	R-51	D-43	R (Coolidge)
1925–1927	69th	R-247	D-183	R-56	D-39	R (Coolidge)
1927–1929	70th	R-237	D-195	R-49	D-46	R (Coolidge)
1929–1931	71st	R-267	D-167	R-56	D-39	R (Hoover)
1931–1933	72nd	D-220	R-214	R-48	D-47	R (Hoover)
1933–1935	73rd	D-310	R-117	D-60	R-35	D (F. Roosevelt)
1935–1937	74th	D-319	R-103	D-69	R-25	D (F. Roosevelt)
1937–1939	75th	D-331	R-89	D-76	R-16	D (F. Roosevelt)
1939–1941	76th	D-261	R-164	D-69	R-23	D (F. Roosevelt)
1941 1943	77th	D-268	R-162	D-66	R-28	D (F. Roosevelt)
1943–1945	78th	D-218	R-208	D-58	R-37	D (F. Roosevelt)

(continued)

(continued)

Year	Congress	House		Senate		President
		Majority party	Principal minority party	Majority party	Principal minority party	
1945–1947	79th	D-242	R-190	D-56	R-38	D (F. Roosevelt) D (Truman)
1947–1949	80th	R-245	D-188	R-51	D-45	D (Truman)
1949–1951	81st	D-263	R-171	D-54	R-42	D (Truman)
1951–1953	82nd	D-234	R-199	D-49	R-47	D (Truman)
1953–1955	83rd	R-221	D-211	R-48	D-47	R (Eisenhower)
1955–1957	84th	D-232	R-203	D-48	R-47	R (Eisenhower)
1957–1959	85th	D-233	R-200	D-49	R-47	R (Eisenhower)
1959–1961	86th	D-283	R-153	D-64	R-34	R (Eisenhower)
1961–1963	87th	D-263	R-174	D-65	R-35	D (Kennedy)
1963–1965	88th	D-258	R-177	D-67	R-33	D (Kennedy) D (L. Johnson)
1965–1967	89th	D-295	R-140	D-68	R-32	D (L. Johnson)
1967–1969	90th	D-247	R-187	D-64	R-36	D (L. Johnson)
1969–1971	91st	D-243	R-192	D-57	R-43	R (Nixon)
1971–1973	92nd	D-254	R-180	D-54	R-44	R (Nixon)
1973–1975	93rd	D-239	R-192	D-56	R-42	R (Nixon) R (Ford)
1975–1977	94th	D-291	R-144	D-60	R-37	R (Ford)
1977–1979	95th	D-292	R-143	D-61	R-38	D (Carter)
1979–1981	96th	D-276	R-157	D-58	R-41	D (Carter)
1981–1983	97th	D-243	R-192	R-53	D-46	R (Reagan)
1983–1985	98th	D-269	R-165	R-54	D-46	R (Reagan)
1985–1987	99th	D-252	R-182	R-53	D-47	R (Reagan)
1987–1989	100th	D-258	R-177	D-55	R-45	R (Reagan)
1989–1991	101st	D-259	R-174	D-55	R-45	R (G. Bush)
1991–1993	102nd	D-267	R-167	D-56	R-44	R (G. Bush)
1993–1995	103rd	D-258	R-176	D-57	R-43	D (Clinton)
1995–1997	104th	R-230	D-204	R-53	D-47	D (Clinton)
1997–1999	105th	R-227	D-207	R-55	D-45	D (Clinton)
1999–2001	106th	R-222	D-211	R-55	D-45	D (Clinton)
2001–2003	107th	R-221	D-212	R-50	R-50	R (G.W. Bush)

Note: Figures are for the beginning of the first session of each Congress. Key to abbreviations: AD—Administration; AM—Anti-Masonic; D—Democratic; DR—Democratic-Republican; F—Federalist; J—Jacksonian; NR—National Republican; Op—Opposition; R—Republican; U—Unionist; W—Whig.

Sources: U.S. Bureau of the Census, *Historical Statistics of the United States, Colonial Times to 1970* (Washington, D.C.: Government Printing Office, 1975); and U.S. Congress, Joint Committee on Printing, *Official Congressional Directory* (Washington, D.C.: Government Printing Office, 1967–); *CQ Weekly,* selected issues.

Election Results, Congress and the Presidency, 1860–2000

Election year	Congress	House Members elected Dem.	Rep.	Misc.	House Gains/losses Dem.	Rep.	Senate Members elected Dem.	Rep.	Misc.	Senate Gains/losses Dem.	Rep.	Presidency Elected	Popular vote Plurality
1860	37th	42	106	28	−59	−7	11	31	7	−27	+5	Lincoln (R)	485,706
1862	38th	80	103		+38	−3	12	39		+1	+8		
1864	39th	46	145		−34	+42	10	42		−2	+3	Lincoln (R)	405,581
1866	40th	49	143		+3	−2	11	42		+1	0	A. Johnson (R)	
1868	41st	73	170		+24	+27	11	61		0	+19	Grant (R)	304,906
1870	42nd	104	139		+31	−31	17	57		+6	−4		
1872	43rd	88	203		−16	+64	19	54		+2	−3	Grant (R)	763,474
1874	44th	181	107	3	+93	−96	29	46		+10	−8		
1876	45th	156	137		−25	+30	36	39		+7	−7	Hayes (R)	−254,235
1878	46th	150	128	14	−6	−9	43	33	1	+7	−6		
1880	47th	130	152	11	−20	+24	37	37	2	−6	+4	Garfield (R)	1,898
												Arthur (R)	
1882	48th	200	119	6	+70	−33	36	40		−1	+3		
1884	49th	182	140	2	−18	+21	34	41		−2	+2	Cleveland (D)	25,685
1886	50th	170	151	4	−12	+11	37	39		+3	−2		
1888	51st	156	173	1	−14	+22	37	47		0	+8	B. Harrison (R)	−90,596
1890	52nd	231	88	14	+75	−85	39	47	2	+2	0		
1892	53rd	220	126	8	−11	+38	44	38	3	+5	−9	Cleveland (D)	372,639
1894	54th	104	246	7	−116	+120	30	44	5	−5	+6		
1896	55th	134	206	16	+30	−40	34	46	10	−5	+2	McKinley (R)	596,985
1898	56th	163	185	9	+29	−21	26	53	11	−8	+7		
1900	57th	153	198	5	−10	+13	29	56	3	+3	+3	McKinley (R)	859,694
1902	58th	178	207		+25	+9	32	58		+3	+2	T. Roosevelt (R)	
1904	59th	136	250		−42	+43	32	58		0	0	T. Roosevelt (R)	2,543,695

Year	Congress	House (D)	House (R)	House (Other)	House D Δ	House R Δ	Senate (D)	Senate (R)	Senate (Other)	Senate D Δ	Senate R Δ	President	Plurality
1906	60th	164	222		+28	−28	29	61		−3	−3		
1908	61st	172	219		+8	−3	32	59		+3	−2	Taft (R)	1,269,457
1910	62nd	228	162	1	+56	−57	42	49		+10	−10		
1912	63rd	290	127	18	+62	−35	51	44	1	+9	−5	Wilson (D)	2,173,945
1914	64th	231	193	8	−59	+66	56	39	1	+5	−5		
1916	65th	210	216	9	−21	+23	53	42	1	−3	+3	Wilson (D)	579,511
1918	66th	191	237	7	−19	+21	47	48	1	−6	+6		
1920	67th	132	300	1	−59	+63	37	59		−10	+11	Harding (R)	7,020,023
1922	68th	207	225	3	+75	−75	43	51	2	+6	−8	Coolidge (R)	
1924	69th	183	247	5	−24	+22	40	54	1	−3	+3	Coolidge (R)	7,333,217
1926	70th	195	237	3	+12	−10	47	48	1	+7	−6		
1928	71st	167	267	1	−28	+30	39	56	1	−8	+8	Hoover (R)	6,429,579
1930	72nd	220	214	1	+53	−53	47	48	1	+8	−8		
1932	73rd	313	117	5	+97	−101	59	36	1	+12	−12	F. Roosevelt (D)	7,068,817
1934	74th	322	103	10	+9	−14	69	25	2	+10	−11		
1936	75th	333	89	13	+11	−14	75	17	4	+6	−8	F. Roosevelt (D)	11,073,102
1938	76th	262	169	4	−71	+80	69	23	4	−6	+6		
1940	77th	267	162	6	+5	−7	66	28	2	−3	+5	F. Roosevelt (D)	4,964,561
1942	78th	222	209	4	−45	+47	57	38	1	−9	+10		
1944	79th	243	190	2	+21	−19	57	38	1	0	0	Roosevelt (D)	3,594,993
1946	80th	188	246	1	−55	+56	45	51		−12	+13	Truman (D)	
1948	81st	263	171	1	+75	−75	54	42		+9	−9	Truman (D)	2,188,054
1950	82nd	234	199	2	−29	+28	48	47	1	−6	+5		
1952	83rd	213	221	1	−21	+22	47	48	1	−1	+1	Eisenhower (R)	6,621,242
1954	84th	232	203		+19	−18	48	47	1	+1	−1		
1956	85th	234	201		+2	−2	49	47		+1	0	Eisenhower (R)	9,567,720
1958	86th	283	154		+49	−47	64	34		+17	−13		

(continued)

Election Results, Congress and the Presidency, 1860–2000 (continued)

Election year	Congress	House Members elected Dem.	Rep.	Misc.	House Gains/losses Dem.	Rep.	Senate Members elected Dem.	Rep.	Misc.	Senate Gains/losses Dem.	Rep.	Presidency Elected	Popular vote Plurality
1960	87th	263	174		−20	+20	64	36		−2	+2	Kennedy (D)	118,574[1]
1962	88th	258	176	1[2]	−4	+2	67	33		+4	−4		
1964	89th	295	140		+38	−38	68	32		+2	−2	L. Johnson (D)	15,951,378
1966	90th	248	187		−47	+47	64	36		−3	+3		
1968	91st	243	192		−4	+4	58	42		−5	+5	Nixon (R)	510,314
1970	92nd	255	180		+12	−12	55	45		−4	+2		
1972	93rd	243	192		−12	+12	57	43		+2	−2	Nixon (R)	17,999,528
1974	94th	291	144		+43	−43	61	38		+3	−3		
1976	95th	292	143		+1	−1	62	38		0	0	Carter (D)	1,682,970
1978	96th	277	158		−11	+11	59	41		−3	+3		
1980	97th	243	192		−33	+33	47	53		−12	+12	Reagan (R)	8,420,270
1982	98th	269	166		+26	−26	46	54		0	0		
1984	99th	253	182		−14	+14	47	53		+2	−2	Reagan (R)	16,877,890
1986	100th	258	177		+5	−5	55	45		+8	−8		
1988	101st	259	174		+2	−2	55	45		+1	−1	G. Bush (R)	7,077,023
1990	102nd	267	167	1	+9	−8	56	44		+1	−1		
1992	103rd	258	176	1	−9	+9	57	43		+1	−1	Clinton (D)	5,805,444
1994	104th	204	230	1	−52	+52	47	53		−8	+8[3]		
1996	105th	207	227	1	+3	−3	45	55		−2	+2	Clinton (D)	8,203,602
1998	106th	211	223	1	+5	−5	45	55		0	0		
2000	107th	212	221	2	+1	−2	50	50		+5	−5	G.W. Bush (R)	−539,898

The seats totals reflect the makeup of the House and Senate at the start of each Congress. Special elections that shifted party ratios in between elections are not noted.

1. Includes divided Alabama elector slate votes.
2. Vacancy—Rep. Clem Miller, D–Calif. (1959–62) died Oct. 6, 1962, but his name remained on the ballot and he received a plurality.
3. Sen. Richard Shelby (Ala.) switched from the Democratic to the Republican Party the day after the election, bringing the total Republican gain to nine.

Votes Cast and Delegates Selected in Presidential Primaries, 1912–2000

Year	Democratic Party			Republican Party			Total	
	Number of primaries	Votes cast	Delegates selected through primaries (%)	Number of primaries	Votes cast	Delegates selected through primaries (%)	Votes cast	Delegates selected through primaries (%)
1912	12	974,775	32.9	13	2,261,240	41.7	3,236,015	37.3
1916	20	1,187,691	53.5	20	1,923,374	58.9	3,111,065	56.2
1920	16	571,671	44.6	20	3,186,248	57.8	3,757,919	51.2
1924	14	763,858	35.5	17	3,525,185	45.3	4,289,043	40.4
1928	16	1,264,220	42.2	15	4,110,288	44.9	5,374,508	43.5
1932	16	2,952,933	40.0	14	2,346,996	37.7	5,299,929	38.8
1936	14	5,181,808	36.5	12	3,319,810	37.5	8,501,618	37.0
1940	13	4,468,631	35.8	13	3,227,875	38.8	7,696,506	37.3
1944	14	1,867,609	36.7	13	2,271,605	38.7	4,139,214	37.7
1948	14	2,151,865	36.3	12	2,653,255	36.0	4,805,120	36.1
1952	16	4,928,006	38.7	13	7,801,413	39.0	12,729,419	38.8
1956	19	5,832,592	42.7	19	5,828,272	44.8	11,660,864	43.7
1960	16	5,687,742	38.3	15	5,537,967	38.6	11,224,631	38.5
1964	16	6,247,435	45.7	16	5,935,339	45.6	12,182,774	45.6
1968	15	7,535,069	40.2	15	4,473,551	38.1	12,008,620	39.1
1972	21	15,993,965	65.3	20	6,188,281	56.8	22,182,246	61.0
1976	27	16,052,652	76.0	26	10,374,125	71.0	26,426,777	73.5
1980	34	18,747,825	71.8	34	12,690,451	76.0	31,438,276	73.7
1984	29	18,009,192	52.4	25	6,575,651	71.0	24,584,868	59.6
1988	36	22,961,936	66.6	36	12,165,115	76.9	35,127,051	70.2
1992	39	20,239,385	66.9	38	12,696,547	83.9	32,935,932	72.7
1996	35	10,947,364	65.3	42	13,991,649	84.6	25,230,334	69.2
2000[1]	40	14,024,664	64.6	43	17,146,048	83.8	31,170,712	70.8

1. The totals for 2000 are based on official returns for most primaries and nearly complete but unofficial returns for others.

Sources: Percentages of delegates selected are from Congressional Quarterly, *Selecting the President: From 1789–1996* (Washington, D.C.: Congressional Quarterly, 1997), 17; and state secretary of state offices.

Sites of Major Party Conventions, 1832–2000

The following chart lists the twenty-one cities selected as the sites of major party conventions and the number of conventions they have hosted from the first national gathering for the Democrats (1832) and the Republicans (1856) through the 2000 conventions. The Democrats have hosted a total of forty-four conventions; the Republicans thirty-seven.

	Total conventions	Democratic conventions		Republican conventions	
		Number	Last hosted	Number	Last hosted
Chicago, Ill.	25	11	1996	14	1960
Baltimore, Md.	10	9	1912	1	1864
Philadelphia, Pa.	8	2	1948	6	2000
St. Louis, Mo.	5	4	1916	1	1896
New York, N.Y.	5	5	1992	0	—
San Francisco, Calif.	4	2	1984	2	1964
Cincinnati, Ohio	3	2	1880	1	1876
Kansas City, Mo.	3	1	1900	2	1976
Miami Beach, Fla.	3	1	1972	2	1972
Cleveland, Ohio	2	0	—	2	1936
Houston, Texas	2	1	1928	1	1992
Los Angeles, Calif.	2	2	2000	0	—
Atlanta, Ga.	1	1	1988	0	—
Atlantic City, N.J.	1	1	1964	0	—
Charleston, S.C.	1	1	1860	0	—
Dallas, Texas	1	0	—	1	1984
Denver, Colo.	1	1	1908	0	—
Detroit, Mich.	1	0	—	1	1980
Minneapolis, Minn.	1	0	—	1	1892
New Orleans, La.	1	0	—	1	1988
San Diego, Calif.	1	0	—	1	1996

Political Party Nominees, 1831–2000

Following is a comprehensive list of major and minor party nominees for president and vice president from 1831, when the first nominating convention was held by the Anti-Masonic Party, to 2000. In many cases, minor parties made only token efforts at a presidential campaign. Often, third-party candidates declined to run after being nominated by the convention, or their names appeared on the ballots of only a few states. In some cases the names of minor candidates did not appear on any state ballots and they received only a scattering of write-in votes, if any.

The basic source for the 1832 to 1972 elections was Joseph Nathan Kane, *Facts About the Presidents,* 6th ed. (New York: H.W. Wilson Co., 1993). To verify the names appearing in Kane, Congressional Quarterly consulted the following additional sources: Richard M. Scammon, *America at the Polls* (Pittsburgh: University of Pittsburgh Press, 1965); Richard M. Scammon, *America Votes 8* (Washington, D.C.: Congressional Quarterly, 1969); Richard M. Scammon, *America Votes 10* (Washington, D.C.: Congressional Quarterly, 1973); Richard B. Morris, ed. *Encyclopedia of American History,* (New York: Harper and Row, 1965); *Dictionary of American Biography,* (New York: Scribner's, 1928–1936); *Facts on File* (New York: Facts on File Inc., 1945–1975); Arthur M. Schlesinger, ed., *History of U.S. Political Parties,* Vols. I–IV, (New York: McGraw Hill, 1971); and *Who Was Who in America, 1607–1968,* Vols. I–V (Chicago: Marquis Co., 1943–1968). The source for the 1976 to 2000 elections was Congressional Quarterly's *America Votes* series, Vols. 12 (1977), 14 (1981), 16 (1985), 18 (1989), 20 (1993), 22 (1997), and 24 (2001) published in Washington, D.C.

In cases where these sources contain information in conflict with Kane, the conflicting information is included in a footnote. Where a candidate appears in Kane *but could not be verified in another source,* an asterisk appears beside the candidate's name on the list.

1832 ELECTION

Democratic Party
President: Andrew Jackson, Tennessee
Vice president: Martin Van Buren, New York

National Republican Party
President: Henry Clay, Kentucky
Vice president: John Sergeant, Pennsylvania

Independent Party
President: John Floyd, Virginia
Vice president: Henry Lee, Massachusetts

Anti-Masonic Party
President: William Wirt, Maryland
Vice president: Amos Ellmaker, Pennsylvania

1836 ELECTION

Democratic Party
President: Martin Van Buren, New York
Vice president: Richard Mentor Johnson, Kentucky

Whig Party
President: William Henry Harrison, Hugh Lawson White, Daniel Webster
Vice president: Francis Granger, John Tyler
The Whigs nominated regional candidates in 1836 hoping that each candidate would carry his region and deny Democrat Van Buren an electoral vote majority. Webster was the Whig candidate in Massachusetts; Harrison in the rest of New England, the Middle Atlantic states, and the West; and White in the South.
Granger was the running mate of Harrison and Webster. Tyler was White's running mate.

1840 ELECTION

Whig Party
President: William Henry Harrison, Ohio
Vice president: John Tyler, Virginia

Democratic Party
President: Martin Van Buren, New York
The Democratic convention adopted a resolution that left the choice of vice-

presidential candidates to the states. Democratic electors divided their vice-presidential votes among incumbent Richard M. Johnson (forty-eight votes), Littleton W. Tazewell (eleven votes), and James K. Polk (one vote).

Liberty Party
President: James Gillespie Birney, New York
Vice president: Thomas Earle, Pennsylvania

1844 ELECTION

Democratic Party
President: James Knox Polk, Tennessee
Vice president: George Mifflin Dallas, Pennsylvania

Whig Party
President: Henry Clay, Kentucky
Vice president: Theodore Frelinghuysen, New Jersey

Liberty Party
President: James Gillespie Birney, New York
Vice president: Thomas Morris, Ohio

National Democratic Party
President: John Tyler, Virginia
Vice president: None
Tyler withdrew in favor of the Democrat, Polk.

1848 ELECTION

Whig Party
President: Zachary Taylor, Louisiana
Vice president: Millard Fillmore, New York

Democratic Party
President: Lewis Cass, Michigan
Vice president: William Orlando Butler, Kentucky

Free Soil Party
President: Martin Van Buren, New York
Vice president: Charles Francis Adams, Massachusetts

Free Soil (Barnburners—Liberty Party)
President: John Parker Hale, New Hampshire
Vice president: Leicester King, Ohio
Later John Parker Hale relinquished the nomination.

National Liberty Party
President: Gerrit Smith, New York
Vice president: Charles C. Foote, Michigan

1852 ELECTION

Democratic Party
President: Franklin Pierce, New Hampshire
Vice president: William Rufus De Vane King, Alabama

Whig Party
President: Winfield Scott, New Jersey
Vice president: William Alexander Graham, North Carolina

Free Soil
President: John Parker Hale, New Hampshire
Vice president: George Washington Julian, Indiana

1856 ELECTION

Democratic Party
President: James Buchanan, Pennsylvania
Vice president: John Cabell Breckinridge, Kentucky

Republican Party
President: John Charles Fremont, California
Vice president: William Lewis Dayton, New Jersey

American (Know-Nothing) Party
President: Millard Fillmore, New York
Vice president: Andrew Jackson Donelson, Tennessee

Whig Party (the "Silver Grays")
President: Millard Fillmore, New York
Vice president: Andrew Jackson Donelson, Tennessee

North American Party
President: Nathaniel Prentice Banks, Massachusetts
Vice president: William Freame Johnson, Pennsylvania
Banks and Johnson declined the nominations and gave their support to the Republicans.

1860 ELECTION

Republican Party
President: Abraham Lincoln, Illinois
Vice president: Hannibal Hamlin, Maine

Democratic Party
President: Stephen Arnold Douglas, Illinois
Vice president: Herschel Vespasian Johnson, Georgia

Southern Democratic Party
President: John Cabell Breckinridge, Kentucky
Vice president: Joseph Lane, Oregon

Constitutional Union Party
President: John Bell, Tennessee
Vice president: Edward Everett, Massachusetts

1864 ELECTION

Republican Party
President: Abraham Lincoln, Illinois
Vice president: Andrew Johnson, Tennessee

Democratic Party
President: George Brinton McClellan, New York
Vice president: George Hunt Pendleton, Ohio

Independent Republican Party
President: John Charles Fremont, California
Vice president: John Cochrane, New York
Fremont and Cochrane declined the nominations and gave their support to the Republicans.

1868 ELECTION

Republican Party
President: Ulysses Simpson Grant, Illinois
Vice president: Schuyler Colfax, Indiana

Democratic Party
President: Horatio Seymour, New York
Vice president: Francis Preston Blair Jr., Missouri

1872 ELECTION

Republican Party
President: Ulysses Simpson Grant, Illinois
Vice president: Henry Wilson, Massachusetts

Liberal Republican Party
President: Horace Greeley, New York
Vice president: Benjamin Gratz Brown, Missouri

Independent Liberal Republican Party (Opposition Party)
President: William Slocum Groesbeck, Ohio
Vice president: Frederick Law Olmsted, New York

Democratic Party
President: Horace Greeley, New York
Vice president: Benjamin Gratz Brown, Missouri

Straight-Out Democratic Party
President: Charles O'Conor, New York
Vice president: John Quincy Adams, Massachusetts

Prohibition Party
President: James Black, Pennsylvania
Vice president: John Russell, Michigan

People's Party (Equal Rights Party)
President: Victoria Claflin Woodhull, New York
Vice president: Frederick Douglass

Labor Reform Party
President: David Davis, Illinois
Vice president: Joel Parker, New Jersey

Liberal Republican Party of Colored Men
President: Horace Greeley, New York
Vice president: Benjamin Gratz Brown, Missouri

National Working Men's Party
President: Ulysses Simpson Grant, Illinois
Vice president: Henry Wilson, Massachusetts

1876 ELECTION

Republican Party
President: Rutherford Birchard Hayes, Ohio
Vice president: William Almon Wheeler, New York

Democratic Party
President: Samuel Jones Tilden, New York
Vice president: Thomas Andrews Hendricks, Indiana

Greenback Party
President: Peter Cooper, New York
Vice president: Samuel Fenton Cary, Ohio

Prohibition Party
President: Green Clay Smith, Kentucky
Vice president: Gideon Tabor Stewart, Ohio

American National Party
President: James B. Walker, Illinois
Vice president: Donald Kirkpatrick, New York

1880 ELECTION

Republican Party
President: James Abram Garfield, Ohio
Vice president: Chester Alan Arthur, New York

Democratic Party
President: Winfield Scott Hancock, Pennsylvania
Vice president: William Hayden English, Indiana

Greenback Labor Party
President: James Baird Weaver, Iowa
Vice president: Benjamin J. Chambers, Texas

Prohibition Party
President: Neal Dow, Maine
Vice president: Henry Adams Thompson, Ohio

American Party
President: John Wolcott Phelps, Vermont
Vice president: Samuel Clarke Pomeroy, Kansas*

1884 ELECTION

Democratic Party
President: Grover Cleveland, New York
Vice president: Thomas Andrews Hendricks, Indiana

Republican Party
President: James Gillespie Blaine, Maine
Vice president: John Alexander Logan, Illinois

Anti-Monopoly Party
President: Benjamin Franklin Butler, Massachusetts
Vice president: Absolom Madden West, Mississippi

Greenback Party
President: Benjamin Franklin Butler, Massachusetts
Vice president: Absolom Madden West, Mississippi

Prohibition Party
President: John Pierce St. John, Kansas
Vice president: William Daniel, Maryland

American Prohibition Party
President: Samuel Clarke Pomeroy, Kansas
Vice president: John A. Conant, Connecticut

Equal Rights Party
President: Belva Ann Bennett Lockwood, District of Columbia
Vice president: Marietta Lizzie Bell Stow, California

1888 ELECTION

Republican Party
President: Benjamin Harrison, Indiana
Vice president: Levi Parsons Morton, New York

Democratic Party
President: Grover Cleveland, New York
Vice president: Allen Granberry Thurman, Ohio

Prohibition Party
President: Clinton Bowen Fisk, New Jersey
Vice president: John Anderson Brooks, Missouri*

Union Labor Party
President: Alson Jenness Streeter, Illinois
Vice president: Charles E. Cunningham, Arkansas*

United Labor Party
President: Robert Hall Cowdrey, Illinois
Vice president: William H.T. Wakefield, Kansas*

American Party
President: James Langdon Curtis, New
York
Vice president: Peter Dinwiddie
Wigginton, California*

Equal Rights Party
President: Belva Ann Bennett Lockwood,
District of Columbia
Vice president: Alfred Henry Love,
Pennsylvania*

Industrial Reform Party
President: Albert E. Redstone, California*
Vice president: John Colvin, Kansas*

1892 ELECTION

Democratic Party
President: Grover Cleveland, New York
Vice president: Adlai Ewing Stevenson,
Illinois

Republican Party
President: Benjamin Harrison, Indiana
Vice president: Whitelaw Reid, New York

People's Party of America
President: James Baird Weaver, Iowa
Vice president: James Gaven Field,
Virginia

Prohibition Party
President: John Bidwell, California
Vice president: James Britton Cranfill,
Texas

Socialist Labor Party
President: Simon Wing, Massachusetts
Vice president: Charles Horatio Matchett,
New York*

1896 ELECTION

Republican Party
President: William McKinley, Ohio
Vice president: Garret Augustus Hobart,
New Jersey

Democratic Party
President: William Jennings Bryan,
Nebraska
Vice president: Arthur Sewall, Maine

People's Party (Populist)
President: William Jennings Bryan,
Nebraska

Vice president: Thomas Edward Watson,
Georgia

National Democratic Party
President: John McAuley Palmer, Illinois
Vice president: Simon Bolivar Buckner,
Kentucky

Prohibition Party
President: Joshua Levering, Maryland
Vice president: Hale Johnson, Illinois*

Socialist Labor Party
President: Charles Horatio Matchett, New
York
Vice president: Matthew Maguire, New
Jersey

National Party
President: Charles Eugene Bentley,
Nebraska
Vice president: James Haywood
Southgate, North Carolina*

National Silver Party (Bi-Metallic League)
President: William Jennings Bryan,
Nebraska
Vice president: Arthur Sewall, Maine

1900 ELECTION

Republican Party
President: William McKinley, Ohio
Vice president: Theodore Roosevelt, New
York

Democratic Party
President: William Jennings Bryan,
Nebraska
Vice president: Adlai Ewing Stevenson,
Illinois

Prohibition Party
President: John Granville Wooley, Illinois
Vice president: Henry Brewer Metcalf,
Rhode Island

Social-Democratic Party
President: Eugene Victor Debs, Indiana
Vice president: Job Harriman, California

**People's Party (Populist—Anti-Fusionist
faction)**
President: Wharton Barker, Pennsylvania
Vice president: Ignatius Donnelly,
Minnesota

Socialist Labor Party
President: Joseph Francis Malloney,
Massachusetts
Vice president: Valentine Remmel,
Pennsylvania

Union Reform Party
President: Seth Hockett Ellis, Ohio
Vice president: Samuel T. Nicholson,
Pennsylvania

United Christian Party
President: Jonah Fitz Randolph Leonard,
Iowa
Vice president: David H. Martin,
Pennsylvania

People's Party
(Populist—Fusionist faction)
President: William Jennings Bryan,
Nebraska
Vice president: Adlai Ewing Stevenson,
Illinois

Silver Republican Party
President: William Jennings Bryan,
Nebraska
Vice president: Adlai Ewing Stevenson,
Illinois

National Party
President: Donelson Caffery, Louisiana
Vice president: Archibald Murray Howe,
Massachusetts*

1904 ELECTION

Republican Party
President: Theodore Roosevelt, New York
Vice president: Charles Warren Fairbanks,
Indiana

Democratic Party
President: Alton Brooks Parker, New York
Vice president: Henry Gassaway Davis,
West Virginia

Socialist Party
President: Eugene Victor Debs, Indiana
Vice president: Benjamin Hanford, New
York

Prohibition Party
President: Silas Comfort Swallow,
Pennsylvania
Vice president: George W. Carroll, Texas

People's Party (Populist)
President: Thomas Edward Watson,
Georgia
Vice president: Thomas Henry Tibbles,
Nebraska

Socialist Labor Party
President: Charles Hunter Corregan, New
York
Vice president: William Wesley Cox,
Illinois

Continental Party
President: Austin Holcomb
Vice president: A. King, Missouri

1908 ELECTION

Republican Party
President: William Howard Taft, Ohio
Vice president: James Schoolcraft
Sherman, New York

Democratic Party
President: William Jennings Bryan,
Nebraska
Vice president: John Worth Kern, Indiana

Socialist Party
President: Eugene Victor Debs, Indiana
Vice president: Benjamin Hanford, New
York

Prohibition Party
President: Eugene Wilder Chafin, Illinois
Vice president: Aaron Sherman Watkins,
Ohio

Independence Party
President: Thomas Louis Hisgen,
Massachusetts
Vice president: John Temple Graves,
Georgia

People's Party (Populist)
President: Thomas Edward Watson,
Georgia
Vice president: Samuel Williams, Indiana

Socialist Labor Party
President: August Gillhaus, New York
Vice president: Donald L. Munro, Virginia

United Christian Party
President: Daniel Braxton Turney, Illinois
Vice president: Lorenzo S. Coffin, Iowa

1912 ELECTION

Democratic Party
President: Woodrow Wilson, New Jersey
Vice president: Thomas Riley Marshall,
Indiana

Progressive Party ("Bull Moose" Party)
President: Theodore Roosevelt, New York
Vice president: Hiram Warren Johnson,
California

Republican Party
President: William Howard Taft, Ohio
Vice president: James Schoolcraft
Sherman, New York
Sherman died October 30; he was re-
placed by Nicholas Murray Butler, New
York.

Socialist Party
President: Eugene Victor Debs, Indiana
Vice president: Emil Seidel, Wisconsin

Prohibition Party
President: Eugene Wilder Chafin, Illinois
Vice president: Aaron Sherman Watkins,
Ohio

Socialist Labor Party
President: Arthur Elmer Reimer,
Massachusetts
Vice president: August Gillhaus, New
York[1]

1916 ELECTION

Democratic Party
President: Woodrow Wilson, New Jersey
Vice president: Thomas Riley Marshall,
Indiana

Republican Party
President: Charles Evans Hughes, New
York
Vice president: Charles Warren Fairbanks,
Indiana

Socialist Party
President: Allan Louis Benson, New York
Vice president: George Ross Kirkpatrick,
New Jersey

Prohibition Party
President: James Franklin Hanly, Indiana
Vice president: Ira Landrith, Tennessee

Socialist Labor Party
President: Arthur Elmer Reimer,
Massachusetts*
Vice president: Caleb Harrison, Illinois*

Progressive Party
President: Theodore Roosevelt, New York
Vice president: John Milliken Parker,
Louisiana

1920 ELECTION

Republican Party
President: Warren Gamaliel Harding, Ohio
Vice president: Calvin Coolidge,
Massachusetts

Democratic Party
President: James Middleton Cox, Ohio
Vice president: Franklin Delano Roosevelt,
New York

Socialist Party
President: Eugene Victor Debs, Indiana
Vice president: Seymour Stedman, Illinois

Farmer Labor Party
President: Parley Parker Christensen, Utah
Vice president: Maximilian Sebastian
Hayes, Ohio

Prohibition Party
President: Aaron Sherman Watkins, Ohio
Vice president: David Leigh Colvin, New
York

Socialist Labor Party
President: William Wesley Cox, Missouri
Vice president: August Gillhaus, New York

Single Tax Party
President: Robert Colvin Macauley,
Pennsylvania
Vice president: R.G. Barnum, Ohio

American Party
President: James Edward Ferguson,
Texas
Vice president: William J. Hough

1924 ELECTION

Republican Party
President: Calvin Coolidge,
Massachusetts
Vice president: Charles Gates Dawes,
Illinois

Democratic Party
President: John William Davis, West Virginia
Vice president: Charles Wayland Bryan, Nebraska

Progressive Party
President: Robert La Follette, Wisconsin
Vice president: Burton Kendall Wheeler, Montana

Prohibition Party
President: Herman Preston Faris, Missouri
Vice president: Marie Caroline Brehm, California

Socialist Labor Party
President: Frank T. Johns, Oregon
Vice president: Verne L. Reynolds, New York

Socialist Party
President: Robert La Follette, New York
Vice president: Burton Kendall Wheeler, Montana

Workers Party (Communist Party)
President: William Zebulon Foster, Illinois
Vice president: Benjamin Gitlow, New York

American Party
President: Gilbert Owen Nations, District of Columbia
Vice president: Charles Hiram Randall, California[2]

Commonwealth Land Party
President: William J. Wallace, New Jersey
Vice president: John Cromwell Lincoln, Ohio

Farmer Labor Party
President: Duncan McDonald, Illinois*
Vice president: William Bouck, Washington*

Greenback Party
President: John Zahnd, Indiana*
Vice president: Roy M. Harrop, Nebraska*

1928 ELECTION

Republican Party
President: Herbert Clark Hoover, California
Vice president: Charles Curtis, Kansas

Democratic Party
President: Alfred Emanuel Smith, New York
Vice president: Joseph Taylor Robinson, Arkansas

Socialist Party
President: Norman Mattoon Thomas, New York
Vice president: James Hudson Maurer, Pennsylvania

Workers Party (Communist Party)
President: William Zebulon Foster, Illinois
Vice president: Benjamin Gitlow, New York

Socialist Labor Party
President: Verne L. Reynolds, Michigan
Vice president: Jeremiah D. Crowley, New York

Prohibition Party
President: William Frederick Varney, New York
Vice president: James Arthur Edgerton, Virginia

Farmer Labor Party
President: Frank Elbridge Webb, California
Vice president: Will Vereen, Georgia[3]

Greenback Party
President: John Zahnd, Indiana*
Vice president: Wesley Henry Bennington, Ohio*

1932 ELECTION

Democratic Party
President: Franklin Delano Roosevelt, New York
Vice president: John Nance Garner, Texas

Republican Party
President: Herbert Clark Hoover, California
Vice president: Charles Curtis, Kansas

Socialist Party
President: Norman Mattoon Thomas, New York
Vice president: James Hudson Maurer, Pennsylvania

Communist Party
President: William Zebulon Foster, Illinois

Vice president: James William Ford, New
York

Prohibition Party
President: William David Upshaw, Georgia
Vice president: Frank Stewart Regan,
Illinois

Liberty Party
President: William Hope Harvey, Arkansas
Vice president: Frank B. Hemenway,
Washington

Socialist Labor Party
President: Verne L. Reynolds, New York
Vice president: John W. Aiken,
Massachusetts

Farmer Labor Party
President: Jacob Sechler Coxey, Ohio
Vice president: Julius J. Reiter, Minnesota

Jobless Party
President: James Renshaw Cox,
Pennsylvania
Vice president: V.C. Tisdal, Oklahoma

National Party
President: Seymour E. Allen,
Massachusetts

1936 ELECTION

Democratic Party
President: Franklin Delano Roosevelt,
New York
Vice president: John Nance Garner, Texas

Republican Party
President: Alfred Mossman Landon,
Kansas
Vice president: Frank Knox, Illinois

Union Party
President: William Lemke, North Dakota
Vice president: Thomas Charles O'Brien,
Massachusetts

Socialist Party
President: Norman Mattoon Thomas, New
York
Vice president: George A. Nelson,
Wisconsin

Communist Party
President: Earl Russell Browder, Kansas
Vice president: James William Ford, New
York

Prohibition Party
President: David Leigh Colvin, New York
Vice president: Alvin York, Tennessee

Socialist Labor Party
President: John W. Aiken, Massachusetts
Vice president: Emil F. Teichert, New York

National Greenback Party
President: John Zahnd, Indiana*
Vice president: Florence Garvin, Rhode
Island*

1940 ELECTION

Democratic Party
President: Franklin Delano Roosevelt,
New York
Vice president: Henry Agard Wallace, Iowa

Republican Party
President: Wendell Lewis Willkie, New York
Vice president: Charles Linza McNary,
Oregon

Socialist Party
President: Norman Mattoon Thomas, New
York
Vice president: Maynard C. Krueger,
Illinois

Prohibition Party
President: Roger Ward Babson,
Massachusetts
Vice president: Edgar V. Moorman, Illinois

Communist Party (Workers Party)
President: Earl Russell Browder, Kansas
Vice president: James William Ford, New
York

Socialist Labor Party
President: John W. Aiken, Massachusetts
Vice president: Aaron M. Orange, New
York

Greenback Party
President: John Zahnd, Indiana*
Vice president: James Elmer Yates,
Arizona*

1944 ELECTION

Democratic Party
President: Franklin Delano Roosevelt,
New York
Vice president: Harry S. Truman, Missouri

Republican Party
President: Thomas Edmund Dewey, New
York
Vice president: John William Bricker, Ohio

Socialist Party
President: Norman Mattoon Thomas, New
York
Vice president: Darlington Hoopes,
Pennsylvania

Prohibition Party
President: Claude A. Watson, California
Vice president: Andrew Johnson,
Kentucky

Socialist Labor Party
President: Edward A. Teichert,
Pennsylvania
Vice president: Arla A. Albaugh, Ohio

America First Party
President: Gerald Lyman Kenneth Smith,
Michigan
Vice president: Henry A. Romer, Ohio

1948 ELECTION

Democratic Party
President: Harry S. Truman, Missouri
Vice president: Alben William Barkley,
Kentucky

Republican Party
President: Thomas Edmund Dewey, New
York
Vice president: Earl Warren, California

States' Rights Democratic Party
President: James Strom Thurmond, South
Carolina
Vice president: Fielding Lewis Wright,
Mississippi

Progressive Party
President: Henry Agard Wallace, Iowa
Vice president: Glen Hearst Taylor, Idaho

Socialist Party
President: Norman Mattoon Thomas, New
York
Vice president: Tucker Powell Smith,
Michigan

Prohibition Party
President: Claude A. Watson, California
Vice president: Dale Learn, Pennsylvania

Socialist Labor Party
President: Edward A. Teichert,
Pennsylvania
Vice president: Stephen Emery, New York

Socialist Workers Party
President: Farrell Dobbs, New York
Vice president: Grace Carlson, Minnesota

Christian Nationalist Party
President: Gerald Lyman Kenneth Smith,
Missouri
Vice president: Henry A. Romer, Ohio

Greenback Party
President: John G. Scott, New York
Vice president: Granville B. Leeke,
Indiana*

Vegetarian Party
President: John Maxwell, Illinois
Vice president: Symon Gould, New York*

1952 ELECTION

Republican Party
President: Dwight David Eisenhower, New
York
Vice president: Richard Milhous Nixon,
California

Democratic Party
President: Adlai Ewing Stevenson II,
Illinois
Vice president: John Jackson Sparkman,
Alabama

Progressive Party
President: Vincent William Hallinan,
California
Vice president: Charlotta A. Bass, New
York

Prohibition Party
President: Stuart Hamblen, California
Vice president: Enoch Arden Holtwick,
Illinois

Socialist Labor Party
President: Eric Hass, New York
Vice president: Stephen Emery, New York

Socialist Party
President: Darlington Hoopes,
Pennsylvania
Vice president: Samuel Herman Friedman,
New York

Socialist Workers Party
President: Farrell Dobbs, New York
Vice president: Myra Tanner Weiss, New York

America First Party
President: Douglas MacArthur, Wisconsin
Vice president: Harry Flood Byrd, Virginia

American Labor Party
President: Vincent William Hallinan, California
Vice president: Charlotta A. Bass, New York

American Vegetarian Party
President: Daniel J. Murphy, California
Vice president: Symon Gould, New York*

Church of God Party
President: Homer Aubrey Tomlinson, New York
Vice president: Willie Isaac Bass, North Carolina*

Constitution Party
President: Douglas MacArthur, Wisconsin
Vice president: Harry Flood Byrd, Virginia

Greenback Party
President: Frederick C. Proehl, Washington
Vice president: Edward J. Bedell, Indiana

Poor Man's Party
President: Henry B. Krajewski, New Jersey
Vice president: Frank Jenkins, New Jersey

1956 ELECTION

Republican Party
President: Dwight David Eisenhower, Pennsylvania
Vice president: Richard Milhous Nixon, California

Democratic Party
President: Adlai Ewing Stevenson II, Illinois
Vice president: Estes Kefauver, Tennessee

States' Rights Party
President: Thomas Coleman Andrews, Virginia
Vice president: Thomas Harold Werdel, California
    Ticket also favored by Constitution Party.

Prohibition Party
President: Enoch Arden Holtwick, Illinois
Vice president: Edward M. Cooper, California

Socialist Labor Party
President: Eric Hass, New York
Vice president: Georgia Cozzini, Wisconsin

Texas Constitution Party
President: William Ezra Jenner, Indiana*
Vice president: Joseph Bracken Lee, Utah*

Socialist Workers Party
President: Farrell Dobbs, New York
Vice president: Myra Tanner Weiss, New York

American Third Party
President: Henry Krajewski, New Jersey
Vice president: Ann Marie Yezo, New Jersey

Socialist Party
President: Darlington Hoopes, Pennsylvania
Vice president: Samuel Herman Friedman, New York

Pioneer Party
President: William Langer, North Dakota*
Vice president: Burr McCloskey, Illinois*

American Vegetarian Party
President: Herbert M. Shelton, California*
Vice president: Symon Gould, New York*

Greenback Party
President: Frederick C. Proehl, Washington
Vice president: Edward Kirby Meador, Massachusetts*

States' Rights Party of Kentucky
President: Harry Flood Byrd, Virginia
Vice president: William Ezra Jenner, Indiana

South Carolinians for Independent Electors
President: Harry Flood Byrd, Virginia

Christian National Party
President: Gerald Lyman Kenneth Smith, Missouri
Vice president: Charles I. Robertson

1960 ELECTION

Democratic Party
President: John Fitzgerald Kennedy, Massachusetts
Vice president: Lyndon Baines Johnson, Texas

Republican Party
President: Richard Milhous Nixon, California
Vice president: Henry Cabot Lodge, Massachusetts

National States' Rights Party
President: Orval Eugene Faubus, Arkansas
Vice president: John Geraerdt Crommelin, Alabama

Socialist Labor Party
President: Eric Hass, New York
Vice president: Georgia Cozzini, Wisconsin

Prohibition Party
President: Rutherford Losey Decker, Missouri
Vice president: Earle Harold Munn, Michigan

Socialist Workers Party
President: Farrell Dobbs, New York
Vice president: Myra Tanner Weiss, New York

Conservative Party of New Jersey
President: Joseph Bracken Lee, Utah
Vice president: Kent H. Courtney, Louisiana

Conservative Party of Virginia
President: C. Benton Coiner, Virginia
Vice president: Edward M. Silverman, Virginia

Constitution Party (Texas)
President: Charles Loten Sullivan, Mississippi
Vice president: Merritt B. Curtis, District of Columbia

Constitution Party (Washington)
President: Merritt B. Curtis, District of Columbia
Vice president: B.N. Miller

Greenback Party
President: Whitney Hart Slocomb, California*
Vice president: Edward Kirby Meador, Massachusetts*

Independent Afro-American Party
President: Clennon King, Georgia
Vice president: Reginald Carter

Tax Cut Party (America First Party; American Party)
President: Lar Daly, Illinois
Vice president: Merritt Barton Curtis, District of Columbia

Theocratic Party
President: Homer Aubrey Tomlinson, New York
Vice president: Raymond L. Teague, Alaska*

Vegetarian Party
President: Symon Gould, New York
Vice president: Christopher Gian-Cursio, Florida

1964 ELECTION

Democratic Party
President: Lyndon Baines Johnson, Texas
Vice president: Hubert Horatio Humphrey, Minnesota

Republican Party
President: Barry Morris Goldwater, Arizona
Vice president: William Edward Miller, New York

Socialist Labor Party
President: Eric Hass, New York
Vice president: Henning A. Blomen, Massachusetts

Prohibition Party
President: Earle Harold Munn, Michigan
Vice president: Mark Shaw, Massachusetts

Socialist Workers Party
President: Clifton DeBerry, New York
Vice president: Edward Shaw, New York

National States' Rights Party
President: John Kasper, Tennessee
Vice president: J.B. Stoner, Georgia

Constitution Party
President: Joseph B. Lightburn, West Virginia
Vice president: Theodore C. Billings, Colorado

Independent States' Rights Party
President: Thomas Coleman Andrews, Virginia
Vice president: Thomas H. Werdel, California*

Theocratic Party
President: Homer Aubrey Tomlinson, New York
Vice president: William R. Rogers, Missouri*

Universal Party
President: Kirby James Hensley, California
Vice president: John O. Hopkins, Iowa

1968 ELECTION

Republican Party
President: Richard Milhous Nixon, New York
Vice president: Spiro Theodore Agnew, Maryland

Democratic Party
President: Hubert Horatio Humphrey, Minnesota
Vice president: Edmund Sixtus Muskie, Maine

American Independent Party
President: George Corley Wallace, Alabama
Vice president: Curtis Emerson LeMay, Ohio
    LeMay replaced S. Marvin Griffin, who originally had been selected.

Peace and Freedom Party
President: Eldridge Cleaver
Vice president: Judith Mage, New York

Socialist Labor Party
President: Henning A. Blomen, Massachusetts
Vice president: George Sam Taylor, Pennsylvania

Socialist Workers Party
President: Fred Halstead, New York
Vice president: Paul Boutelle, New Jersey

Prohibition Party
President: Earle Harold Munn Sr., Michigan
Vice president: Rolland E. Fisher, Kansas

Communist Party
President: Charlene Mitchell, California
Vice president: Michael Zagarell, New York

Constitution Party
President: Richard K. Troxell, Texas
Vice president: Merle Thayer, Iowa

Freedom and Peace Party
President: Richard Claxton (Dick) Gregory, Illinois
Vice president: Mark Lane, New York

Patriotic Party
President: George Corley Wallace, Alabama
Vice president: William Penn Patrick, California

Theocratic Party
President: William R. Rogers, Missouri

Universal Party
President: Kirby James Hensley, California
Vice president: Roscoe B. MacKenna

1972 ELECTION

Republican Party
President: Richard Milhous Nixon, California
Vice president: Spiro Theodore Agnew, Maryland

Democratic Party
President: George Stanley McGovern, South Dakota
Vice president: Thomas Francis Eagleton, Missouri
    Eagleton resigned and was replaced on August 8, 1972, by Robert Sargent Shriver Jr., Maryland, selected by the Democratic National Committee.

American Independent Party
President: John George Schmitz, California
Vice president: Thomas Jefferson Anderson, Tennessee

Socialist Workers Party
President: Louis Fisher, Illinois
Vice president: Genevieve Gunderson, Minnesota

Socialist Labor Party
President: Linda Jenness, Georgia
Vice president: Andrew Pulley, Illinois

Communist Party
President: Gus Hall, New York
Vice president: Jarvis Tyner, New York

Prohibition Party
President: Earle Harold Munn Sr., Michigan
Vice president: Marshall Uncapher

Libertarian Party
President: John Hospers, California
Vice president: Theodora Nathan, Oregon

People's Party
President: Benjamin Spock, New York
Vice president: Julius Hobson, District of Columbia

America First Party
President: John V. Mahalchik
Vice president: Irving Homer

Universal Party
President: Gabriel Green
Vice president: Daniel Fry

1976 ELECTION

Democratic Party
President: James Earl (Jimmy) Carter Jr., Georgia
Vice president: Walter Frederick Mondale, Minnesota

Republican Party
President: Gerald Rudolph Ford, Michigan
Vice president: Robert Joseph Dole, Kansas

Independent candidate
President: Eugene Joseph McCarthy, Minnesota
Vice president: none[4]

Libertarian Party
President: Roger MacBride, Virginia
Vice president: David P. Bergland, California

American Independent Party
President: Lester Maddox, Georgia
Vice president: William Dyke, Wisconsin

American Party
President: Thomas J. Anderson, Tennessee
Vice president: Rufus Shackleford, Florida

Socialist Workers Party
President: Peter Camejo, California
Vice president: Willie Mae Reid, California

Communist Party
President: Gus Hall, New York
Vice president: Jarvis Tyner, New York

People's Party
President: Margaret Wright, California
Vice president: Benjamin Spock, New York

U.S. Labor Party
President: Lyndon H. LaRouche Jr., New York
Vice president: R. W. Evans, Michigan

Prohibition Party
President: Benjamin C. Bubar, Maine
Vice president: Earl F. Dodge, Colorado

Socialist Labor Party
President: Jules Levin, New Jersey
Vice president: Constance Blomen, Massachusetts

Socialist Party
President: Frank P. Zeidler, Wisconsin
Vice president: J. Quinn Brisben, Illinois

Restoration Party
President: Ernest L. Miller
Vice president: Roy N. Eddy

United American Party
President: Frank Taylor
Vice president: Henry Swan

1980 ELECTION[5]

Republican Party
President: Ronald Wilson Reagan, California
Vice president: George Herbert Walker Bush, Texas

Democratic Party
President: James Earl (Jimmy) Carter Jr., Georgia
Vice president: Walter Frederick Mondale, Minnesota

National Unity Campaign
President: John B. Anderson, Illinois
Vice president: Patrick Joseph Lucey, Wisconsin

Libertarian Party
President: Edward E. Clark, California
Vice president: David Koch, New York

Citizens Party
President: Barry Commoner, New York
Vice president: LaDonna Harris, New Mexico

Communist Party
President: Gus Hall, New York
Vice president: Angela Davis, California

American Independent Party
President: John Richard Rarick, Louisiana
Vice president: Eileen M. Shearer, California

Socialist Workers Party
President: Andrew Pulley, Illinois
Vice president: Matilde Zimmermann
President: Clifton DeBerry, California
Vice president: Matilde Zimmermann
President: Richard Congress, Ohio
Vice president: Matilde Zimmermann

Right to Life Party
President: Ellen McCormack, New York
Vice president: Carroll Driscoll, New Jersey

Peace and Freedom Party
President: Maureen Smith, California
Vice president: Elizabeth Barron

Workers World Party
President: Deirdre Griswold, New Jersey
Vice president: Larry Holmes, New York

Statesman Party
President: Benjamin C. Bubar, Maine
Vice president: Earl F. Dodge, Colorado

Socialist Party
President: David McReynolds, New York
Vice president: Diane Drufenbrock, Wisconsin

American Party
President: Percy L. Greaves, New York
Vice president: Frank L. Varnum, California
President: Frank W. Shelton, Utah
Vice president: George E. Jackson

Middle Class Party
President: Kurt Lynen, New Jersey
Vice president: Harry Kieve, New Jersey

Down With Lawyers Party
President: Bill Gahres, New Jersey
Vice president: J.F. Loghlin, New Jersey

Independent Party
President: Martin E. Wendelken

Natural Peoples Party
President: Harley McLain, North Dakota
Vice president: Jewelie Goeller, North Dakota

1984 ELECTION[6]

Republican Party
President: Ronald Wilson Reagan, California
Vice president: George Herbert Walker Bush, Texas

Democratic Party
President: Walter Fritz Mondale, Minnesota
Vice president: Geraldine Anne Ferraro, New York

Libertarian Party
President: David P. Bergland, California
Vice president: Jim Lewis, Connecticut

Independent Party
President: Lyndon H. LaRouche Jr., Virginia
Vice president: Billy Davis, Mississippi

Citizens Party
President: Sonia Johnson, Virginia
Vice president: Richard Walton, Rhode Island

Populist Party
President: Bob Richards, Texas
Vice president: Maureen Kennedy Salaman, California

Independent Alliance Party
President: Dennis L. Serrette, New Jersey
Vice president: Nancy Ross, New York

Communist Party
President: Gus Hall, New York
Vice president: Angela Davis, California

Socialist Workers Party
President: Mel Mason, California
Vice president: Andrea Gonzalez, New York

Workers World Party
President: Larry Holmes, New York
Vice president: Gloria La Riva, California
President: Gavrielle Holmes, New York
Vice president: Milton Vera

American Party
President: Delmar Dennis, Tennessee
Vice president: Traves Brownlee, Delaware

Workers League Party
President: Ed Winn, New York
Vice presidents: Jean T. Brust, Helen
Halyard, Edward Bergonzi

Prohibition Party
President: Earl F. Dodge, Colorado
Vice president: Warren C. Martin, Kansas

1988 ELECTION[7]

Republican Party
President: George Herbert Walker Bush,
Texas
Vice president: James "Dan" Quayle,
Indiana

Democratic Party
President: Michael Stanley Dukakis,
Massachusetts
Vice president: Lloyd Millard Bentsen Jr.,
Texas

Libertarian Party
President: Ronald E. Paul, Texas
Vice president: Andre V. Marrou, Nevada

New Alliance Party
President: Lenora B. Fulani, New York
Vice president: Joyce Dattner

Populist Party
President: David E. Duke, Louisiana
Vice president: Floyd C. Parker

Consumer Party
President: Eugene Joseph McCarthy,
Minnesota
Vice president: Florence Rice

American Independent Party
President: James C. Griffin, California
Vice president: Charles J. Morsa

National Economic Recovery Party
President: Lyndon H. LaRouche Jr.,
Virginia
Vice president: Debra H. Freeman

Right to Life Party
President: William A. Marra, New Jersey
Vice president: Joan Andrews

Workers League Party
President: Edward Winn, New York
Vice president: Barry Porster

Socialist Workers Party
President: James Warren, New Jersey
Vice president: Kathleen Mickells

Peace and Freedom Party
President: Herbert Lewin
Vice president: Vikki Murdock

Prohibition Party
President: Earl F. Dodge, Colorado
Vice president: George D. Ormsby

Workers World Party
President: Larry Holmes, New York
Vice president: Gloria La Riva, California

Socialist Party
President: Willa Kenoyer, Minnesota
Vice president: Ron Ehrenreich

American Party
President: Delmar Dennis, Tennessee
Vice president: Earl Jepson

Grassroots Party
President: Jack E. Herer, California
Vice president: Dana Beal

Independent Party
President: Louie Youngkeit, Utah

Third World Assembly
President: John G. Martin, District of
Columbia
Vice president: Cleveland Sparrow

1992 ELECTION[8]

Democratic Party
President: Bill Clinton, Arkansas
Vice president: Albert Gore Jr., Tennessee

Republican Party
President: George Herbert Walker Bush,
Texas
Vice president: James "Dan" Quayle,
Indiana

Independent
President: H. Ross Perot, Texas
Vice president: James Stockdale,
California

Libertarian Party
President: Andre V. Marrou, Nevada
Vice president: Nancy Lord, Georgia

America First Party (Populist)
President: James "Bo" Gritz, Nevada
Vice president: Cyril Minett

New Alliance Party
President: Lenora B. Fulani, New York
Vice president: Maria E. Munoz, California

U.S. Taxpayers Party
President: Howard Phillips, Virginia
Vice president: Albion W. Knight, Maryland

Natural Law Party
President: John Hagelin, Iowa
Vice president: Mike Tompkins, Iowa

Peace and Freedom Party
President: Ron Daniels, California
Vice president: Asiba Tupahache

Independent
President: Lyndon H. LaRouche Jr., Virginia
Vice president: James L. Bevel

Socialist Workers Party
President: James Warren, New Jersey
Vice president: Willie Mae Reid, California

Independent
President: Drew Bradford

Grassroots Party
President: Jack E. Herer, California
Vice president: Derrick P. Grimmer

Socialist Party
President: J. Quinn Brisben, Illinois
Vice president: Barbara Garson

Workers League Party
President: Helen Halyard, Michigan
Vice president: Fred Mazelis, Michigan

Take Back America Party
President: John Yiamouyiannas
Vice president: Allen C. McCone

Independent
President: Delbert L. Ehlers
Vice president: Rick Wendt

Prohibition Party
President: Earl F. Dodge, Colorado
Vice president: George D. Ormsby

Apathy Party
President: Jim Boren
Vice president: Will Weidman

Third Party
President: Eugene A. Hem
Vice president: Joanne Roland

Looking Back Party
President: Isabell Masters, Oklahoma
Vice president: Walter Masters, Florida

American Party
President: Robert J. Smith
Vice president: Doris Feimer

Workers World Party
President: Gloria La Riva, California
Vice president: Larry Holmes, New York

1996 ELECTION[9]

Democratic Party
President: Bill Clinton, Arkansas
Vice president: Albert Gore Jr., Tennessee

Republican Party
President: Robert Dole, Kansas
Vice president: Jack Kemp, New York

Reform Party
President: H. Ross Perot, Texas
Vice president: Pat Choate, District of
Columbia

Green Party
President: Ralph Nader, District of
Columbia
Vice president: Winona LaDuke,
Minnesota

Libertarian Party
President: Harry Browne, Tennessee
Vice president: Jo Anne Jorgensen, South
Carolina

U.S. Taxpayers Party
President: Howard Phillips, Virginia
Vice president: Herbert W. Titus, Virginia

Natural Law Party
President: John Hagelin, Iowa
Vice president: Mike Tompkins, North
Carolina

Workers World Party
President: Monica Moorehead, New Jersey
Vice president: Gloria La Riva, California

Peace and Freedom Party
President: Marsha Feinland, California
Vice president: Kate McClatchy,
Massachusetts

Independent
President: Charles E. Collins, Florida
Vice president: Rosemary Giumarra

Socialist Workers Party
President: James E. Harris Jr., Georgia
Vice president: Laura Garza, New York

Grassroots Party
President: Dennis Peron, Minnesota
Vice president: Arlin Troutt, Arizona

Socialist Party
President: Mary Cal Hollis, Colorado
Vice president: Eric Chester,
Massachusetts

Socialist Equality Party
President: Jerome White, Michigan
Vice president: Fred Mazelis, Michigan

American Party
President: Diane Beall Templin, California
Vice president: Gary Van Horn, Utah

Prohibition Party
President: Earl F. Dodge, Colorado
Vice president: Rachel Bubar Kelly, Maine

Independent Party of Utah
President: A. Peter Crane, Utah
Vice president: Connie Chandler, Utah

America First Party
President: Ralph Forbes, Arkansas

Independent Grassroots Party
President: John Birrenbach, Minnesota
Vice president: George McMahon, Iowa

Looking Back Party
President: Isabell Masters, Oklahoma
Vice president: Shirley Jean Masters,
California

Independent
President: Steve Michael, District of
Columbia

2000 ELECTION

Republican Party
President: George W. Bush, Texas
Vice president: Richard Cheney, Wyoming

Democratic Party
President: Albert Gore Jr., Tennessee
Vice president: Joseph Lieberman,
Connecticut

Green Party
President: Ralph Nader, District of
Columbia
Vice president: Winona LaDuke,
Minnesota

Reform Party
President: Patrick J. Buchanan, Virginia
Vice president: Ezola Foster, California

Libertarian Party[10]
President: Harry Browne, Tennessee
Vice president: Art Olivier, California
President: L. Neil Smith, Arizona

Constitution Party
President: Howard Phillips, Virginia
Vice president: J. Curtis Frazier II, Missouri

Natural Law Party
President: John Hagelin, Iowa
Vice president: Nat Goldhaber, California

Socialist Party
President: David McReynolds, New York
Vice president: Mary Cal Hollis, Colorado

Socialist Workers Party
President: James E. Harris Jr., Georgia
Vice president: Margaret Trowe, Minnesota

Workers World Party
President: Monica Moorehead, New
Jersey
Vice president: Gloria La Riva, California

Independent
President: Cathy Gordon Brown,
Tennessee
Vice president: Sabrina R. Allen,
Tennessee

Vermont Grassroots Party
President: Dennis I. Lane, Vermont
Vice president: Dale Wilkinson, Minnesota

Independent
President: Randall A. Venson, Tennessee
Vice president: Gene Kelley, Tennessee

Prohibition Party
President: Earl F. Dodge, Colorado
Vice president: W. Dean Watkins, Arizona

Independent
President: Louie Youngkeit, Utah
Vice president: Robert Leo Beck, Utah

NOTES

*Candidates appeared in Joseph Nathan Kane, *Facts About the Presidents,* 4th ed. (New York: H.W. Wilson, 1981), but could not be verified in another source.

1. 1912: Arthur M. Schlesinger's *History of American Presidential Elections* (New York: McGraw-Hill, 1971) lists the Socialist Labor Party vice-presidential candidate as Francis. No first name is given.

2. 1924: Richard M. Scammon's *America at the Polls* (Pittsburgh: University of Pittsburgh Press, 1965) lists the American Party vice-presidential candidate as Leander L. Pickett.

3. 1928: *America at the Polls* lists the Farmer Labor Party vice-presidential candidate as L.R. Tillman.

4. 1976: McCarthy, who ran as an independent with no party designation, had no national running mate, favoring the elimination of the office. But as various state laws required a running mate, he had different ones in different states, amounting to nearly two dozen, all political unknowns.

5. 1980: In several cases vice-presidential nominees were different from those listed for most states, and the Socialist Workers and American Party nominees for president varied from state to state. For example, because Pulley, the major standard-bearer for the Socialist Workers Party was only twenty-nine years old, his name was not allowed on the ballot in some states (the Constitution requires presidential candidates to be at least thirty-five years old). Hence, the party ran other candidates in those states. In a number of states, candidates appeared on the ballot with variants of the party designations listed, without any party designation, or with entirely different party names.

6. 1984: Both Larry Holmes and Gavrielle Holmes were standard-bearers of the Workers World Party. Of the two, Larry Holmes was listed on more state ballots. Milton Vera was Gavrielle Holmes's vice-presidential running mate in Ohio and Rhode Island. The Workers League Party had three vice-presidential candidates: Jean T. Brust in Illinois; Helen Halyard in Michigan, New Jersey, and Pennsylvania; and Edward Bergonzi in Minnesota and Ohio.

7. 1988: The candidates listed include all those who appeared on the ballot in at least one state. In some cases, a party's vice-presidential candidate varied from state to state. Candidates' full names and states were not available from some parties.

8. 1992: The candidates listed include all those who appeared on the ballot in at least one state. In some cases a party's vice-presidential candidate varied from state to state. Candidates' states were not available from some parties.

9. 1996: The candidates listed include all those who appeared on the ballot in at least one state. In some cases a party's vice-presidential candidate varied from state to state. Candidates' states were not available from some parties.

10. 2000: L. Neil Smith ran as the Libertarian Party's presidential candidate in Arizona only. Harry Browne ran as the party's candidate in the other forty-nine states.

National Party Chairs, 1848–2001

Name	State	Years of Service
Democratic Party		
B.F. Hallett	Massachusetts	1848–1852
Robert McLane	Maryland	1852–1856
David A. Smalley	Virginia	1856–1860
August Belmont	New York	1860–1872
Augustus Schell	New York	1872–1876
Abram S. Hewitt	New York	1876–1877
William H. Barnum	Connecticut	1877–1889
Calvin S. Brice	Ohio	1889–1892
William F. Harrity	Pennsylvania	1892–1896
James K. Jones	Arkansas	1896–1904
Thomas Taggart	Indiana	1904–1908
Norman E. Mack	New York	1908–1912
William F. McCombs	New York	1912–1916
Vance C. McCormick	Pennsylvania	1916–1919
Homer S. Cummings	Connecticut	1919–1920
George White	Ohio	1920–1921
Cordell Hull	Tennessee	1921–1924
Clem Shaver	West Virginia	1924–1928
John J. Raskob	Maryland	1928–1932
James A. Farley	New York	1932–1940
Edward J. Flynn	New York	1940–1943
Frank C. Walker	Pennsylvania	1943–1944
Robert E. Hannegan	Missouri	1944–1947
J. Howard McGrath	Rhode Island	1947–1949
William M. Boyle Jr.	Missouri	1949–1951
Frank E. McKinney	Indiana	1951–1952
Stephen A. Mitchell	Illinois	1952–1954
Paul M. Butler	Indiana	1955–1960
Henry M. Jackson	Washington	1960–1961
John M. Bailey	Connecticut	1961–1968
Lawrence F. O'Brien	Massachusetts	1968–1969
Fred Harris	Oklahoma	1969–1970
Lawrence F. O'Brien	Massachusetts	1970–1972
Jean Westwood	Utah	1972
Robert Straus	Texas	1972–1977
Kenneth Curtis	Maine	1977–1978
John White	Texas	1978–1981
Charles Manatt	California	1981–1985
Paul Kirk	Massachusetts	1985–1989
Ronald H. Brown	Washington, D.C.	1989–1993
David Wilhelm	Illinois	1993–1994
Christopher Dodd (general chair)	Connecticut	1994–1997
Donald Fowler	South Carolina	1994–1997

(continued)

(continued)

Name	State	Years of Service
Roy Romer (general chair)	Colorado	1997–1999
Steven Grossman	Massachusetts	1997–1999
Ed Rendell (general chair)	Pennsylvania	1999–2001
Joe Andrew	Indiana	1999–2001
Terrence McAuliffe	New York	2001–
Republican Party		
Edwin D. Morgan	New York	1856–1864
Henry J. Raymond	New York	1864–1866
Marcus L. Ward	New Jersey	1866–1868
William Claflin	Massachusetts	1868–1872
Edwin D. Morgan	New York	1872–1876
Zachariah Chandler	Michigan	1876–1879
J. Donald Cameron	Pennsylvania	1879–1880
Marshall Jewell	Connecticut	1880–1883
D.M. Sabin	Minnesota	1883–1884
B.F. Jones	Pennsylvania	1884–1888
Matthew S. Quay	Pennsylvania	1888–1891
James S. Clarkson	Iowa	1891–1892
Thomas H. Carter	Montana	1892–1896
Mark A. Hanna	Ohio	1896–1904
Henry C. Payne	Wisconsin	1904
George B. Cortelyou	New York	1904–1907
Harry S. New	Indiana	1907–1908
Frank H. Hitchcock	Massachusetts	1908–1909
John F. Hill	Maine	1909–1912
Victor Rosewater	Nebraska	1912
Charles D. Hilles	New York	1912–1916
William R. Willcox	New York	1916–1918
Will Hays	Indiana	1918–1921
John T. Adams	Iowa	1921–1924
William M. Butler	Massachusetts	1924–1928
Hubert Work	Colorado	1928–1929
Claudius H. Huston	Tennessee	1929–1930
Simeon D. Fess	Ohio	1930–1932
Everett Sanders	Indiana	1932–1934
Henry P. Fletcher	Pennsylvania	1934–1936
John Hamilton	Kansas	1936–1940
Joseph W. Martin Jr.	Massachusetts	1940–1942
Harrison E. Spangler	Iowa	1942–1944
Herbert Brownell Jr.	New York	1944–1946
B. Carroll Reece	Tennessee	1946–1948
Hugh D. Scott Jr.	Pennsylvania	1948–1949

(continued)

National Party Chairs, 1848–2001 *(continued)*

Name	State	Years of Service
Republican Party *(continued)*		
Guy George Gabrielson	New Jersey	1949–1952
Arthur E. Summerfield	Michigan	1952–1953
C. Wesley Roberts	Kansas	1953
Leonard W. Hall	New York	1953–1957
H. Meade Alcorn Jr.	Connecticut	1957–1959
Thruston B. Morton	Kentucky	1959–1961
William E. Miller	New York	1961–1964
Dean Burch	Arizona	1964–1965
Ray C. Bliss	Ohio	1965–1969
Rogers C.B. Morton	Maryland	1969–1971
Robert Dole	Kansas	1971–1973
George Bush	Texas	1973–1974
Mary Louise Smith	Iowa	1974–1977
William Brock	Tennessee	1977–1981
Richard Richards	Utah	1981–1983
Paul Laxalt (general chair)	Nevada	1983–1986
Frank Fahrenkopf Jr.	Nevada	1983–1989
Lee Atwater	South Carolina	1989–1991
Clayton Yeutter	Nebraska	1991–1992
Rich Bond	New York	1992–1993
Haley Barbour	Mississippi	1993–1997
Jim Nicholson	Colorado	1997–2001
James Gilmore	Virginia	2001–

Sources: Hugh A. Bone, *Party Committees and National Politics* (Seattle: University of Washington, 1958), 241–243; Congressional Quarterly, *The President, the Public, and the Parties,* 2nd ed. (Washington, D.C.: Congressional Quarterly, 1997), 21; and various issues of the *CQ Weekly Report.*

index